FINANCIAL STEWARDSHIP of CHARITIES

Maximising impact in times of uncertainty

Adrian Poffley

DIRECTORY OF SOCIAL CHANGE

Published by
The Directory of Social Change
24 Stephenson Way
London NW1 2DP
tel.: 020 7209 5151, fax: 020 7391 4804
e-mail: books@dsc.org.uk
from whom further copies and a full publications list are available.

The Directory of Social Change is a Registered Charity no. 800517

ISBN 1 903991 17 X

British Library Cataloguing in Publication Data
A catalogue record for this book is available from the British Library

Cover design by Russell Stretten

Edited by Myra Bennett

Text designed and typeset by GreenGate Publishing Services, Tonbridge

Printed and bound by Page Bros, Norwich

Other Directory of Social Change departments in London:
Courses and Conferences tel: 020 7209 4949
Charity Centre tel: 020 7209 1015
Publicity tel: 020 7391 4900
Research tel: 020 7391 4880

Directory of Social Change Northern Office:
Federation House, Hope Street, Liverpool L1 9BW
Courses and Conferences tel: 0151 708 0117
Research tel: 0151 708 0136

Contents

PART 2   FINANCE STRATEGY

Acknowledgements

Grateful acknowledgement is made to the following for permission to reprint previously published material:

John Argenti. Association of Chief Executives of Voluntary Organisations (ACEVO), 83 Victoria Street, London SW1H 0HW, tel. 0845 345 8481 website: www.acevo.org.uk. BDO Stoy Hayward. British Overseas NGOs for Development (BOND). The Chartered Institute of Management Accountants (CIMA). Elsevier Science for excerpts from 'Long Range Planning', Vol. 26, No.1, *Strategy as Order Emerging from Chaos* by Ralph Stacey, copyright 1993, with permission from Elsevier Science. Harvard Business School Press for excerpts from *The Balanced Scorecard* by Robert Kaplan and David Norton, Boston, MA 1996, copyright © 1996 by Harvard Business School Publishing Corporation, all rights reserved; excerpts from *The Strategy-Focused Organization* by Robert Kaplan and David Norton, Boston, MA 2001, copyright © 2001 by Harvard Business School Publishing Corporation, all rights reserved; excerpts from Adaptive Enterprise by Stephan Haeckel, Boston, MA 1999, copyright © 1999 by Harvard Business School Publishing Corporation, all rights reserved; excerpts from *Harvard Business Review*, November/December 1996, pp.61–78, 'What is Strategy?' by Michael Porter, copyright 1996 by Harvard Business School Publishing Corporation, all rights reserved. Andrew Hind. Jeremy Hope and Robin Fraser. Kogan Page. Neil McBride. National Council of Voluntary Organisations (NCVO). Osmosis Publications for excerpts from *The Genghis Khan Guide to Business* by Brian Warnes, London, 1984, copyright © 1984 by Osmosis Publications, reprinted with permission of the author, tel. 020 8852 6560; e-mail business.dynamics@btinternet.com. PKF. Penguin Books Limited for excerpts from *Business @ The Speed of Thought* by Bill Gates, copyright © 1999 by Penguin Group; excerpts from *Managing without Profit* by Mike Hudson, copyright © 1999 by Penguin Group; excerpts from *An Insight into Management Accounting (2nd edition)* by John Sizer, copyright © 1979. Plaza Publishing for permission to use material of the author previously published in *NGO Finance* magazine and *Charity Finance* magazine. The Ramblers Association. The British Refugee Council. Sho-net Systems. Sight Savers International. John Wiley & Sons, Inc. for excerpts from *Strategic Planning for Public and Nonprofit Organizations* by John Bryson, copyright © 1995 by Jossey-Bass. This material is used with permission of John Wiley & Sons, Inc.

Crown copyright material is reproduced with the permission of the Controller of HMSO and the Queen's Printer for Scotland.

About the author

Adrian Poffley has worked in charity finance since 1990, as Chief Accountant for Voluntary Service Overseas and, since 1998, as Director of Finance and Support Services for Sight Savers International. He was Honorary Treasurer for The Refugee Council from 1994 to 2001 and is a regular speaker and writer on charity finance, strategy and governance. He is a Fellow of the Chartered Institute of Management Accountants.

About the Directory of Social Change

The Directory of Social Change (DSC) is an independent voice for positive social change, set up in 1975 to help voluntary organisations become more effective. It does this by providing practical, challenging and affordable information and training to meet the current, emerging and future needs of the sector.

DSC's main activities include:

- researching and publishing reference gudies and handbooks'
- providing practical training courses;
- running conferences and briefing sessions;
- organising Charityfair, the biggest annual forum for the sector;
- encouraging voluntary groups to network and share information;
- campaigning to promote the interests of the voluntary sector as a whole.

The Directory of Social Change
24 Stephenson Way
London
NW1 2DP

Federation House
Hope Street
Liverpool
L1 9BW

Publications and subscriptions
tel: 020 7209 5151
fax: 020 7391 4804

Publicity
tel: 020 7391 4900

Research
tel: 020 7391 4880
tel: 0151 708 0136

Courses and conferences
tel: 020 7209 4949
tel: 0151 708 0117

Charityfair
tel: 020 7209 4949
tel: 020 7209 1015 (exhibitors)

website: www.dsc.org.uk
e-mail: books@dsc.org.uk

Preface

Between the Chair and the SOFA

This book has its roots in two places.

First, it reflects my own experiences as a paid finance specialist and honorary treasurer based in the middle of medium-sized charities trying to apply best practice, comply with changing statute, satisfy my own curiosity and having to live with the consequences. It is the product of several strands of thought that I have pursued for many years, and on which my contemplation continues. How should you plan when so much of the future is uncertain? What is the value of using a budget that is out of date? How can trustees exhibit effective governance on financial matters? What is a finance strategy? It sounds impressive, but what actually is it? How can you empower individuals with financial responsibility without losing control? How can you get non-financial specialists to be comfortable with a balance sheet and a statement of financial activities (SOFA)? These are the sort of issues that I have grappled with, from the dual perspectives of Finance and Support Services Director of Sight Savers International and Honorary Treasurer of The Refugee Council, two charities exhibiting almost diametrically opposite characteristics. Sight Savers International, 75 per cent unrestricted funding each year, long-term stability, tried and tested methods of service delivery, uncontroversial cause; The Refugee Council, 80 per cent restricted funding, short-term agreements, long-term uncertainty, a recent history of huge changes in its service provision, highly political cause.

In 1998 Sight Savers International set out to design and implement an approach to financial management to tackle the dilemma of managing projects that require long-term funding security within an uncertain operating environment. Our traditional annual budgeting and variance reporting systems were ineffective and unpopular internally. Just as our ideas and concepts were crystalising I met the Beyond Budgeting Round Table (BBRT), a consortium of mainly large European commercial organisations funding research into performance management systems in the post-industrial age of uncertainty and discontinuous change. Increasingly the evidence of this research has suggested that traditional fixed plans and budgets are barriers to success. Sight Savers International prepared its last annual budget in 1999 and, in June 2000, became the first charity to join the BBRT. Sitting alongside some of the best known and most successful companies in Europe, its rolling financial management methodology has led Sight Savers International to be recognised within the consortium as one of the barrier breakers. The methodology outlined in Part 3 of the book describes the approach developed and implemented by the charity, the refinement of which has been strongly influenced by the thinking and experiences of fellow BBRT member organisations.

Second, this book has evolved from the appeals that are frequently made by trustees and senior managers for clarity and guidance on the apparently incomprehensible matter of charity finance, their discomfort with the subject exacerbated by the language of the accountant. As awareness of the financial responsibilities of charity leaders has increased, so has the urgency and frequency of such appeals. Inspired by my colleagues on the board at The Refugee Council, I have written this very much with the interests of trustees and senior managers in mind: those people who need to understand what critical matters have to be addressed if a charity is to be properly stewarded financially. *Financial Stewardship of Charities* is an attempt to get to the heart of what financial stewardship is about in charities in a language that is intelligible to those responsible for its discharge. It aims to provide a complete, yet straightforward, guide on how to use a charity's financial resources to maximum effect *despite* uncertainty.

• • • • •

Having served my accounting apprenticeship in the dog-eat-dog world of PLCs I have often marvelled since joining the charity sector in 1990 at the genuine willingness of those engaged within it to offer advice and support to each other. I have been the fortunate and grateful recipient of such guidance on many occasions and I offer this book in that spirit. I owe a great deal to many people within the sector, not least my dedicated colleagues at Sight Savers International and The Refugee Council, many of whose insights are implicit in this text. Both organisations make fantastic contributions to those they exist to serve. Let me acknowledge my deep gratitude within the sector to Ken Caldwell, Naaz Coker, Nick Hardwick, Melinda Letts, Dick Porter and Julia Unwin, each of whom have contributed significantly to my own development through their encouragement, challenge and leadership. Outside the sector, this is an opportunity to pay tribute to the work of Robin Fraser and Jeremy Hope, the research fellows of BBRT, and to their support of Sight Savers International as we endeavour to apply principles of which they can be proud. The experiences, ideas and support of fellow member organisations of the BBRT have also been immensely valuable and stimulating.

Whilst writing this book has been a very satisfying experience for me it has also placed demands on others without whom it could not have been completed. I am grateful to many friends and colleagues for their encouragement to keep going when progress felt slow and to my editor at the Directory of Social Change, Alison Baxter, for her advice and faith in the book. Dick Porter, Executive Director at Sight Savers International and Naaz Coker, Chair of The Refugee Council, both offered unqualified support for the book, and willingly consented to the organisations' material and experiences being shared with a wider audience. Myra Bennett, Barbara Frost, Andrew Hind, Mike Hudson, Richard Poffley, Kate Sayer and Julia Unwin voluntarily waded through drafts of the text and made invaluable suggestions whilst Jenny Crosskey provided essential administrative support. They must all take their share of any credit which the book may receive. Any errors and ambiguities that exist, however, are entirely my responsibility.

The biggest demands however have been placed on my wife Mariela and our young children Jonathan and Alison. They have all donated much precious time together to the book's cause and I dedicate it to them hopeful that the outcome justifies the considerable impositions it made. I also dedicate it to my parents and brothers, each of whom has given me a lifetime of love, support and, in their very different fields, inspiration.

Adrian Poffley, February 2002

Foreword

I have been looking forward to such a book as this for many years. Ever since I became involved in the charity sector many years ago, I have been looking for better ways of dealing with some of the issues that are fundamental to the proper management and governance of charities.

The whole of the accounting world has evolved to deal with the commercial world and the questions asked in the for-profit sector. These questions seem trivial and easy to answer when you move to the charity world. In business, the over-riding objective is to maximise shareholder value. Everything else comes back to this. In the charity world, the over-riding objective is for the charity to achieve its objectives. Sounds simple, but these are different for each charity and we find it difficult to measure whether the objectives have been met. The aspirations of charities are not easily translated into measures such as profit per share.

So this book comes as a massive encouragement, as we learn that charities really are trying to develop performance management models that will enable them to be responsive to the major challenges such as meeting their beneficiaries' needs and to make an impact. The models and approaches described are real and can be implemented. They move away from bureaucratic rigidity and towards a more intuitive management style. In keeping with this style, the approaches are flexible and you may wish to try some things and not others. You will know what will suit your charity best.

I look forward to discussing the approaches with other charities and to seeing others implementing aspects of the methods described in this book.

Kate Sayer, February 2002
Partner, Sayer Vincent, Accountants

Introduction

How should charities steward the financial resources at their disposal in order to maximise the impact they have over time, whilst operating in an environment of increasing uncertainty? This book offers a number of propositions.

- A charity's goal is to maximise the beneficial impact over time for those it exists to serve.
- Excellence in financial stewardship is essential if it is to do this. It has to be clear what it is trying to achieve financially if it is to succeed operationally.
- Such stewardship can only be exercised in the context of a corporate framework defining how the charity intends to act in furthering its objects.
- Maximising impact *over time* requires a charity to spend *and* save. Understanding when to do each, and managing the competing demands of the two is critical.
- The degree of uncertainty facing a charity is such that it must be organised to react and adapt. Detailed, overly prescriptive planning and control tools, including annual budgeting, must be replaced by much more nimble, informative systems.
- Good financial stewardship is not complicated; it is not the same as accountancy and is much nearer common sense than rocket science. Trustees and senior managers need to be competent financial stewards, and can be using only a few critical tools.

What is stewardship?

At its simplest, financial stewardship refers to the responsible use of financial resources. It has three components.

- A finance **strategy**, giving a clear sense of where the organisation is trying to get to financially and how it intends to get there.
- Good **management** processes, to enable those responsible for the charity's overall performance to execute that strategy.
- An appropriate internal **environment**, if those processes are to be managed effectively.

These three components are each dependent on the one beneath it (see Figure A). Successful strategy implementation, for example, depends on good management processes, which in turn require an appropriate environment. The process of financial stewardship is a series of cause and effect relationships: the environment provides the inputs, and the management processes transform those inputs into strategic outputs and outcomes. This book devotes one part to each of the three components in order to create, step by step, a financial stewardship 'map'. Key building blocks make up each component: finance strategy for example has four blocks (income, funds, assets and expenditure); environment has three (structure, capabilities and information systems), and a chapter is given to each 'block'. Key stewardship questions that need to be addressed are listed at the end of each chapter.

Part 1

Part 1 looks at strategy and starts with the question of what is meant by strategy and where it fits into the overall corporate management of organisations. Since finance is simply one of the resources used to deliver charitable impact, a key tenet of the book's core argument is that it is not possible to write or implement a sensible *finance* strategy without first having determined the organisation's *corporate* strategy. Chapter 1 therefore discusses what value a corporate strategy has, what should be included in one and what process might be used to develop one. It also challenges the extent to which detailed, accurate planning is possible. So many factors influence performance, and many of these are not only out of the control of the organisation but entirely unpredictable. For international organisations, for example, natural disasters, political and economic crises in the countries of operation occur with depressing frequency and yet are impossible to reflect accurately in operational or financial planning. The degree of uncertainty present in an organisation's operating environment emerges as being critical in determining an appropriate approach to corporate strategy, and thereby to financial stewardship. The variety of approaches available can be considered through a spectrum of increasing operational uncertainty, ranging from rational planning to chaos management, with proponents of the latter questioning the whole value of traditional strategic planning:

> 'It is impossible for managers to plan or envision the long-term future of an innovative organisation. Instead, they must create and discover an unfolding future, using their ability to learn together in groups and to interact politically in a spontaneous, self-organising manner.'[1]

[1] Stacey (1993) p.10.

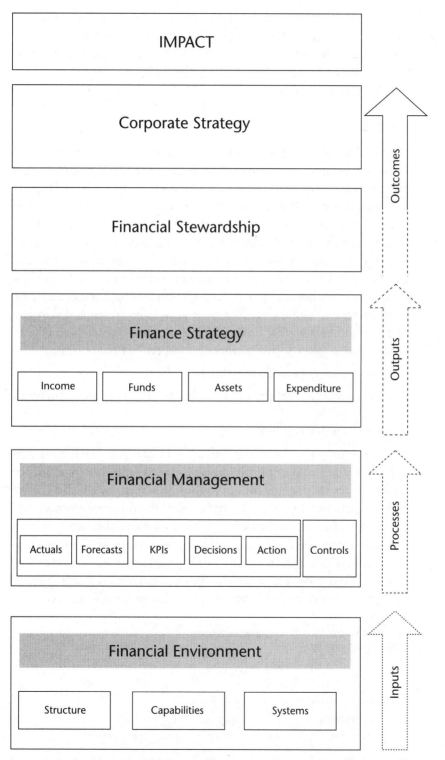

Figure A The financial stewardship map

The approaches to corporate strategy adopted by The Refugee Council and Sight Savers International are outlined in Chapter 2, each exhibiting some elements of the models of the previous chapter. Sight Savers International's adaptation of the Balanced Scorecard into a strategy map is described.

Part 2

Having discussed strategy and financial stewardship in the context of corporate strategy Part 2 moves onto finance strategy, beginning with a preliminary outline in Chapter 3 of what is meant by the term. What is a finance strategy? Few organisations have one, or at least an explicit one that is written and complete, and there is no consensus as to what a finance strategy should include. Charities do usually have a picture of what the financial position of the organisation will be at some point in the future, but it is often unclear whether that projection reflects what is expected or what is required. Expectation and requirement may be very different. In either case, the figures are seldom accompanied by any narrative to explain what financial steps the charity intends to take to achieve that result, which is a crucial ingredient of finance strategy.

A finance strategy must do two things:

1 it must explain *what* financial results the organisation is aiming to achieve and

2 *how* it intends to achieve them.

The three primary statements included in the Annual Report and Accounts of any charity provide a ready-made framework for a finance strategy, since they are the means, statutorily at least, by which a charity defines its financial results. The structure of the three statements – the statement of financial activities (SOFA), the balance sheet and the cash flow statement – defines the financial performance of charities from four perspectives: income, funds, assets (including cash) and expenditure (see Figure B). These are the four perspectives that any finance strategy must address and Chapters 4 to 7 devote thought to each.

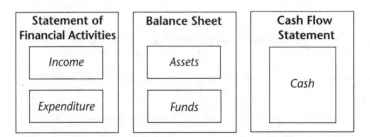

Figure B The structure of the primary statements

Part 3

Part 3 then considers what *processes* must be in place to deliver the outputs, and what activities the charity should be undertaking on a daily basis to deliver the objectives of the finance strategy. It focuses on two sets of processes:

1 the crucial decision-making processes by which the financial resources of the charity should be managed
2 the control processes that need to be in place.

At the heart of the argument is a detailed explanation of a financial management methodology appropriate for conditions of uncertainty. The principles and processes by which charities should make decisions about how they spend their funds within very uncertain operating environments are explained. The methodology follows a simple cycle of MONITOR–AIM–PLAN–ACT behaviour, and is designed to be lightweight but highly effective in guiding decision-makers' actions. Its philosophy is one of adaptability, of recognising that, whether planned or not, organisations have to respond to the circumstances they find themselves in as follows.

■ Understand where you are now.
■ Look ahead to see what is in front of you.
■ Decide where you want to get to.
■ Determine how you intend to get there.
■ Set off towards your intended direction.

This methodology promotes a rolling approach to resource management in place of conventional annual budgeting which tends to absorb a huge amount of time and energy and yet has considerable flaws as a resource management tool. To take an analogy, a pedestrian walks down a street with a destination in mind but still has to react to unexpected events. To have made laborious efforts to predict in detail what might arise on the journey would be a waste of time. So it is with financial management in conditions of uncertainty: an organisation needs to have a clear sense of where it is trying to get to, and how, but it cannot plan for the unknown. As a charity heads in the general direction intended, it must be ready to react to the unexpected and uncontrollable events (good and bad) that it finds in its path.

Chapters 9 to 13 outline the five stages of the continuous decision-making cycle that any organisation must follow.

Applying these steps to the task of managing a charity's funds builds a financial management process that is logical and effective. Part 3 guides the reader through the five stages, starting with determining what information to collect in order to understand the current financial position of the charity. The characteristics of successful management accounts, the foundation of any management information system, are described. The role of forecasts and the importance of understanding what financial commitments the charity already has is then explored. The concept of mapping future available resources against current commitments is introduced and the role of key performance indicators as the main yardsticks against which actual results are assessed is explained. Actual results, forecasts, commitments and key performance indicators combine to create a toolkit with which to make effective decisions on how to use the charity's funds.

A well-designed finance decision-making process gives a charity considerable management control over its finances. It is after all a performance management tool that should enable decision-makers to apply the resources at their disposal in an optimal way at the time the decision is made, and flag when that does not occur. This is the acid test for internal control processes: do they guide decision-makers to deploy resources to maximum effect in a secure way? It raises questions about what controls should be in place. The final chapter of Part 3 explores this subject in terms of risk management and internal audit, reflecting the recent attention to risk promoted by, amongst other things, the Statement of Recommended Practice, *Accounting and Reporting by Charities*, published in October 2000 (SORP 2000).

Understanding the financial risks that face the organisation, and what steps it is appropriate to take to manage, but not necessarily minimise, those risks is a key element of good financial stewardship. Yet it is one of those subjects that can envelop every aspect of the charity's work, and needs to be handled pragmatically. Similar comments apply to internal audit, a function that management should be able to use to give it independent verification of the adequacy of the systems and processes used by the charity, including the financial ones. In practice, the relationship between internal audit and management is rarely straightforward. Chapter 14 therefore explores what role internal audit can usefully play in controlling the risks of financial stewardship, how the relationship with management should be defined, and promotes the importance of internal audit etiquette to ensure that all parties know what to expect.

Part 4

If good financial stewardship is to be demonstrated, both a sound finance strategy and good financial management processes are necessary. But they are not sufficient. Nothing will happen without the tools provided by an appropriately designed and maintained environment within which strategy is implemented and management exercised. Part 4 therefore focuses on the prerequisites, or *inputs*, which must be in place if the financial management of the organisation is to be effective in delivering its strategic aims. The first input is that of organisational *structure*. Crucially this is about who does what. What should be the respective roles of trustees, the honorary treasurer, the finance director, finance specialists, and operational management in stewarding the finances of the charity? There are several important lines in the sand to be drawn between these players and Chapter 15 endeavours to do this.

Second comes the matter of *capabilities*. Even with the right structure the charity has to recruit and retain staff with the appropriate financial capability. This poses challenges for any charity's reward, performance management and professional development strategies, requiring it to compete in an open market place against employers in all sectors searching for the same skills, whilst honouring values as an organisation created for public, not private, benefit. Chapter 16 highlights the principles needed to underpin the reward strategy in order to manage the tension between market forces and internal values. Thirdly comes the question of *systems*. Effective and reliable finance systems underpin the whole stewardship model. But like any other system they need to be well designed, implemented, used, supported and reviewed. This systems management cycle is outlined in the final chapter.

A finance environment that is built around appropriate structures, capabilities and systems provides the foundations for excellence in financial stewardship. Management processes appropriate for conditions of uncertainty that are designed and maintained in this environment give the decision-makers the information needed to deliver the aims of the finance strategy. Thus the financial stewardship map is complete, providing a critical tool for successful implementation of corporate strategy, and thereby maximum beneficiary impact.

PART 1

CORPORATE STRATEGY

1 What is corporate strategy and how can it serve an organisation?

A corporate strategy is nothing more than a description of how an organisation intends to get to where it wants to be. There are, however, many definitions to choose from, each placing a distinct slant on what distinguishes strategy and its planning from other management activities and tools (see Box 1.1).

Does your organisation need to prepare a corporate strategy? The answer is unequivocally 'Yes!'. Whether it ends up being pulled together into a document called a strategic plan or not, high level thinking about the *raison d'être* of the organisation and how, in broad terms, it intends to meet its mandate, must be carried out periodically. Otherwise there will be no coherence or rationale to the activities undertaken.

1.1 Definitions of strategy

The essence of strategy is in the activities – choosing to perform activities differently or to perform different activities than rivals....

Strategy renders choices about what not to do as important as choices about what to do.
Source: Porter (1996) p.77 and p.64

A pattern of purposes, policies, programs, actions, decisions, or resource allocations that define what an organization is, what it does, and why it does it.
Source: Bryson (1995) p.32

Strategies are means not ends. Strategies are actions, they are what an organization *does*, not what it is *for*. The *sole* justification for a strategy is its effect on achieving the purpose or conduct.
Source: Argenti (1993) p.41

Strategy is one step in a logical continuum that moves an organization from a high-level mission statement to the work performed by frontline and back office employees.
Source: Kaplan and Norton (2001) p.72

What should a corporate strategy describe?

Reference to any business section of the library or bookshop would quickly confirm that there is a whole myriad of theories and models on offer to guide the budding strategist. There is no right way to do it and there is a real risk of trying to shoehorn the organisation and its unique circumstances into one particular theory. No two organisations' management systems look the same, nor does any system mirror perfectly any of the theoretical models expounded by the academics, consultants, advisers or theorists. In practice most organisations mix and match elements of different models, tailoring them to be effective in their particular environment.

Crucially, whatever strategy tools are used they must enable the organisation to:

- understand why it exists and how it intends to meet its purpose
- define what success looks like
- share that understanding with others – staff, supporters, donors, partners and beneficiaries
- monitor how the charity is getting on within a framework.

It does not matter what the corporate strategy looks like, nor how it is prepared, as long as its implementation enables the organisation to meet its purpose. The track record of organisations in implementing strategic plans may not be good according to some research.[1] However, to the extent that they do succeed, one could ask the question as to whether that is *in spite* of their strategic planning or *because* of it. Prior to engaging in the exercise of strategic planning, which can achieve much, but also prove to be a major distraction to the charity, it is worth being absolutely clear about the purpose of the exercise. Bryson (1995) very helpfully articulates the role that the process of strategic planning has in the future in this world of uncertainty and rapid change. Strategic planning he says is 'a disciplined effort to produce fundamental decisions and actions that shape and guide what an organization is, what it does, and why it does it' (Bryson, 1995 pp.4–5). If Bryson is right, by the end of a strategic planning process the charity should have:

- a clear sense of direction
- some defined organisational priorities

---

[1] Kaplan and Norton (2001) p.1 quote research placing strategy implementation failure rates at between 70–90%.

- an understanding of what it intends to do about the key issues facing it
- a sense of the internal and external environment in which the charity is operating
- clarity about responsibilities.

The benefits of strategic planning

Bryson (1995 p.7) defines four overriding benefits that should result from engaging in strategic planning.

1 The promotion of strategic thought and action which leads to clarification of the organisation's future direction and the establishment of organisational priorities for action.
2 Improved decision-making. Strategic planning focuses attention on the crucial issues and challenges an organisation faces, and it helps key decision-makers to plan how to cope with them.
3 Enhanced organisational responsiveness and improved performance, i.e. organisations engaging in strategic planning will be better placed to respond wisely to internal and external demands and pressures, and deal effectively with rapidly changing circumstances.
4 Effective fulfilment of roles and responsibilities by policy-makers and key decision-makers. Teamwork and expertise are likely to be strengthened.

Hind (1995 pp.85–6) highlights three benefits, amongst others, that should come from strategic planning.

1 A set of objectives, which provide focus for an organisation's activities and increase the commitment of the charity's donors, volunteers, staff and trustees.
2 A basis on which resource allocation decisions can be made, by prioritising the charity's proposed activities.
3 A benchmark against which progress can subsequently be measured, by clearly setting out the charity's objectives.

Where does strategic planning fit into the management cycle?

Kaplan and Norton offer a graphical presentation of where strategic planning fits into the management cycle, together with easy to remember definitions for the potentially confusing terms (see Figure 1a). A central theme to their approach – that strategic planning is not a

Source: Adapted from Kaplan and Norton (2001) p.73

Figure 1a Translating a mission into desired outcomes

single event but part of a continuous process – is particularly pertinent, and reflects the fact that strategic planning can be of greatest value in periods of operating uncertainty. Continual adaptation is now the name of the game.

To a lesser or greater extent all planning, including determining corporate strategies, can be described in some form of the basic performance management cycle (see Figure 1b). Goals are set to confirm what the organisation is trying to achieve in the context of where it is now; a plan of action is agreed that it is believed will achieve the goals; the plan is implemented; results are monitored and goals and plans are either revised or confirmed. There is a continuous process of looking ahead, establishing a destination and a plan of how to get there, setting off and monitoring progress, in the light of which goals or plans might need to be changed. The planning and control cycle that has been promoted for many years (Figure 1c) is a derivative of this.

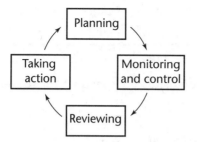

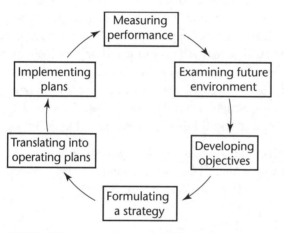

Figure 1b The basic performance management cycle

Source: Sizer (1985) p.22

Figure 1c The stages in a planning and control cycle

The process of developing a strategic plan

There are many sources of material available to the reader to guide their thinking about how to design and manage a strategic planning process. It can be helpful to try to determine where the organisation fits on an unpredictability spectrum since the type of strategic planning that would be most appropriate is crucially influenced by the extent to which the charity is looking forward in an environment of certainty or uncertainty. The more certain the organisation's future the more it can plan with confidence, adopting a rational, logical approach. The greater the uncertainties the more the plan, and the process by which it is written and agreed, must adopt flexible characteristics. The spectrum can be illustrated by reference to three types of strategic planning model: rational, political and chaotic.

Rational planning	Political decision-making	Chaos management

Increasing unpredictability

Figure 1d The unpredictability spectrum for strategic planning

The rational planning model

In this model, objectives are determined sequentially from goals, plans from objectives, and actions from plans. Goals are determined first, from which objectives are established over a defined period to meet those goals. With clear objectives in place plans are then written outlining how the objectives will be met. All very neat and tidy, and logical, but heavily dependent on there being consensus amongst the parties on each of these steps. In practice, the steps can be reiterative involving several refinements of thought before being agreed. This model reflects the basic planning and control model presented in Figure 1b.

Hind (1995 p.88) lays out a very logical, easy to follow, set of chronological steps by which to build a corporate strategy, which essentially follows the rational approach (see Figure 1e):

1 the vision
2 the direction or mission statement
3 environmental analysis leading to corporate strategies
4 financial policies leading to a financial plan
5 key tasks
6 specific actions.

The political decision-making model

Recognising that in most organisations there is not such consensus, Bryson (1995) promotes an alternative model – the 'political decision-making model'. This he describes as follows.

'It begins with issues, which by definition involve conflict, not consensus. The conflicts may be over ends, means, timing, location, political advantage, reasons for change, or philosophy, and the conflicts may be severe. As efforts proceed to resolve these issues, policies and programs emerge to address them that are politically rational; that is, they are politically acceptable to involved or affected parties. Over time, more general policies may be formulated to capture, frame, shape, guide, or interpret the policies and programs developed to deal with the issues. The various policies and programs

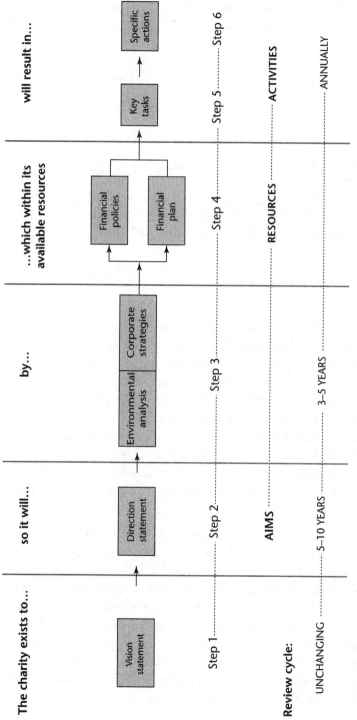

Source: Hind (1995) p.88

Figure 1e The six steps in charity strategic planning

are, in effect, treaties among the various stakeholder groups. And while they may not exactly record a consensus, at least they represent a reasonable level of agreement among stakeholders.' (p.11)

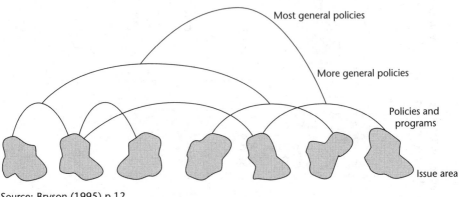

Source: Bryson (1995) p.12

Figure 1f Political decision-making model

The political dimension of planning in the not-for-profit organisation must be recognised head on. One of the sector's great strengths is the commitment of its employees, volunteers, supporters and other groups not only to their job but also to the cause. Stakeholders are precisely that: they have a stake in the outcome and very often their commitment is fuelled by deep-rooted ideology or conscience. With that commitment comes passion, intellect, but rarely consensus. Issues have to be put on the table and discussed. Bryson (1995) takes the reader through the ten steps in detail and includes many practical exercises that can be undertaken with the various stakeholders to complete each step (see Box 1.2).

Much of Bryson's book is spent detailing this ten-step strategic planning process – he calls it the Strategic Change Cycle – and it has much to commend it. It is in essence how Sight Savers International went about developing its Strategic Framework 2001–2003 and much of the work undertaken under the direction of Chief Executive Nick Hardwick at The Refugee Council mirrors Bryson's Strategic Change Cycle model closely. The Refugee Council undertook a very well structured, and participatory, approach to developing a strategic plan for the period 2001–2006 (see Chapter 2). Bryson (p.23) asserts that any not-for-profit organisation can follow this process if two conditions exist:

1 a majority of participants in the process support the process (Bryson calls it the 'dominant coalition') and

2 there is an individual willing and able to lead the organisation through it ('the process champion').

Hence step one of the ten – the 'planning to plan' stage. Most of the steps are self-explanatory from the descriptions in Box 1.2, but Step 2, 'identify organisational mandates', might not be. This simply refers to the need, early in the process, to identify what obligations the charity has, legal or informal, and to clearly understand what area is not legitimate territory for it to enter. Bryson (1995) makes a salutory observation in defence of this step:

'Most organizations make one or all of the following three fundamental mistakes. First, not knowing what they must do, they are unlikely to do it. Second, they may believe they are more tightly constrained in their actions than they actually are. Third, they may assume that if they are not explicitly told to do something, they are not allowed to do it.' (p.26)

One other question may stand out in considering the ten steps in Box 1.2, certainly when compared to the rational planning model. Why is 'establish an effective organisational vision' as late as step 8 of the ten-step process? Bryson has a very pragmatic answer. If the organisation is able to define a generally accepted vision of success earlier in the process then all well and good. Some organisations may indeed be able to kick off the whole process by agreeing its vision. Yet many others will not. This will only come when participants in the process have sorted out the

---

1.2 Bryson's ten-step strategic planning process

1 Initiate and agree on a strategic planning process
2 Identify organizational mandates
3 Clarify organizational mission and values
4 Assess the organization's external and internal environments to identify strengths, weaknesses, opportunities and threats
5 Identify the strategic issues facing the organization
6 Formulate strategies to manage these issues
7 Review and adopt the strategic plan or plans
8 Establish an effective organizational vision
9 Develop an effective implementation process
10 Reassess strategies and the strategic planning process

Source: Bryson (1995) p. 23

difference between what they want and what they can have. It may be, as a result, that the real value of an inspiring vision is not to help strategy *formulation* but its *implementation*. It is interesting to note that Kaplan and Norton (Figure 1a), Hind (Figure 1e) and Bryson (Box 1.2) each offer a different perspective on where mission and vision fit in the strategic planning processes. There is not even agreement about which precedes the other, thereby confirming, perhaps, that there are no hard and fast rules.

The chaos management model

There is a school of thought that goes further than Bryson's political decision-making model: that of chaos management. One of its strongest proponents is Professor Ralph Stacey of Hertfordshire University Business School. Stacey argues that management's task is to create unstable conditions from which learning will take place. Strategy emerges, in the Stacey model, spontaneously 'from the chaos of challenge and contradiction through a process of real time learning and politics' (Stacey, 1993 p.12). Stacey articulates a coherent case, arguing that there is plenty of evidence that the strategic change introduced by organisations reflects their reaction to the uncertainty that they faced (i.e. the learning they experienced) rather than the implementation of predetermined plans.

> 'As soon as we claim that we can envision and plan, that is, determine the long-term future of an organisation, we make the unquestioned assumption that there are identifiable links in organisational life, at least in principle, between a cause and an effect, between an action and an outcome. We could not possibly believe that a plan of action (for example, action A now, followed by action B next year and action C the year after) could lead to, say, a dominant market share, unless we were confident that there were causal links between an action now and a market share in five years' time. *It is no longer possible to avoid questioning that assumption about causality and when we do, we have to revise our views on how organisations develop strategically.*'

> 'The new frame of reference exposes much of the received wisdom on strategic management to be a fantasy defence against anxiety, and points instead to the essential role of managers, in creating the necessary unstable conditions required for that effective learning and political interaction from which new strategic directions may or may not emerge.' (Stacey, 1993 p.11)

The application of chaos theory to organisations may provide explanations for much of the behaviour of companies and the performance they achieve. There is certainly evidence to support one of the key ideas emerging from chaos theory – that small, apparently insignificant, actions can have major implications in an unpredictable way (see the Y2K compliance example in Box 1.3). All of us can probably recognise that the distinctions between, for example, competing products can be very small, but crucially affect our long-term preferences for one over the other. Why do we exhibit such strong brand loyalty? Poor service received once can lead to permanent disaffection with a company and its products and that is equally true of a charity. The more sophisticated fundraising charities have recognised the importance of lifetime value just as commercial organisations did some time ago. Such organisations appreciate very well that it is not the value of the individual transaction/donation that is key; it is the value of those transactions/donations over the lifetime of the relationship between the customer/donor and the supplier/charity. Considerable effort is now being devoted to develop better measures of fundraising return on investment than the inadequate 12-month cost-income ratios.[2] Long-term return on investment is what counts.

1.3 Emergent behaviour – the consequences of chaos theory

The discovery that an editorial system within a newspaper was not year 2000 compliant has led to the procurement of a new state-of-the-art commercial package for the editorial department. The procurement was not intended and went against established practice that all systems should be developed in-house for reasons based on costs. This unexpected procurement has resulted in a recognition that the nature of the editorial task can be changed significantly, changed motivation and orientation to jobs and a spreading dissatisfaction with the existing technology within other organisational functions whose shortcomings are highlighted when compared to the new system. Furthermore, changes in motivation are leading to changes in dress and attitude, according to the managing director. These changes are ongoing and may lead to even more significant changes on the business in the future. Thus a small technical event – the lack of year 2000 compliance – may lead through a trail of events to dramatic organisational changes: all amplified by feedback.

Source: McBride (1999) p.7

---

[2] See for example Aldrich (1999).

Stacey (1993) gives an illuminating insight into how organisations will have to behave if they are to succeed in the uncertain future. He summarises this by contrasting two frames of reference – the current and the new (see Figure 1g). The new frame challenges many of the deep-rooted conventions of how organisations should be run, particularly in value-driven, not-for-profit organisations that are stewarded on a culture of participation and reaching consensus. Are you sure you need a single shared vision throughout the organisation, Stacey asks? Is a strongly shared culture desirable? Isn't it better to steward the organisation on the basis of self-policing learning rather than management by objectives? But what would the chaos management approach to running organisations look like in practice? How does the Stacey model translate into action? What processes would be in place? Stacey (pp.16–17) offers an eight-step guide to help create the internal environment that will enable new strategic direction to emerge.

1 Develop new perspectives on the meaning of control by accepting learning as a form of control so that a sequence of actions will only continue in a particular direction while those espousing that direction continue to enjoy sufficient support.
2 Design the use of power to encourage open questioning and public testing of assertions rather than competitive win/lose solutions.
3 Encourage self-organising groups, avoiding the temptation to set objectives, terms of reference, or promoting a particular predetermined outcome.
4 Provoke multiple cultures by rotating people between functions or hiring experienced staff from other organisations.
5 Present ambiguous challenges instead of clear long-term objectives or visions so that the emotion and conflict needed to encourage an active search for new ways of doing things is provoked.
6 Expose the business to challenging situations rather than running for cover.
7 Devote explicit attention to improving group learning skills so that personal anxieties associated with uncomfortable learning experiences are overcome.
8 Create resource slack so that learning and political interaction have time to take place properly.

It is not necessary to subscribe wholesale to the chaos management model to appreciate the potential value that some of the processes listed above could bring an organisation. What is increasingly recognised in organisations in all sectors is that any strategic plan must be flexible so that unexpected circumstances (opportunities and obstacles) can be managed

Today's frame of reference	A new frame of reference
Long-term future is predictable to some extent	Long-term future is unknowable
Visions and plans are central to strategic management	Dynamic agendas of strategic issues are central to effective strategic management
Vision: single shared organisation-wide intention. A picture of a future state	Challenge: multiple aspirations, stretching and ambiguous. Arising out of current ill-structured and conflicting issues with long-term consequences
Strongly shared cultures	Contradictory counter cultures
Cohesive teams of managers operating in a state of consensus	Learning groups of managers, surfacing conflict, engaging in dialogue, publicly testing assertions
Decision-making as purely logical, analytical process	Decision-making as exploratory, experimental process based on intuition and reasoning by analogy
Long-term control and development as the monitoring of progress against plan milestones. Constraints provided by rules, systems and rational argument	Control and development in open-ended situations as a political process. Constraints provided by need to build and sustain support. Control as a self-policing learning
Strategy as the realisation of prior intent	Strategy as spontaneously emerging from the chaos of challenge and contradiction, through a process of real-time learning and politics
Top management drives and controls strategic direction	Top management creates favourable conditions for complex learning and politics
General mental models and prescriptions for many specific situations	New mental models required for each new strategic situation
Adaptive equilibrium with the environment	Non-equilibrium, creative interaction with the environment

Source: Stacey (1993) p.12

Figure 1g Changing the frame of reference for strategic management

appropriately at the time. The challenge is to design a corporate strategy with enough clarity of thought about the vision of the future, and how that vision will be turned into reality, to guide decision-making effectively rather than simply creating a strait jacket that forces inappropriate decisions or a document that is simply irrelevant. More and more, organisations are looking to adapt strategy continuously but within the context and with the guidance of some principles, beliefs or values that critically define the organisation, what it is about and what it stands for.

The presentation in this chapter of contrasting approaches to strategic planning aims to encourage the charity's stewards to think carefully and creatively about the best method of developing and implementing a corporate strategy in their organisation. The result, almost certainly, will be a composite of various theories and models. That is fine, if it maximises the impact achieved with the resources at the charity's disposal.

Key stewardship questions – corporate strategy

1 Does the charity have a corporate strategy outlining how it intends to meet its purpose in the next X years?
2 What role does the corporate strategy play in the overall management of the charity?
3 Is the type of corporate strategy the most appropriate one given the degree of uncertainty prevalent in the charity's operating environment?
4 What strategic planning process best serves the charity – rational, political or chaotic?

2 Case studies on strategic planning

The Refugee Council Strategic Plan 2001–2006

The following pages outline the process used by The Refugee Council to develop its Strategic Plan 2001–2006. Whilst it perhaps most closely resembles the political decision-making model (see page 16) it also has some characteristics of both rational and chaos management models. Key to an understanding of the process is recognition that the organisation is operating in a politically controversial arena (refugees and asylum seekers) and was writing the plan at a time of great change. The increasingly widespread migration of people worldwide and major legislative changes associated with asylum support in the UK are but two aspects of this change.

The development of The Refugee Council's Strategic Plan 2001–2006 followed a number of clear stages.

1 Trustees and senior staff determined the purpose, core beliefs, initial strategic directions that the organisation should follow at a two-day workshop. These were presented graphically (see Figure 2a) in a format that became a powerful communication tool with the *raison d'être*, values and intended directions giving a corporate perspective on one page.

2 These were shared and debated at a staff conference before a project group (of staff and trustees) then carried out a detailed assessment of the Council's strategic position and the main strategic choices that it faced.

3 External stakeholder analysis was completed, out of which a number of common themes emerged; all were issues that needed to be resolved in order to move forward.

4 An assessment was made of the organisation's strategic fit, of its internal capacity to meet the challenges of the future.

5 Recognising the volatility of the environment in which it operates, the Council developed four possible scenarios for what the future might hold. As the consultation document used in the process stated 'the point of this exercise is not to predict the future but to ensure

PURPOSE

The Refugee Council gives practical help and promotes refugees' rights in Britain and abroad.

Our objective is to ensure refugees' rights are respected and they have access to safety, dignity, the means to live and the opportunity to reach their full potential.

We apply this to:
- The international human rights framework
- Causes of flight to Britain
- The journey and arrival
- The asylum determination process
- Support for asylum seekers
- Settlement and return

We achieve our objectives by:
- Providing direct services to individual refugees and asylum seekers
- Supporting other agencies who provide services for refugees
- Providing information about refugees
- Influencing the policies of government and other organisations that affect refugees

Our priorities are:
- Refugees and asylum seekers in Britain
- Actual and potential refugees in their main countries of origin

BELIEFS

- A commitment to Human Rights and that asylum is a fundamental human right
- Valuing diversity: staff, users, refugee community organisations, sector
- Impartiality: non-partisan, boundaries, transparency, confidentiality
- Integrity: finance, information, advocacy
- Making a difference: direct and indirect services, quality, advocacy, relations with Government

STRATEGIC DIRECTIONS

1 Become a truly national organisation:
- Direct and indirect services
- Campaigning
- Members and supporters

2 Develop a thriving and diverse refugee voluntary sector with Refugee Community Organisations at its heart

3 Provide and develop high quality direct services where The Refugee Council can provide:
- Services to meet a national need, or
- Economies of scale and temporarily fill gaps which complement the services of smaller organisations or
- Specialist expertise, and
- Influence on relevant policies and legislation

4 Maintain the UK's commitment to the Geneva Convention on Refugees and extend our influence in Britain, Europe, and internationally

5 Extend support to other organisations with effectively marketed second tier services

6 Strengthen our financial position through investment in fundraising, increasing our trading income, diversifying our funding and building our reserves

7 Be a model of good practice in the voluntary sector in developing staff and volunteers

8 Strengthen internal and external communication with IT

Source: Adapted from The Refugee Council (2001)

Figure 2a The Refugee Council purpose, beliefs and strategic directions 2001–2006

that our plans are robust enough to cope with the range of scenarios.'[1] The scenarios were assessed both in terms of external drivers (using the PEST categories – political, economic, social and technical) and in terms of impact (such as on refugee numbers and public attitudes). Simple bullet point predictions under the scenarios were documented.

6 A Gap Analysis was undertaken, giving an initial identification of gaps in provision to refugees and asylum seekers not fully met by the services of the Council or other providers for each of the main groups with whom the charity works.

7 All the information garnered from the above stages of the process were then summarised into an advanced Strengths/Weaknesses/Opportunities/Threats (SWOT) analysis.

8 Out of the SWOT analysis emerged six key questions facing the Council (see Box 2.1). The trustees met for a day-long facilitated session to consider, in depth and with consideration for the values and *raison d'être* of the charity, what answers it would give to each question.

9 The analysis of the Council's strategic position, its choices, and the summary of purpose, beliefs and strategic directions, then formed the framework on which the more detailed, and shorter-term planning was done. Each key task of the plan linked directly back to one of the strategic directions (see Figure 2b for an example). A draft strategy was drawn up in light of these decisions and was the subject of further detailed external and internal consultation. A final version of the strategy was agreed at the meeting of the Board of Trustees in November 2000 and subsequently distributed to all relevant parties.

---

[1] Refugee Council Consultation Document.

2.1 The Refugee Council's strategic choices

1 **Should The Refugee Council develop new services to meet unmet needs?**
The Council will establish criteria for the development of new services that reflect both where we can make the most effective contribution and the objective of strengthening the refugee sector as a whole. Within these criteria the Council will seek to consolidate its direct services in London and develop its capacity in the regions whilst retaining its ability to respond to sudden changes in its environment.

2 **Should we develop our existing policy of devolving/sub-contracting some of our existing activities (where funding arrangements allow) to other organisations?**
Where appropriate and in the light of evaluation of current initiatives, The Refugee Council will seek to maximise the funding and support available to the sector by developing new partnerships and subcontracting relationships with its refugee sector partners.

3 **What should the priorities be for the use of our unrestricted income?**
The Refugee Council defines itself as 'a service delivery organisation that campaigns' rather than 'a campaigning organisation that also delivers services'. Within that context we will prioritise funding for activity to influence the climate of public and political opinion in which we work. We will also seek to make a modest contribution to our reserves each year until they reach best practice levels as described in our reserves policy.

4 **How centralised/decentralised should the organisation be?**
We will ensure that our internal structures reflect the development of our activity in the regions. We will develop new relationships with Regional and National Refugee Councils to ensure this activity remains accountable and appropriate.

5 **Should we develop an effective individual supporter base?**
We will not become a 'mass membership' organisation. However, we will harness the substantial support there is for refugees and asylum seekers by piloting and then rolling out as appropriate the development of a large, effective, national individual supporter base. We will work to develop a more productive relationship with our members.

6 **Should we extend the remit of The Refugee Council to include all forced migrants?**
We will maintain the focus of The Refugee Council on refugees and asylum seekers. We will not extend our remit to cover other sorts of migrants. However, we will retain the flexibility to address other migration issues where they impact on our core concerns.

Source: Adapted from The Refugee Council (2001) pp.13–15

Strategic direction	Objectives	Key tasks	Year 1	Year 2–3	Year 4–5
7 Be a model of good practice in the voluntary sector in developing staff and volunteers	7.1 Staff training, development and reward sufficient to recruit and retain staff to meet the needs of the organisation	1 Agree and implement HR strategy	●	●	●
		2 Define and maintain an appropriate organisational 'culture'		●	●
		3 Increase proportion of staff costs allocated to training and development each year.	●	●	●
		4 Implement staff supervision and appraisal policies	●		
		5 Salary and job evaluation review			●
	7.2 Diversity reflected in all parts of the organisation	1 Diversity targets set and met	●	●	●
		2 Review recruitment policy		●	
		3 Implement staff audit		●	●
		4 Review flexible working policies		●	●

Source: The Refugee Council

Figure 2b Extract from The Refugee Council Annual Plan 2001

Sight Savers International Strategic Framework 2001–2003

Historically strategic plans have been weighty tomes, laying out in great detail what an organisation intends to happen over a period of, typically, three to five years. However, often after the great effort to produce such a plan and the collective sigh of relief that greets its completion the organisation gets back to work, stopping only to refer to the plan in order to meet pre-arranged reporting deadlines. In fact, the very articulation in a quantifiable form of what the organisation aims to look like by the end of the plan period can become a millstone round the authors' necks rather than an inspiration. In hindsight, the plan can appear to have hardly influenced future actions.

In 1997–1998, under the very able stewardship of its Chief Executive, Melinda Letts, the National Asthma Campaign (NAC) wrote a different kind of strategic plan. Actually it wasn't a *plan*; it was a strategic *framework* providing a context within which shorter-term plans and actions could be determined. It was readable, honest and inspiring. That same approach greatly influenced Sight Savers International, which during 2000 prepared a framework document, based on the NAC model, looking forward three years. The Sight Savers Framework includes a number of core components.

- A vision statement – an inspirational, easy to remember statement of what the world could look like.
- A mission statement – a statement of how the charity intends to contribute to the advancement towards the vision (see Box 2.2)
- A statement of values – those values that underpin all the work of the charity and guide its decision-makers.
- Key strategic themes that the charity needs to focus on during the defined period.
- Some measures by which the work of the charity can be assessed.

There is no doubt that the Framework is a crucial document for Sight Savers International.

- Its preparation has forced the organisation's decision-makers to reflect on the very issues Bryson's definition of strategic planning highlights (see page 12), and to look afresh and reaffirm or redefine what contribution – indeed *unique* contribution – the organisation can make. In the Framework the charity sets out not only its vision and mission but also its distinct features: those characteristics of the organisation that distinguish it from others working in the same

2.2 Sight Savers International's Mission

Sight Savers International is dedicated to combating blindness in developing countries, primarily in the Commonwealth, by working with partner organisations in poor and the least served communities to support on-going activities that prevent and cure blindness, restore sight, and provide services to blind people.

The distinctive features of SSI's mission are:

- The development of comprehensive eye care services amongst the target populations where we work. This is SSI's core model and is based on an integrated approach, which combines prevention, treatment and services to blind people. It provides a continuum of care to people with preventable, curable and non-curable eye conditions.
- The commitment to establishing sustainable programmes, which will continue to serve communities as SSI reduces its support. This involves helping our partners develop their capacity in whatever respect necessary to become viable, independent organisations and integrating services into the local communities.
- Our focus on Commonwealth countries.

Source: Sight Savers International (2001a)

field. This not only helps guide decision-making but also acts as a powerful communication tool with potential donors and supporters.

- The charity has articulated its values, those inviolable principles that underpin everything it does. Strategies, plans, tactics, activities, decisions: all have to be consistent with those values.
- The Framework has described in narrative form ten strategic themes, which will guide Sight Savers International's thinking over the next three years (see Box 2.3). The themes are not prescriptive but, rather, indicative of what work the charity will focus on. Each theme – to which typically 500 words, no more, are devoted – is described in terms of the broad rationale for its inclusion, the type of strategic activities that will support it, and the type of performance indicators that will be used to measure progress. The themes do not specify what work will be completed, for example, year by year, country by country or project by project. However, all activities are expected to be consistent with, and support progress in relation to, one or more of the themes.

2.3 Sight Savers International's ten strategic themes

SSI will:

1 continue to direct its support to poor and under-served communities
2 further the aims of Vision 2020[1] by tackling the disease priorities and by increasing support to all levels of human resource development
3 continue to support integrated and community-based models in eye care, promoting eye health, preventing blindness, and working with blind and visually impaired people
4 seek to ensure that communities receiving services are involved in their design, delivery and evaluation
5 continue to work with its partners to deliver services and build their capacity to ensure that those services can be maintained in the long term
6 seek to influence the policies and practices of people, organisations and institutions to prevent and cure blindness, both in the UK and in countries where we work
7 continue to seek a higher profile for the charity and raise awareness of the issue of avoidable blindness, both in the UK and in countries where we work
8 continue to generate additional funds so that the quantity and quality of programme activity can be systematically increased over the next three years
9 aim to improve continually its effectiveness by ensuring that its decisions are informed by what it learns from its own and others' experience and other knowledge and by sharing such expertise using high-quality information management practices
10 continue to develop, promote and support internal structures and processes that enable the charity to maximise its impact on delivering its mission.

Source: Sight Savers International (2001a)

- Sight Savers International has asserted that the Framework will help guide the determination of appropriate strategies and initiatives, (i.e. those that are consistent with the organisation's values and contribute to the advancement of the themes over the three-year period), rather than serve as the blueprint of a pre-determined three-year plan. It becomes a constant reference document for the decision-makers, continually reinforcing what the charity is about and what it is not about.

---

[1] A global initiative to eliminate avoidable blindness by the year 2020 run under the auspices of The World Health Organisation (WHO) and the International Agency for the Prevention of Blindness (IAPB).

■ The Framework is not a 'plan'. It offers guiding parameters, not pre-determined prescriptions of what will be done, and has been a flagship from which to lead a major change in organisational culture. A new style of planning has been introduced based on continual reaction and adaptation within the constraints and stimulus of the Framework. This has extended into the financial planning conducted internally, the process of which will be outlined in Part 3.

Sight Savers International's business context

The precision with which an organisation can anticipate how it will meet its beneficiaries' needs is a crucial factor in determining what strategy is adopted. The more a charity knows about what its beneficiaries and donors want the more it can concentrate on meeting those needs more effectively. The strategy becomes one of maximising the efficiency of what in industrial terms would be the make and sell model, i.e. the organisation makes product and then sells it to a customer, in each case as efficiently as possible (Haeckel, 1999). Sight Savers International is essentially offering a make and sell model with regard to its service delivery. Its product, an increasingly well-honed model of community-based health, has been developed over a long period, has a successful track record, and a reliable future demand. The latter stems from the overwhelming need of its beneficiaries, far greater than the charity and other international and local organisations in the same field can meet. In these circumstances the strategy has to be one of meeting the entirely predictable beneficiary needs with solutions that are known to work increasingly effectively.

The greater the unpredictability of the needs of beneficiaries and donors the more a charity's strategy must reflect a 'sense and respond' model, obliging the organisation concerned to develop systems capable of responding quickly to changing beneficiary requirements. In many cases the customer requirements may well be fairly predictable (long-term development for example is precisely that – long term). However, the needs and requirements of donors are likely to be far less predictable. As Figure 2c shows the reality may be that within the charity there are two business operations, fundraising and service delivery, that have very distinct characteristics.

In Sight Savers International's case, on the service delivery side, the needs of beneficiaries are predictable: the world's major eye diseases are well-known and unlikely to change quickly. The solutions that will prevent and cure eye disease are tried and tested: they have been developed and

Characteristic	Service delivery	Fundraising
Customer needs (beneficiary/donor)	Predictable	Unpredictable
Products	Tried and tested. Stable, incremental change	New products. Innovative, rapid change
Market lead time	Long	Short
External relationships	Collaborative	Competitive

Figure 2c Sight Savers International's business context

refined over many years and are known to work. The lead-time to bring a new product onto market to replace existing products, to reach new beneficiaries or to develop new relationships with partners is lengthy. And far from being in a competitive environment with other eye care providers, Sight Savers International participates in highly collaborative relationships with those providers to ensure that resources are spread to reach as many beneficiaries as possible and to design best practice models of service delivery that are replicable.

Contrast this service-delivery environment with the charity's fundraising environment. The needs of the donor are relatively unpredictable and, as a result, estimating future income levels can be difficult. New, innovative ways to attract and retain donor support have to be tried continuously if the symptoms of donor fatigue are not to be exhibited. The fundraising environment operates with very short lead-times, requiring the charity to be opportunistic, reacting quickly to unexpected circumstances. And the fundraising market place is certainly competitive, with charities competing for the attention, sympathy, loyalty and money of statutory, corporate and individual donors.

However, the changing world of service provision, of the contract culture, may well mean that the charity is obliged, by donor requirements rather than beneficiary needs, to offer significantly different services to those provided not so long ago. The Refugee Council, sudden recipients of a Home Office request to run a major element of the new Asylum Support Programme in 2000, with an accompanying grant totalling several million pounds, is a case in point. Many not-for-profit organisations grapple with the question of who is really the customer: is it the donor or is it the beneficiary of the services, a judgement that Kaplan and Norton (2001) call 'Solomon–like'.[2]

---

[2] Kaplan and Norton (2001) p.135.

Sight Savers International's Balanced Scorecard and strategy map

Kaplan and Norton's Balanced Scorecard has received much publicity and plaudits since its introduction in 1995 and not without foundation. Many commercial organisations can demonstrate impressive performance improvements following the introduction of a Balanced Scorecard approach to business management. Initially introduced as a means to ensure that the performance measurements of an organisation focused executive attention not only on financial measures but also non-financial ones, the Scorecard is now promoted as a tool for managing strategy (see Box 2.4).

2.4 The Balanced Scorecard

The Balanced Scorecard (BSC) translates an organization's mission and strategy into a comprehensive set of performance measures that provides the framework for a strategic measurement and management system. The scorecard measures organizational performance across four balanced perspectives: financial, customers, internal business processes, and learning and growth. The BSC enables companies to track financial results while simultaneously monitoring progress in building the capabilities and acquiring the intangible assets they need for future growth.

The BSC is not merely a collection of financial and non-financial measurements. The scorecard should be the translation of the business' strategy into a linked set of measures that define both the long-term strategic objectives, as well as the mechanisms for achieving those objectives.

Source: Kaplan and Norton (1996) p.2 and p.32

Since developing the scorecard concept Kaplan and Norton have analysed the patterns of companies' scorecards, and mapped them on a framework that they call a strategy map (see Box 2.5).

2.5 The strategy map

A strategy map for a Balanced Scorecard makes explicit the strategy's hypotheses. Each measure of a Balanced Scorecard becomes embedded in a chain of cause-and-effect logic that connects the desired outcomes from the strategy with the drivers that will lead to the strategic outcomes.

Source: Kaplan and Norton (2001) p.69

The power of the strategy map is twofold. First, by presenting the critical initiatives of a strategy in relation to the mission of the organisation *graphically* on one sheet of paper, the map offers a method of communicating and describing strategy in a digestible form to all employees and supporters. However well written that is unlikely to be true of a narrative- or figure-dominated document. Even the Sight Savers International Strategic Framework 2001–2003 extends to 16 pages, and requires some effort to digest. Secondly, the map requires the assumed cause-and-effects of the various initiatives to be defined. Crucially, this enables the links between the initiatives to be understood and offers the scope for every employee or volunteer to understand where and how their contribution fits into the delivery of charitable purpose. The chaos management theorists (see page 20) would perhaps challenge the degree to which the cause-and-effect of initiatives can be predicted and Kaplan and Norton recognise this by acknowledging that strategy is a *hypothesis* of cause-and-effect, which should be constantly refined in the light of experiences and new ideas.

'The key for implementing strategy is to have everyone in the organization clearly understand the underlying hypotheses, to align resources with the hypotheses, to test the hypotheses continually, and to adapt as required in real time.' (Kaplan and Norton, 2001 p.76)

Slowly the Scorecard is being applied to the not-for-profit sectors and being adapted for use in government departments, in other public sector bodies and in voluntary organisations. As Kaplan and Norton (2001 ch.5) themselves acknowledge, adapting a model that was written with commercial organisations in mind does require some careful thought. The financial drivers that underpin the Scorecard for the private sector do not similarly influence charities. However, increasingly there are examples, especially in the US, where voluntary organisations have developed a Balanced Scorecard and mapped it successfully.

In searching for a means of communicating strategy and forcing the charity to articulate its hypotheses about what initiatives would best enable purpose to be met, Sight Savers International translated its Strategic Framework 2001–2003 onto a Strategy Map. This is reproduced in Figure 2d. The Map represents the intended strategy of Sight Savers International from differing perspectives, outlining how the organisation must look in each case if it is to succeed in delivering mission. As with Kaplan and Norton's generic architecture it is designed with a top-down logic. The order reflects cause and effect but not importance.

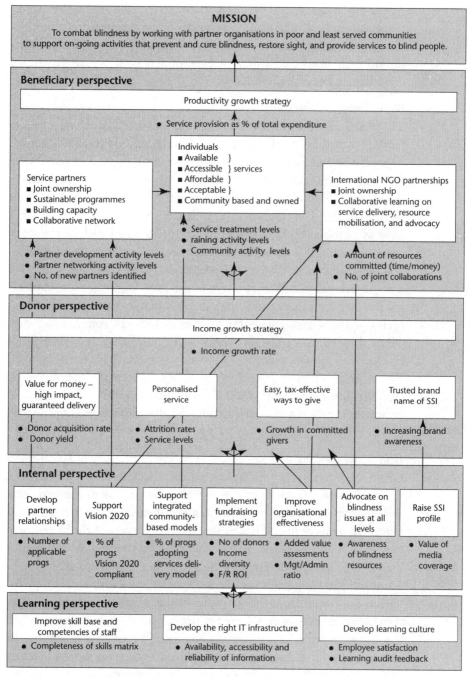

MISSION

To combat blindness by working with partner organisations in poor and least served communities to support on-going activities that prevent and cure blindness, restore sight, and provide services to blind people.

Beneficiary perspective

Productivity growth strategy

- Service provision as % of total expenditure

Individuals
- Available }
- Accessible } services
- Affordable }
- Acceptable }
- Community based and owned

Service partners
- Joint ownership
- Sustainable programmes
- Building capacity
- Collaborative network

International NGO partnerships
- Joint ownership
- Collaborative learning on service delivery, resource mobilisation, and advocacy

- Service treatment levels
- raining activity levels
- Community activity levels

- Partner development activity levels
- Partner networking activity levels
- No. of new partners identified

- Amount of resources committed (time/money)
- No. of joint collaborations

Donor perspective

Income growth strategy

- Income growth rate

Value for money – high impact, guaranteed delivery

Personalised service

Easy, tax-effective ways to give

Trusted brand name of SSI

- Donor acquisition rate
- Donor yield

- Attrition rates
- Service levels

- Growth in committed givers

- Increasing brand awareness

Internal perspective

Develop partner relationships	Support Vision 2020	Support integrated community-based models	Implement fundraising strategies	Improve organisational effectiveness	Advocate on blindness issues at all levels	Raise SSI profile
• Number of applicable progs	• % of progs Vision 2020 compliant	• % of progs adopting services delivery model	• No of donors • Income diversity • F/R ROI	• Added value assessments • Mgt/Admin ratio	• Awareness of blindness resources	• Value of media coverage

Learning perspective

Improve skill base and competencies of staff	Develop the right IT infrastructure	Develop learning culture
• Completeness of skills matrix	• Availability, accessibility and reliability of information	• Employee satisfaction • Learning audit feedback

Source: Sight Savers International

Figure 2d Sight Savers International Strategy Map 2001–2003

37

At the top of the Map is the mission, the overriding aim of the organisation, towards which all the objectives and initiatives are ultimately directed. Since the charity exists to serve beneficiaries, how the charity should look from a *beneficiary perspective* if it is to succeed is shown immediately beneath the mission.

Beneficiary perspective

The beneficiary perspective identifies the individuals receiving eye care services as the key beneficiary group of the charity's work, but acknowledges the importance of two other beneficiary groups: service partners (through whom services are provided) and international NGO partnerships (with whom the global strategy of eye care service delivery is co-ordinated). The characteristics that Sight Savers International's work is expected to have from the point of view of each of the three groups is defined. Individual beneficiaries, for example, want services that are available, accessible, affordable, and acceptable and which are community-based and owned. Amongst other things service partners are looking for programmes that are sustainable, whilst international NGO partners want collaborative relationships not competitive ones. All of these aims are sought within an overall beneficiary strategy of productivity growth over the next three years; the charity expects to be able to increase its impact through an increase in the quantity and, crucially, the *quality* of its work. For each beneficiary, key performance indicators are shown, identifying how the charity will measure whether it is meeting their needs.

Donor perspective

Given the intended beneficiary outcomes, the Map next outlines how the charity must look from a *donor perspective* if it is to succeed. The donor perspective answers the question of how the charity must be perceived by its donors if it is to support the delivery of the beneficiary demands. It addresses the issue of the value proposition 'which defines how the company differentiates itself to attract, retain and deepen relationships with targeted customers' (Kaplan and Norton, 2001 p.76). This it does in terms of the attributes of the products and services that the charity offers donors, the type of relationship it seeks to develop and the image it wants to promote. The strategy promotes a number of propositions. First, that donors are looking for value for money in terms of having confidence that their funds will reach the intended destination and have the desired high impact when they get there. Secondly, that donors are looking for a personalised service, where the charity tailors its interaction with the donor to reflect the latter's individual wishes (in terms, for example, of the frequency and type of communication that they would like to receive from the charity). Understanding this from the donor's point of view is critical in determining what sort of service the charity will offer and how it will organise itself to deliver it. Thirdly, the donor wants easy-to-administer, tax-effective ways to give to the charity.

Finally, the perspective acknowledges the importance of developing and promoting the charity brand name, recognising the importance to donors of being confident that their funds are placed in the hands of a trustworthy, professional and highly effective organisation. The logic of the Map defines these donor requirements within an income growth strategy for the next three years. It is through the provision of fundraising products that meet defined requirements of the donors that the charity intends to generate the growing income stream that will be needed to finance the increased growth and productivity of services to beneficiaries.

Internal perspective

Whilst the first two perspectives identify the major outcomes to be sought by the strategy, the remaining two describe how it is intended that these are achieved. The *internal perspective* highlights those activities that are critical to the delivery of the value proposition that the donors are looking for, and the services and relationships that the beneficiaries wish to have. Seven strategic initiatives are shown, all of which are included in the ten strategic themes (see Box 2.3, page 32) included in the Strategic Framework. These are the corporate processes that the management must focus its attention on.

Learning perspective

The *learning perspective* descibes the key competencies, technologies and internal culture/climate that will support the implementation of the strategic initiatives of the internal perspective. From this, attention and resource gets applied to developing and implementing a comprehensive professional development programme for staff, to investing in IT infrastructure, and to creating a learning culture whereby future policy and practice is driven by best practice knowledge and experience. Without these learning strategies, the ultimate mission will flounder.

Cause-and-effect relationships

The arrows on the Map indicate the key cause-and-effect relationships in the strategy. Whilst the logic is designed top-down, the cause and effect works bottom-up.

General remarks: on implementing strategy

Whatever process is used for developing a corporate strategy, and however that strategy is ultimately presented, it will have no value if it does not guide the day-to-day implementation of activities in pursuit of furthering the mission. The agreement and articulation of a strategy is just the start of the process of managing the organisation rather than the completion of a discrete piece of work.

The strategy must be at the heart of senior management and trustee agendas. They must keep their eyes on the big picture and focus on what the organisation's mission is, how well the organisation is doing in delivering mission, and what strategic decisions need to be taken. The typical agenda however is considerably more operational than this. Kaplan and Norton (2001) quote research suggesting that 85 per cent of management teams spend less than one hour a month discussing strategy.[3] The organisation has to find a way to allow the senior management and trustees to devote the necessary time to thinking strategy, and it may be necessary to take specific action to ensure that this happens (see Box 2.6 for example). Stewardship of the corporate direction requires careful consideration of the big strategic issues facing the charity. It requires a team of individuals who are comfortable thinking big pictures, challenging each other, disagreeing, and assuming collective responsibility for the decisions made. Determining who should attend such a forum is not, however, straightforward. As

---

2.6 Sight Savers International's Strategic Management Forum

At Sight Savers International we concluded that the normal Senior Management Team (SMT) meeting of the directors was not an adequate place to oversee the Strategic Framework in terms both of who was at the meeting or the style and format of that tightly agended, minuted meeting. We established a Strategic Management Forum with an explicit remit and a wider membership than the SMT. Its terms of reference are to determine and monitor the implementation of activities in the context of the Strategic Framework. Its composition includes not only the four directors but also other members of staff whose perspective or expertise was felt to add significant value to the ability of the SMT to steward the organisation appropriately within the Framework.

---

[3] Kaplan and Norton p. 13.

Hudson (1999 p.211) notes 'everyone wants a seat at the top table'. Those who are not invited to participate have to understand why, and be offered other channels through which to influence corporate action.

Everyone in the organisation needs to understand the strategy and how their contribution fits into it. The internal communication of corporate strategy needs to be explicitly addressed rather than assuming that this will be achieved through the line management cascade process, particularly if major corporate change is being sought. Personal and team objectives, plans and performance measures must fully complement the corporate strategy. The sum of these sub-plans must equal the corporate total: between them the sub-plans must deliver the corporate whole. Again, this is where a graphic representation of the corporate plan can help, reducing the risk that the interaction of the strategic initiatives is not understood or that a key area of activity is overlooked.

Key stewardship questions – case studies

1 What strategic planning lessons can be learnt from the experiences of The Refugee Council and Sight Savers International?
2 What directions or themes should be at the heart of the strategy, and what values should underpin it?
3 Could tools such as the Balanced Scorecard and strategy mapping help design, communicate and monitor implementation of the strategy?
4 How can trustees and senior managers best steward the implementation of the strategy?

PART 2

FINANCE STRATEGY

3 The purpose and components of a finance strategy

If strategic planning is about producing 'fundamental decisions and actions that shape and guide what an organization is, what it does, and why it does it' (Bryson, 1995 p.4–5), what is the purpose of finance strategy? What are its key components? What questions need to be answered? Whilst there is a very well defined set of guidelines and regulations for how an organisation should report its financial position *historically*, such as the Statement of Recommended Practice (SORP) *Accounting and Reporting by Charities*, there are no such guidelines about how it should lay out its financial *intentions*. The answer is that there is no best practice in terms of describing a finance strategy, and most charities have not written one.[1]

Defining the finance strategy

The purpose of a finance strategy must be to define how the organisation intends to get to the financial position it believes it should be in if it is succeeding in meeting its mission. There are three prerequisites for the successful definition of a finance strategy.

1 The organisation must have a mission and a corporate strategy describing how it intends to deliver that mission.
2 There must be an understanding about what the financial picture – as expressed in statements such as the statement of financial activities (SOFA), balance sheet and cash flow – would look like if the charity were delivering the mission optimally.
3 There must be an understanding about how the charity intends to get from its current financial position to the ideal one.

---

[1] At a presentation on finance strategy by the author at the Charity Accountants' Conference in September 2001 only about 5% of the audience of 70 admitted to having a written finance strategy.

The finance strategy should describe how the organisation intends to get from its *current* financial performance and position to its *intended* performance and position (see Figure 3a).

Figure 3a The dynamic of finance strategy

The financial position at a particular date is described by the balance sheet: it is a snapshot *in* time. Performance, which is achieved *over* time, is reflected in both the SOFA and the cash flow statement. They describe how the balance sheet position has been reached and are therefore an historical record that can no longer be influenced. By contrast, the balance sheet is still 'live', defining the financial resources that still have to be stewarded as at the date at which the statement is prepared.

The role of financial stewardship

Financial stewardship is about managing the financial resources at the disposal of the charity and these are defined on the balance sheet. The distinction between financial *performance* and *position* highlights the continual need for the charity to manage two principal, competing, demands on its financial resources – spending them to meet charitable purpose today versus investing or retaining them in order to be able to meet purpose in the future. The steward's finance strategy must explain how the charity intends to manage its financial resources optimally so that it both maximises its impact today whilst maintaining the organisation as a going concern, so that it can have impact tomorrow. The aim is to maximise impact *over time* not just today. Ultimately this simplifies the key decision of the financial steward – what should be done with the financial resources at their disposal – down to one of four choices (see Figure 3b).

1 Should the resources be spent on activities (including grant giving) in furtherance of the charity's objects?

2 Should they be spent on the management and administration of the charity?

3 Should they be devoted to activities to generate future income (i.e. fundraising activities)?

4 Should they be retained, for use at a later date, so as to maintain the charity as a going concern?

Other than giving the funds back to the donor which, in certain circumstances the charity may be required to do, there are no other choices.

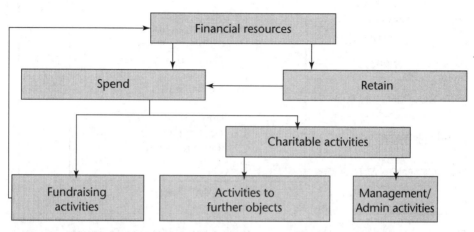

Figure 3b Choices of the financial steward

How to read SOFAs and balance sheets

Good financial stewardship does not require advanced knowledge of accountancy as this book endeavours to demonstrate. Nevertheless, it does demand a willingness and an ability to understand and to work with financial concepts. Those readers who are unfamiliar with the construction of statements of financial activities and balance sheets may find some of Part 2 of the book difficult. Persevere and the penny will drop! As a start, study Figure 3c, and Box 3.1 following it, which together describe how to work your way round the SOFA and balance sheet primary statements.

The balance sheet in Figure 3c shows two snapshot financial positions as at a particular date (in the example this is 31 December) and the SOFA outlines what has happened in the middle, to get from one balance sheet to the other. The easiest way to understand the two statements is to place them side by side and read them in the order indicated by the arrows as in Figure 3c. For guidance, refer to the notes in Box 3.1 as indicated by the reference numbers.

Statement of Financial Activities for the 12 months ended 31 December Year 2			Balance Sheet as at 31 December Year 2		
	Year 2	Year 1		Year 2	Year 1
Incoming resources			Fixed assets		
Resources expended	3		Current assets		
			Current liabilities		2
NET IN/OUT RESOURCES			Long-term liabilities		
Gains/(losses) on investments	4		NET ASSETS		
NET MOVEMENT IN FUNDS	5				
			Unrestricted funds		
Fund balances at start of year			Designated funds		
			Restricted funds		
FUND BALANCES AT END YEAR	6				
			TOTAL FUNDS	6	1

Figure 3c Interpreting the financial statements in statutory accounts

3.1 Reading the SOFA and balance sheet

1   The current year starts with the balance sheet as at the end of year 1. The total fund balances held by the trustees at the start of the year are shown in the bottom half of the year 1 balance sheet column. In this example the balances are categorised into three types of fund reflecting the nature of any restriction imposed on the fund by either the donor (restricted funds) or the trustees (designated funds).

2   The form in which those fund balances were held is shown in the top half of the balance sheet. Each fund balance must be in the form of fixed assets, current assets or long- or short-term liabilities.

3   Moving to the SOFA the left-hand column shows the income raised and expenditure incurred in the lastest year (year 2). Normally this column would be split into three with unrestricted, designated and restricted funds shown separately. Income raised in the year adds to the fund balances, expenditure incurred depletes them. Comparable figures for the preceding 12 months (year 1) are shown in the right hand column.

4   The fund balances are affected not only by income and expenditure but also by changes in the value of any market investments held by the trustees. Gains in investments (whether realised or not) add to fund balances, losses in investments reduce them.

5 The combined impact of income raised, expenditure incurred and gains/losses on investment charged results in a net movement in fund balances in the year, showing by how much the opening fund balances have increased or fallen in the current year. These are the closing fund balances.

6 The same closing fund balances appear on the bottom half of the left-hand column of the balance sheet. Under the heading Year 2, the left-hand column shows the fund balance position as at the balance sheet date (31 December Year 2). The bottom half of the balance sheet shows the fund balances by type of fund and the top half the asset form in which the fund balances are held.

Using the financial statements

To define the objectives of a finance strategy, it is necessary to look at the financial statements included in the annual statutory accounts (the primary statements), acknowledging that these objectives only have relevance in relation to the organisation's purpose. It is not possible to write a finance strategy without reference to the corporate strategy; it is the continuum of the same, single, strategic planning process. Hind's diagram (Figure 1e, page 17) shows this clearly. Determining a finance strategy therefore is about deciding how the organisation plans to use the financial resources available now and in the future to deliver the intended results of the corporate strategy, and what that will mean the charity looks like in financial terms.

These intended results should be defined in terms of the statement of financial activities and the balance sheet. As discussed above, to do so assumes the financial strategist understands how these statements are constructed, what information they give, and what information they do *not* give. The statements tell the story of the flow of funds from receipt to expenditure, identifying what income has been received, what is done with the funds until they are applied, and finally how they are spent. However, financial information alone cannot tell the reader how *effective* the expenditure is, what impact it has. Measuring impact involves the collection and interpretation of information about the charity's services, and the effect of those services on addressing the charity's cause. The financial statements tell the reader no more than what funds have been received, and how they have been applied. They do this from the perspective of income, funds, assets and expenditure. These are the key areas that any finance strategy must address (see Box 3.2).

3.2 The four perspectives of the primary statements

Statement of Financial Activities:

Income
The SOFA defines what income has been received during the period being accounted for, categorised into several groups that define the broad sources of receipt.

Expenditure
The SOFA shows what funds have been expended and in what broad directions, as a minimum split between charitable activity, including management and administration of the charity, and reinvestment in further income-generating activities

Balance Sheet:

Assets
The funds held at the balance sheet date are classified in terms of the form in which they are held.

Funds
The balance sheet confirms what income already received has not yet been spent, categorised in terms of the extent to which the donor has applied some restriction as to how the funds can be used by the charity.

The following four chapters consider these four areas, the order reflecting the flow of funds through the charity from their arrival as income, their management as fund balances and assets, through to their expenditure in furtherance of the charity's purpose.

Key stewardship questions – finance strategy

1 What future financial position should the charity reach?
2 How does it intend to get there?
3 How does the charity intend to manage the competing demands of spend versus retain?
4 Do the charity's stewards understand the primary statements?

4 The level, type and source of income

The financial steward must first ask the following question.

- Is the charity generating appropriate levels of income, of the right type, from sufficiently varied sources?

There are three key characteristics of income to be sought. First, there is the *level* of income. It must be sufficient to enable the charity to meet its purpose; it must cover all the costs that are going to be incurred in undertaking the activities by which the charitable purpose is delivered. Second, there is the *type* of income, which crucially refers to the extent to which the donor imposes a restriction on how the charity can apply the funds received. Third, there is the *source* of the income; here it is safe to suggest that any charity should aim to have a diversity of income sources in order to avoid the risks associated with putting all the eggs in one basket.

A charity's income generation strategy must reflect all three requirements and an understanding of the trade-offs between them. Arguably there is an opportunity cost associated with any fundraising activity since resources devoted to generating income from one source could otherwise be deployed to generate income from another. The charity must be sure, for example, that the benefits of restricted income exceed the opportunity cost of missing out on potential unrestricted income. One such benefit could be that of risk management, of diversifying income sources in order to reduce the reliance on unrestricted income. At times it may be a sensible strategy to trade off unrestricted income for restricted. However, once the true costs of servicing the requirements of the restricted funder are understood, the charity may conclude that it would be better to raise, say, £75 of unrestricted income than £100 of income with restrictions attached that are difficult to comply with.

Level of income

Two issues in relation to the *level* of income raised are worthy of some discussion here: those of generating contribution and covering core costs.

Generating income contribution

As any experienced steward of commercial organisations knows, 'gross margin not sales constitutes the real income of a business' (Warnes, 1984 p.27). Similarly, for a charity, the resources needed to finance the charitable work by which its purpose is served are provided by the income *contribution* that is generated from the fundraising activities, not from the gross income.

Income contribution can be defined as the net income available for charitable use once the costs of generating the income have been deducted, and a charity's income-generating aim must be to maximise the contribution made available for charitable purpose over time. It is important to remember that fundraising activities only 'break-even' once the contribution from them covers the management and administration costs incurred by the charity (such as audit fees), many of which will be fixed (or change in discrete steps) irrespective of the levels of charitable activity. The *real* income of the charity is the income that is available for activities that further the charity's objects (i.e. after income that is reinvested in further fundraising activities or used to pay for management and administration costs is deducted). A periodic review of the charity's break-even point, the level of income at which the contribution covers the fixed costs, is worth doing.[1] If it is rising over time, one or both of two phenomena must be occurring: the profitability of income-generating activities must be falling, and/or the level of fixed costs must be rising. Either occurrence is worthy of attention.

Crucially, the charity needs to understand that the solution to the problem of how to increase the contribution available to finance charitable activity revolves around reducing the break-even point, not necessarily increasing income. Conceptually, this is a fundamental point to understand. If a charity wishes to increase the funds available for activities that further its objects, it must either make fundraising activities more profitable, or it must reduce management and administration costs. It may make sense to *reduce* gross income if that enables unprofitable fundraising activities to be eliminated and the management and administrative effort required in support to be scaled down.

It costs money to generate income, and the charity needs to know how much. Sustaining or increasing the level of charitable activity requires available resources to increase over time, which in turn depends on continual investment in income-generating activities. Some of the

---

1 Break-even point = management and admin costs/gross margin percentage from fundraising activities.

charity's funds must be directed towards marketing and publicising the organisation to current and potential donors. Different fundraising activities incur very different costs and the charity must reassure itself that the income contribution generated by each is adequate and improving. Any deterioration needs to be identified and understood carefully. This assumes that the costs associated with generating income can be attributed to each separate fundraising activity accurately. That can be difficult, not least because of the time lag between fundraising activity and receipt of income. Assessing the return on legacy promotional activity is perhaps the extreme example of this: the return on investment may not be realised for several years. The investment may not all be borne up front either, with administrative costs conceivably incurred throughout the life of the activity for which the funding was given, in order to meet reporting requirements for example.

At a strategic level, however, it should be possible for financial stewards to reassure themselves that, during any period of time, the charity is not investing too little or too much in fundraising and publicity activities (see Chapter 7). Monitoring the relationship between income raised in a period and the level of funds invested in income generating activities during that same period (the cost:income ratio) can be a misleading performance indicator, implying a direct relationship between the two. More sophisticated analyses are now being developed within the sector to measure lifetime value better. Nevertheless tracking the *trend* of the cost:income ratio over time can be very valuable. The return on investment will come through at some point if the investment was sound, with a consequent improvement in the cost:income ratio. Prudent trustees and management would be wise not to accept too long a lag before expecting to see this occur. Relatively early paybacks on fundraising investments are appropriate given the alternative, charitable use to which the funds invested could have been used.

Funding core costs

There is now a generally accepted definition of core costs, based on a list of 22 types of cost. These include 'management, research and development, and support services such as premises, IT and finance as well as administrative, personnel and training charges' (Unwin, 2001 p.10–11). There are donors, major ones at that, who are unwilling to finance any core costs and often the charity has little choice or negotiating strength over the matter. Such a stance from the funder may seem naïve, unrealistic and even infuriating to the charity but it would be worth understanding the funder's perspective. Julia Unwin's excellent report,

Funding Our Future: Core Costs Revisited,[2] which provides a comprehensive overview of the current funding environment for voluntary organisations, offers a perceptive insight into the concerns funders have about funding core costs (see Box 4.1).

4.1 Why are many funders reluctant to provide funding for core costs?

1 Funders find it difficult to be satisfied that the grant is good value for money and achieving desired outcomes. There is anxiety about the ways in which 'backroom' costs can be justified.

2 Support for core costs has no easily understood justification for being time-limited. Funding programmes that have long-term or open-ended commitments restrict funders from being responsive to new and emerging needs.

3 Funders fear that they will be captured by the organisation to which they are making such a central contribution, from which it will be politically or emotionally difficult to disengage.

4 Funding core costs offers considerable scope for double or even triple funding of certain costs.

5 Offering support for core costs distorts the pricing structure of voluntary organisations offering services, which are purchased hiding the real cost of the services being bought.

Source: Unwin (2001) pp.23–4

Whilst charities can legitimately insist that the activities generating core costs are an essential component of their work, they also have an obligation to manage those costs tightly in order to address the understandable funder concerns listed in Box 4.1. Whilst every charity should unquestionably apply whatever pressure and influence it can on the funder to include an element in the funding for core costs, ultimately it will face a take-it-or-leave-it choice. If it takes it, it must do so with a clear understanding of how the core costs required to support the activity will be financed. There may be risks to take. The charity may have sufficient unrestricted funding to be able to finance the core costs of an activity for a certain length of time but no longer, and perhaps less than the natural length of the activity. Should it even start the activity in this circumstance? That involves a judgement about how likely it is that it will be able to raise funds to finance the core costs of the remaining period of the activity, and on the implications of stopping the

---

[2] First published by ACEVO in 1999 as *Who Pays for Core Costs?*

activity in mid-stream. Unwin's research has identified four 'survival' strategies for financing core costs (Unwin, 2001 pp.15–16).

1 Cost recovery – the price charged to the funder covers the full cost of activities, including an appropriate allocation of core costs.
2 Cost diversion – activities incurring core costs are packaged to funders in the form of discrete projects (e.g. the reception desk activity is marketed as an information service; the policy department is broken down into a number of research projects).
3 Cost donation – voluntary, unrestricted income is raised which can be used for core costs financing.
4 Cost reduction – the level of core costs is driven down thereby reducing the funding requirement.

All these strategies assume that the core costs are known and that there is a reasonable basis for apportioning them over the charitable activities. The latter is not easy, and requires both a good understanding within the charity of at least the basic techniques of activity-based costing and accounting, and a well-designed and maintained accounting system to capture the costs in the most appropriate way.

Recognising the concerns of funders with regard to core costs, Unwin (2001 p.8) proposes three possible funding strategies.

1 Full project funding, in which all reasonable associated costs are met as part of a funding package.
2 Development funding through which an organisation's infrastructure costs are met for a time in order to enable it to develop and grow.
3 Strategic funding through which the funder recognises the need for an organisation to exist – in order to meet its own objectives – and is prepared to contribute over an agreed period of time.

Significantly, the government now promotes these three funding models, with funders strongly encouraged to adopt one of them. Its Compact on Relations between Government and the Voluntary and Community Sector in England includes a Code of Good Practice on Funding (Home Office 2000) in which it recognises the need for core costs to be met if charities are to operate efficiently and effectively. Prudently, the Code also counsels that 'regardless of the funding approach taken, it is important that the funded organisation has an "exit strategy" in the event that a particular source of funding should cease.'(p.6)

Ultimately, much energy has to be devoted to developing and maintaining relationships between the charity and the funder and Unwin appeals for funders and funded to forge a new 'win–win' partnership – a settlement (see Box 4.2). This offers much food-for-thought to both charities and funders.

4.2 A new funder/funded settlement

It is in the interests of funders and operating voluntary organisations to reach a new settlement. This will have implications for both funders and funded organisations. It will require voluntary organisations to:

1 Improve internal accounting, financial management and business planning
2 Develop benchmarking on overhead costs
3 Demonstrate effectiveness and capacity
4 Develop their own ways of measuring effectiveness and organisational change.

It will require funders to:

1 Meet the overhead costs associated with managing a piece of work
2 See their funding as part of a programme of long term investment
3 Manage change within their portfolio of grants
4 Develop new ways of evaluating effectiveness.

Source: Unwin (2001) p.6

Type of income

Generating unrestricted income

What should be the charity's strategy with regard to generating unrestricted income? Clearly the more discretion the trustees have over the funds placed in their trust, the greater the extent to which they can expend those funds as they see fit in furtherance of the charity's objects. The ideal income is unrestricted – where the donor places no restriction, within the objects of the charity, on how those funds are applied. Unrestricted income is the most precious income of all, and charities should adopt a FILO principle with respect to such income – *first in last out* – where generating unrestricted income is treated as a first priority and spending it a last resort. The latter should occur only once any of the restricted funds that could be spent financing the same activity have been exhausted.

The donor's perspective

Whilst no one would doubt the value from the charity's point of view of having the discretion that unrestricted income provides, the donor perspective will be different. One of the core aims of any proposition to donors will be to reassure them that their financial contribution will have impact; that it will make a difference. It is understandably attractive for funders to be able to trace their particular contribution through to the charitable impact. And there lies the tension. The charity wants unrestricted income in order to maximise its flexibility; the donor wants to see as precisely as possible what their funds will be used for and may be comforted by placing a restriction on their use to ensure that they *are* used as they intended.

The charity's perspective

The reality for charities is that they cannot rely solely on unrestricted income to finance their activities, but nor should they. Morally, every charity has an obligation to generate whatever funds it can in order to further alleviate the need for which the organisation was established, as long as it can do so cost effectively. This means endeavouring to source income that will be subject to restrictions from statutory funders such as government departments and European Union institutions, and from non-statutory sources such as the private sector, trusts and foundations. However, the implications of sourcing restricted income need to be clearly understood. Any restricted income raised should be *in addition to* unrestricted income not *instead* of it. Since the greater the restriction, the less discretion a charity has over how the funds are used, the organisation needs to be sure that sourcing restricted income does not detract from the organisation's ability to attract unrestricted income.

If the donor does require restrictions the charity should seek to make them as broad as possible to give it maximum discretion over the use of the funds. Whatever happens, the charity must be sure it is willing and able to comply with the terms of the restriction. There may be onerous reporting requirements to be met and the right decision may be not to accept the funds being offered in these circumstances. Such a decision could be difficult for a fundraiser with stiff income targets to meet. The decision-making process by which funds on offer are accepted or refused may be worth reviewing so that the fundraiser does not feel undue pressure to accept income proposals whatever the cost. It is worth understanding whether there is an incentive for a fundraiser to turn down restricted income. There will also be accounting requirements associated with tracking restricted funds (discrete coding for example) which, equally, need to be understood. Endowment funds can be particularly administratively burdensome. They may need to be held in separate bank accounts, and require separate disclosure and explanation in published accounts, irrespective of their size. They may last in perpetuity, creating problems years down the line when the original trustees of the fund, and relevant paperwork, are no longer accessible. And they may set awkward conditions, for example, requiring the charity to accumulate the interest earned on the capital sum for the first five years, expend the interest earned on the capital in years 6 to 10, accumulate interest in years 11 to 15, and so on.

The accounting implications of accepting restricted funds must not be forgotten. Yet the challenge of complying with the demands of statute or recommended and best practice on fund accounting relates less to questions about how to account and manage the fund income than to how it is expended. There may be questions about which fund to charge income to if the nature of any restriction overlaps with existing funds but it ought to be possible to ensure that the details of income received are entered into the accounting system under the fund which that income relates to. The charity must be able to determine at the time the income is received whether it has received funds with a restriction placed on them or whether they are unrestricted, some of which may need to be designated in accordance with trustee instructions.

Of course every organisation would much prefer to raise unrestricted funds, thereby giving itself maximum freedom to make choices within its mandate about resource allocation. But that seems to be increasingly difficult. Take statutory funding for example. Those reliable grants with undemanding conditions from statutory funders are fast being replaced by increasingly stringent funding contracts from Whitehall departments, the European Union and the like. Increasingly detailed applications now have to be prepared, giving considerable detail about the proposed activity; lengthy processing times have to be endured before decisions are made. It may be necessary, effectively, to underwrite projects that need to begin for which a funding application decision is awaited. That can of course only be done if the charity has funds available to use at its discretion in the event of the application being denied and careful consideration of the risks of commencing activities without funding secured must be made.

In such circumstances, the importance of unrestricted reserves as a strategic financial tool cannot be over-estimated. Funds may be received well after the expenditure to which they relate is incurred which can cause some serious cash flow and accounting headaches. How should the charity account for restricted income received retrospective to the expenditure that it has been granted to cover, expenditure which, precisely because of the delay in confirmation of funding, has had to be treated as unrestricted in an earlier accounting period? The answer may be a rather-difficult-to-explain transfer between restricted and unrestricted funds in order to show the income and expenditure in the same column (see Box 4.3).

4.3 Accounting for retrospective income

- Expenditure is incurred in year one and has to be shown against *un*restricted funds because the decision on the funding application (which if successful would be classified as restricted income against which the expenditure would be matched) is outstanding.
- In year two the funding application is approved by the statutory funder (subject to stringent conditions). Income is either received or accrued, in either case as restricted income, the grant only being eligible to finance the activities of the charity detailed in the application.
- No expenditure is incurred in year two (having been completed in year one). The restricted income recognised in the year drops down the SOFA and falls into the restricted fund balances. Except there is no future expenditure to finance that meets the terms of the restriction! The income sits in one fund whilst unrestricted funds remain depleted by the expenditure incurred in year one. Hence the transfer. The restricted fund balance is transferred to the general fund, replenishing it to its previous level. The more attentive reader of the accounts might question what the trustees are doing moving funds that donors have given with restrictions attached into the unrestricted funds where no such constraints exist? Barely adequate explanations can be given in the notes to the accounts.
- From a fund balance point of view all is well. General funds are at the right level and the restricted fund is empty. Note however that, at the end of year two, both income and its matching expenditure ended up being treated as *un*restricted. Not ideal by any means.

The fundraising appeal determination process

Managing the tension between the charity's desire for unrestricted income and the donor's interest in attributing their funds to specific activities has become highly professionalised within the major fundraising charities, with advanced marketing techniques used to appeal to the donor. Appeals are designed around a particular theme, maybe using examples of the impact on individual beneficiaries' lives that the charity's work has, in order to focus the donor's attention on how their contribution will help. However, they are in fact carefully worded to ensure that, in practice, the charity can treat the income generated from the appeal as unrestricted and use it as they see fit, quite possibly on an activity not explicitly referred to at all in the appeal. In such cases strict attention needs to be paid to the wording of the appeal to make sure that it can be treated as unrestricted funds both legally *and* *morally* without diminishing the impact of the message. It may be, of course, that an appeal's image does encourage some donors to respond with a request that their funds are restricted to use only for the nature of the work highlighted in the appeal. An unrestricted appeal may generate restricted income.

The process by which appeals material is determined internally, be it printed literature for door drops, billboard or television advertising and so on, needs to be defined and supported by all the relevant individuals. In most charities there will be some tensions to manage between the perspectives offered by fundraising staff and those responsible for the delivery of the charitable services. The images and messages of the charity's appeals have to promote the organisation's beneficiaries in a dignified, unpatronising way in keeping with the charity's values but without unduly compromising the power of the fundraising image. By way of illustration, Box 4.4 quotes from a Statement of Principles signed by a network of 220 UK-based voluntary organisations working in international development, the British Overseas NGOs for Development (BOND).

4.4 Using responsible fundraising methods

In their fundraising activities, BOND members aim to portray the realities and complexities of the situations with which they are involved, as inappropriate methods, simplistic images and messages can undo the positive impact of their work. BOND members recognise that the stereotypical image of Southern people and countries held by many in the UK is often simplistic and potentially damaging. BOND members' fundraising publicity aims to avoid exploiting and reinforcing these stereotypes, and aims where possible to challenge them. BOND members aim to control all fundraising activities carried out on their behalf.

Source: British Overseas NGOs for Development (BOND) Statement of Principles, February 2001

The role of auditors

Add in the question of determining the degree of restriction on the funding and it is easy to see how important the appeal design sign-off process is. There is a great deal of sense in the inclusion of the charity's auditors in this decision-making process prior to finalising the design. At the time of the statutory audit the auditors will make their own judgement on the nature of any income raised, on the degree to which that income should be restricted in use. It would be better, therefore, to have that judgement *before* plans are finalised than after the income is raised or, worst of all, spent. However that rarely seems to happen. The most appropriate split of responsibilities would be for auditors to determine the nature of any restriction and for the charity to determine the distribution of income within the boundaries of the restriction. In extreme cases the auditors may not feel qualified to judge and may wish to refer to a legal opinion. Invariably, creating new fundraising appeal designs is a process which seems to operate to tight deadlines. Nevertheless, time must be given to enable auditors to comment on how any income raised from the appeal would need to be classified. If the relationship with the auditors is a good one this needn't take long – a 48 hour turn-around time for an opinion is realistic.

Source of income

Diversifying sources of income is common sense, simply to avoid over-dependence on any one source. That is a well-established strategy of managing risk. It reflects the fact that no income source is 100 per cent secure indefinitely: the four funding strategies promoted by Unwin (see page 55) to enable charities to get core costs covered are all time limited; Government funding can change with the political climate, and so on. But since diversification has its costs (increased management effort, etc.) the charity must understand at what point the benefits of additional diversification are outweighed by the drawbacks. Each source imposes its own particular management demands and income sources that are inappropriately costly or restrictive can easily be chosen in order to reduce risk through diversification. Certainly the more diverse the income sources the more likely that, at any time, one of those sources will be a cause for concern. The charity may wish to impose some parameters that place an indicative ceiling on the proportion of total income that should come from any one source.

Key stewardship questions – income

1 Is the charity generating sufficient income to cover all the costs facing it including core costs?
2 Are the income-generating activities profitable enough? Are they making a sufficient contribution?
3 Is the break-even level of income low enough?
4 Are the charity's funders giving the organisation sufficient discretion over how the income is applied?
5 Does the charity have an adequate number of income sources? Does it have too many?
6 What should be the trade-off points between the levels, types and sources of income?
7 How does the charity intend to achieve these aims?

5 The level, form and matching of funds

Funds are nothing more than income already raised that has not yet been spent; what the SORP 2000 defines as 'a pool of unexpended resources' (Charity Commission, 2000 appendix 1.12). These unexpended resources are the capital of the company, the injections of funds that will finance the future activities and assets of the charity. The only way that funds can be created is by generating income that is not (yet) spent. It is often assumed that charities aim to deliver a balanced bottom line each year, with income and expenditure offsetting each other. In reality, what inflow or outflow of resources is desirable on the statement of financial activities depends on the existing funds position and on the cash situation. It may be appropriate instead to either add to or deplete the existing funds or cash balances. Cash management is considered in the following chapter, on page 81.

Once income has been raised, thereby becoming part of the fund balances, attention should be turned to the issue of how those fund balances should be managed. What level of balances is it appropriate to hold, in what form, and how should the balances best be spent in line with the wishes of the donor (if defined)? These are the questions the finance strategy has to answer.

The level of fund balances

Fund balances should be kept (rather than spent) until it is appropriate to spend the funds in accordance with the wishes of the donor. In the unusual circumstance that it is not possible to comply with a donor's wishes their funds should be returned. Permanent endowment funds are an exception, where the trustees are not permitted to spend the fund but instead must maintain it permanently.[1]

---

[1] Normally the income derived from such a fund *is* expendable.

Restricted funds

In the case of restricted funds the challenge is how best to match income with expenditure given the likely circumstance that more than one restricted fund will be eligible to finance a particular activity (see Matching funds and activities, page 74). Once it is clear which activity a fund will be used to finance, the question of when to spend that fund is a relatively straightforward one, determined by terms of the funding agreement and/or the needs of the activity. The appropriate level of restricted fund balances to hold, therefore, is entirely related to expenditure on the activities to which they are restricted.

Unrestricted funds

Unrestricted fund balances however pose bigger questions. The charity has to maintain itself as a going concern in order to have impact over time, as well as in the present, and achieving this will require it to build and maintain a financial reserve. Unless the terms of the restriction dictate otherwise, restricted fund balances are inappropriately used as such reserves. Unrestricted fund balances will therefore have to be used and, as a result, their level will be determined not only by the expenditure demands of the charity but also its need to continue as a going-concern.

Why hold reserves?

Increasingly trustees are being encouraged or required to explain their reserves policy and to justify the level of reserves held by the charity. In 1997 the Charity Commission published new guidelines in its booklet *Charities' Reserves* (CC19) which emphasise that responsibility for establishing a reserves policy rests with the trustees, and that a charity should be judged on whether its level of reserves, whatever that level, is justified and clearly explained. SORP 2000 recommended that the Trustees' Report should include a description of 'the charity's policy on reserves stating the level of reserves held and why they are held' (paragraph 31e). Neither publication, however, offers guidance to the charity steward on determining appropriate reserves levels.

There are four main reasons to hold reserves (see Box 5.1). For most charities the first of the objectives, maintaining the continuity of the charity's work, will be the most significant in monetary terms. A strategy of building unrestricted funds is a crucial way of guaranteeing continuity so that even in the event of disappointing income, expenditure can be financed from reserves. Not that this is a long-term option

5.1 Why hold reserves?

Charities need to hold reserves in order to:

1 protect the continuity of the charity's work, in spite of uncertain future income streams, i.e. to provide a source of funding in the event of unexpected funding shortfalls

2 protect the charity's funds from loss in value of the asset form in which they are held. If the charity's trustees choose to hold the funds placed in their trust in a form that can lose value as well as gain it, such as market investments, it must have contingency funding available so that in the event of the former happening the fund value can be restored. This is particularly true of endowment and restricted funds, which by definition have been donated for a specific purpose

3 provide the capital needed to finance expansion of the charity. If the charity is to grow it needs injections of money to finance investment in fundraising for example. It can either borrow this money or use its own funds

4 provide the funds needed to replace assets where the historic cost of the asset understates its replacement cost. This is a relatively technical matter and for the purposes of good financial stewardship of the organisation it is sufficient to recognise that in order to replace computers, vehicles and other fixed assets the charity needs funds. Unless the purchase of the assets is itself charitable activity, it is unlikely that specific (restricted) funding will be found for such investments. The charity must therefore generate unrestricted income that is not spent on operational activities, i.e. unrestricted fund balances, or reserves.

– reserves can only be spent once. Eventually the funds will be exhausted unless they are replenished. Reserves management therefore demands also that the decision-makers have a clear enough understanding of future income flows to anticipate when reserves are likely to be needed to honour expenditure commitments. In a period when committed expenditure is running higher than income (and therefore reserves are falling) the charity must be sure that any further expenditure commitments can be financed without reserves being excessively depleted or, worse still, exhausted. Unless the charity wishes to reduce the level of its reserves, it is going to have to know when to stop spending.

The public attention paid to the issue of reserves is appropriate in the context of public accountability for funds placed in the trust of trustees (hence the latter's name) both from the point of view of donors and beneficiaries. The Charity Commission specifically addresses the concern expressed by many that some charities' reserves are too high (see the wording of paragraph 31e of SORP 2000 quoted on page 64). High profile charities are often quoted in this context and, justifiably or not, this inevitably influences public perception of the issue for the sector as a whole. But for the majority of charities the problem is quite the reverse. For them the priority is to find a way to generate unrestricted income that would give the trustees discretion, not to spend the income, but to build an appropriate level of reserves. The level of reserves must be necessary as the Charity Commission rightly stresses but equally importantly it must be *sufficient*. There must be enough reserves to meet the objectives stated in Box 5.1. For charities with insufficient reserves, discussions about what to do with unrestricted funds must take into account the legitimacy and importance of building those reserves alongside the more exciting expenditure options. Again this highlights the importance of maximising impact over time. Regrettably, most charities do have to consider how they will have impact tomorrow as well as today – the cause will not have disappeared. There is much education to do in the public domain to legitimise the building of reserves.

How are reserves defined?

SORP 2000 defines reserves as:

> 'Resources the charity has or can make available to spend, for any of the charity's purposes, once it has met its commitments and covered its other planned expenditure. More specifically this defines reserves as income, which becomes available to the charity, and is to be spent at the trustees' discretion in furtherance of any of the charity's objects but which is not yet spent, committed or designated (i.e. is "free").' (Appendix 1.27)

This definition mirrors that used by the Charity Commission in *Charities' Reserves* and therefore excludes endowment funds and restricted funds from reserves. Understandably so, since such funds clearly are not available to be spent at the trustees' discretion. Interestingly, the definition also excludes designated funds, i.e. those funds earmarked by the trustees for a particular purpose. Presumably this is to recognise that funds which have been designated, even though that is *by the trustees* rather than the donors, are not available to be spent in furtherance of *any* of its charitable objects, only those for which the designation has been made. There is some logic to this. Funds that have been designated to protect those assets held in a form that could only be realised if disposed of, clearly are not available for general use by the trustees. However in many cases trustees designate funds into a continuity reserve, precisely in order to provide a bank of resources to draw on in the event of unforeseen difficulties or opportunities arising. The purpose of the designation is to ensure that maintenance of such a reserve is kept in mind, and that such funds are not inadvertently spent but only after careful trustee consideration. To conclude unilaterally that all designated funds are not reserves is too crude a judgement. Consideration needs to be given as to why the designation has been made, and in what form such funds are held. Ignoring designated funds that could be used by the trustees in extreme circumstances would encourage the trustees to build higher reserves than are necessary.

Determining what reserves to hold

Determining the appropriate size of reserves – sufficient *and* necessary – must be related to the four objectives listed in Box 5.1, page 65. The first two objectives relate to the management of two risks. First, there is the risk that the continuity of activities cannot be sustained because of unexpected shortfalls in income. Secondly, there is the risk that funds held in asset forms might lose market value. The exposure to market value losses (objective 2) can be easily assessed. What would be the monetary value of a loss of, say, 20 per cent in market prices of investments? The need for judgement comes in when assessing how big a possible market drop to protect against. Similarly, calculating how much funding will be needed to finance expansion (objective 3) or pay for the replacement of fixed assets (objective 4) ought to be uncomplicated, based on a rudimentary business plan outlining what will need to be purchased and the anticipated costs of doing so.

Determining the exposure to unexpected falls in income (objective 1), however, is more difficult. Gillingham and Tame (1997) propose a number of ways to consider this including actuarial forecasting, risk assessment and scenario planning. Each has its merits although most charities would find the risk assessment or scenario planning approaches most logical and practical to undertake, and suitable to quote when explaining the level of reserves held or targeted. Relatively crude judgements can be made; this does not have to be a complicated, scientific exercise. After all, the aim of the exercise is only to give the charity an indicative feel for the size of funds it ought to put to one side in case an uncertain event happens in the future.

The risk assessment approach assesses how much the charity can rely on having available funding to cover the costs of its planned activities, and therefore how much it faces a risk from funding that it cannot yet rely on. Determining what level of reserves to hold is done by completing a three-stage process. In simple terms the charity assesses what funds it needs, compares this to how much it can already rely on, and makes a judgement about the risk attached to the remainder. Such an assessment could change frequently as new expenditure commitments are made or funding agreements signed, and the charity must adopt the discipline of reviewing its funding exposure regularly, once a year as a minimum. The annual discipline of writing the Trustees' Report (see Chapter 15, page 202) should encourage this.

Stage one – identifying funding requirement

This is a question of identifying the charity's expenditure commitments; these can be assessed from three levels, each level subsuming the previous one.

1 At a minimum, the first level, there will be costs that it has to incur in the future in order to honour its legal commitments. These would include, for example, the costs that would have to be incurred by the charity in the event of the organisation being closed down, such as meeting staff statutory and contractual terms of employment.

2 The second level of commitment relates to those costs that the charity is morally committed to, even if there is no legal obligation. Project or grant agreements are often of this type, where the charity is contracted to provide defined services or funding over a stipulated period of time, but subject to clauses that enable the contract to be terminated in the event of particular unforeseen circumstances arising. These *force majeure* clauses can include funding shortfalls as grounds to end a contract. The charity may conclude that it is morally obliged to complete all activities currently being undertaken, which will be a mixture of those activities with a finite life and general activity that is ongoing.

3 Level three assumes the most liberal definition of funding need, including not only legal and current commitments but future commitments too. This refers to costs that the charity *intends* to incur but to which it is not yet committed. Level three therefore assumes that the charity wishes to continue as planned, completing current activities and starting new ones as well. It therefore reflects the charity's overall expenditure plans.

Both levels two and three require the charity to make some judgement about the timeframe for the funding of running costs such as payroll for permanent staff, which continue indefinitely. Since the general activity is undertaken in support of the specific project-based activities, the length of the project sets the timeframe for the charity's funding requirement. This in turn requires the charity's management information systems to be set up to provide costed data over activity-based timeframes. They may well not be set up like this. An alternative might be to exclude from consideration those activities that will only be undertaken if specific, and therefore by definition, restricted funding is received. With such activities, reserves are not needed: the contingency plan is that, without funding, the activity does not happen.

Whilst acknowledging the relevance of considering activity-based timeframes and ignoring restricted-funding dependent activities, for many charities it will be adequate to determine their funding requirement by simply using the forecast total costs of the charity over, say, the next 12 months. They can be confident that one year's cover will provide ample lead-time to reduce commitments in the event of a funding downturn, even if that means terminating some existing commitments prior to their completion.

Stage two – identifying funding secured

Identifying funding that is already secure ought to be straightforward. By definition, there should be some form of written agreement that confirms the commitment of the donor to make an income payment to the charity. The exercise can be completed by considering what funding agreements are in place, either by donor or by activity. This stage should also identify any endowment, restricted and possibly designated fund balances that are available to fund the proposed activities.

Stage three – identifying funding risk

The final stage in the reserves determination process is to consider the risk of failing to generate the balance of funding required. Two tasks must be completed. First, the charity must identify the funding sources from which it anticipates generating the income. Again, this may best be done by activity, particularly for those charities reliant on restricted funding. Then a judgement must be made against each possible funding source on the degree of risk associated with the funding. This is expressed as a percentage of the total funding required from the source. It may be very low. For example, the income from individual donors whose donation is made in a committed, indefinite form such as direct debit might be considered to be a very low risk given the low rates at which such donors typically withdraw their support. Other funding sources, such as legacy income, will need to be regarded as a much higher risk given the uncertainty associated with them. Once the degree of risk has been judged, the value of funding at risk by source can be calculated.

For ease of presentation and discussion it is worth laying out the three stages at a summary level in a simple matrix (see Figure 5a). This could be annotated to explain to the reader, for example, what rationale was used to identify a particular degree of risk.

	A		B	C = A − B	D	E = C × D
Activity	Total funding required £'000	Income source	Secure funding £'000	Total at risk £'000	Degree of risk %	Risk £'000
Specific activity 1	200	Funder X	120	80	30	24
Specific activity 2	100	Restricted fund Y	100	0	0	0
General activity 3	300	Funder Z	200	100	50	50
TOTAL	**600**		**420**	**180**		**74**

Activity	Identification of the activities on which the charity incurs cost. This will be a mixture of specific activities and general activity such as departmental running costs.
Total funding required	The total cost of the activity over the defined time period.
Income source	Identification of the funder or existing fund balance from which the funds will be sourced to cover the cost.
Secure funding	The income from the source that is already secure and can be relied on because it has already been received or for which the funder has a contractual commitment.
Total at risk	The balance of the total funding that is therefore not secure.
Degree of risk	The percentage of the insecure funding that is at risk.
Risk	The exposed insecure funding expressed in monetary terms.
Total exposure	The exposed insecure income less relevant opening restricted or designated balances.

Figure 5a Estimating funding risk

Writing a reserves policy

Under the SORP trustees are advised to explain their thinking on reserves and to justify the levels held. The articulation of a reserves policy should explain to the reader:

- what level of reserves the trustees believe it is appropriate to hold, and
- in what form.

The policy should show clearly how this ideal appropriate reserves holding compares with the current reserves position; it should also outline what action is proposed if the current position is not as intended.

Expressing reserves in relation to expenditure

Typically reserves are expressed in relation to expenditure, given that the main rationale for holding reserves is to counter the risk to expenditure from uncertain funding. Often the expression is in terms of the length of time that the reserves would cover the expenditure – weeks, months or, in extreme cases, years. Less often the calculation is rightly expressed in relation to expected *future* expenditure, rather than actual *historic* expenditure. It needs to be the former. In the example in Figure 5a, the level of free reserves required (to cover the funding risk of £74,000) would be expressed in relation to the funding requirement (£600,000) i.e. 12.3 per cent. If the funding requirement referred to, say, a 12-month period the percentage could then be re-expressed as 45 days' cover.

The reserves are the piggy bank available for the future and, in a period of rapid change in expenditure levels (either up or down), expressing reserves in relation to historic expenditure may be misleading. Trustee bodies should express reserves in relation to expenditure in a way that gives a clear guide as to their intentions without inhibiting their ability to make judgements in the light of the particular circumstances that they might find themselves in. This means avoiding setting rigid absolute maximum or minimum reserves levels (for example, stating that 'reserves should be no more than/no less than three months of future expenditure'). Given that the purpose of holding reserves in the first place is to substitute for income that has not been generated, there may be an occasion in which the reserves are actually used, resulting in low reserves. Equally, the reserves policy should not inhibit trustees from allowing reserves to increase to a high level at a particular time as a result of the sudden and unexpected receipt, say, of a sizeable legacy. If the reserves are viewed just after the receipt of such a donation, they might justifiably look high. The reserves policy therefore should indicate what level of reserves is expected and desired whilst acknowledging that actual circumstances may leave them higher or lower than this. The Trustees' Report should explain this circumstance and what action is proposed to get the reserves to the desired level.

5.2 Extract from a reserves policy

The trustees are of the opinion that to safeguard the continuing work and commitments of the charity, the level of free reserves (i.e. unrestricted general funds) at the balance sheet date should normally equate to not less than 25% of the projected total resources due to be expended from these funds in the following year.

Source: Sight Savers International Annual Report and Accounts 2000

The inclusion of the word 'normally' in Box 5.2 leaves the reader with a clear sense of what is expected whilst implying that unusual circumstances may leave the reserves at a different level at any snapshot in time. Note also from the statement that the policy seeks to cover only a percentage of that future expenditure likely to be spent from unrestricted funds, rather than all expenditure. Future expenditure from restricted funds is explicitly excluded from the policy in recognition of the fact that, in the event of income not being generated to finance such activities, they would either be financed from opening restricted fund balances or be discontinued.

The form of fund balances

The greater the degree of restriction, the greater the importance of ensuring that the fund is held in the right form. The acceptance of income with restrictions imposes obligations on the charity, certainly in terms of how such funds are spent, but quite possibly also in terms of how they are protected until they are spent. The charity will have an obligation to return the funds to their donor if they cannot be used in accordance with the terms of any restriction imposed by the latter. It therefore has to ensure that the funds do not end up in a form that makes them difficult to realise, or worse still, are spent on an activity that falls outside the restrictions. It may be necessary to hold the funds in a discrete asset form, such as a separate bank account, to guarantee their protection. Certainly the charity must be looking to keep such fund balances in as liquid and realisable a form as possible. They cannot therefore be held in the form, say, of tangible fixed assets that could only be realised if sold, thereby preventing the charity from functioning effectively.

It is worth spending time understanding the note in the charity's statutory accounts that classifies the fund balances by asset form (see Figure 5b). Ask the question: how easily could the fund balance be converted from its present asset form into cash?

	General	Designated	Restricted
Fixed assets			
Current net assets			
TOTAL NET ASSETS			

In the above table only the shaded box representing general unrestricted funds held in an asset form other than fixed assets – can genuinely be defined as 'free', truly at the discretion of the trustees. The assessment of the health of a balance sheet can change markedly if funds prove to be in a form that is either unrealisable, or if the timing of the realisation of the fund is not solely at the discretion of the trustees. Consider, for example, what would happen if the trustees were holding the funds either in a market based form that had lost value at the time that the funds were needed or in a fixed asset that couldn't be sold without affecting the operating capacity of the charity.

Figure 5b Understanding fund balances by asset category

Dealing with movements in market values

What if the charity holds funds in an asset form that is shown on the balance sheet at market value rather than historic cost? What should it do if the market value drops? Potentially it is going to have to replenish the fund balances to the previous value. Will it be able to say to the donor that the fund balance has reduced, not because of expenditure, but because of lost market value? This will depend on the terms under which the funds were given. Unless there is the explicit agreement of the donor that their funds can be invested in assets that may fall in value, the charity may believe that there is a moral obligation at least to replenish the fund for any market value losses attributable to it. Unless explicitly agreed to the contrary it might assume that the donor does not wish their funds to be 'spent' on, say, investment losses. On the other hand it may make its judgement in the light of movements in the market value of the funds' assets in prior years. A legitimate stance if a year of losses follows several years of gains, which were attributed to the restricted fund, may be to charge the loss to the fund in the exceptional year in which it occurs.

Protecting fixed assets

Having protected the charity's restricted and endowment funds, what is the nature of the assets that are left which, by definition, will represent the designated and unrestricted funds? Very sensibly many trustee bodies are choosing to designate funds equal in value to those assets that cannot be realised without jeopardising the ability of the charity to continue to function (see Box 5.3 below). This minimises the risk that general funds are depleted, whether intentionally or not, to such an extent that restricted and/or endowment fund balances end up being held in the form of fixed assets that cannot be easily realised. It is consequently much easier for everyone – trustees, management, and actual and potential supporters – to see what unrestricted funds are genuinely at the trustees' disposal.

5.3 Establishing a fixed asset designated fund

Once The Refugee Council's trustees had decided to establish a fixed asset designated fund at the end of the 1999/2000 financial year they found themselves transferring all but £4,000 of the general reserves into this fund. The level of reserves at the disposal of the trustees was, in practice, all but zero. Rightly, therefore the trustees recognised the importance of building reserves over the following few years, endeavouring to make contributions to the general fund each year.

Matching funds and activities

If all the charity's funds are unrestricted, the issue of which funds to use for which activity does not arise. Similarly where the charity has funds with tight restrictions that have been given specifically for one precise purpose there is no decision to make about how those funds are spent once the funds have been accepted. Managed prior to use yes, but expended no. But how then should a charity best decide to use all the funds that fall somewhere between these two extremes? A process for making decisions about which funds are used to finance which activities is needed. It must be clear what is paying for what. If not there is considerable risk that particular activities will either be double-funded (or even treble-funded) or not funded at all. As Unwin (2001) indicated this risk was one of the reasons given by funders for their reluctance to finance core costs (see Box 4.1, page 54).

Ideally, the attribution of expenditure to fund would occur at the time the expenditure is incurred. This would ensure that at any time it was clear what balance was held in each fund. In practice it is rarely that straightforward. How should the charity account for an activity that costs more than any restricted funding received for that purpose, for example? At least some of these costs will have to be met from another fund, perhaps from the unrestricted fund, which raises the following question when any particular expenditure is incurred: which of the funds is being depleted? Often the terms of the restriction do leave room for choices about which project to finance. A donor may, for example, simply impose a geographic restriction requiring the funds to be spent only in, say, Africa. Any of the charity's activities that are undertaken in Africa would be eligible to be funded from the fund. The choice as to which fund will be used may well not be one that the charity wishes to make at the time the expenditure is incurred. It may prefer to wait, for example, until the end of the financial year (when a choice will have to be made) when the complete funding and expenditure picture is clear. That decision is not simply a political issue, but a financial stewardship one too. Guided by the principle that the unrestricted funds should be spent last, the charity should assign the expenditure to the fund with the tightest restriction whose criteria it matches. However, it may wish to assign it to a highly restricted fund that it has not yet received hence the preference to avoid matching cost to fund until the latest possible moment.

Some central co-ordination of the matching process to include the service delivering, fundraising and financing involved is essential. This co-ordination will help to manage the jostling between fundraisers within the charity, who compete to get first call on the more marketable projects. Such a co-ordinating body, (e.g. Sight Savers International's Fund Management Committee, see Box 5.4, page 77), serves as forum at which the fundraisers and the service deliverers meet to co-ordinate the matching of income and expenditure. Costed activities are matched to funds. To an observer it might resemble a market square, where stall-holders (the service deliverers) endeavour to sell their wares (the charitable activities) to the customers (the fundraisers). A brokering process is conducted. Participants inform themselves as to which activities currently being undertaken or planned do not have secured funding attached to them and fundraisers, cognisant of the expectations, wishes and interests of their donors bid to secure/reserve these available activities. At any time the following information must be clear.

- The cost of the activities (actual or proposed) to be covered. This reiterates the importance of understanding the true cost of each activity. The structure of most accounting systems make it easy to slip into believing that the direct costs[2] of undertaking an activity are the only costs that need to be covered, leaving all the indirect costs unfunded. Activity-based costing is needed.
- The timeframe over which the funding is needed. It is helpful to know how much expenditure requires finance, from the start of the activity to its finish however long that is, and whether the expenditure fits neatly into one financial year or straddles several. It is the costs of the complete activity that the charity should be appealing to donors to finance. It may be helpful to think in terms of the donor timeframes. Funders such as the institutional funders will think in financial years – their financial years not the charity's – and without question the charity will have to appeal for funds and report on actual expenditure in financial years. Unless the charity is lucky, those periods will not coincide with its own financial year, and as a result it makes sense to think in terms of periods that are divisible in any financial year, such as quarters.
- Which donor and fund(s) is expecting to finance an activity.
- How much funding is predicted from that donor (and therefore what balance, if any, is still likely to be unfunded).
- What the status of the financing is. In Sight Savers International each activity has one of four descriptors against it, indicating the proximity of secure funding being received:
  - available: no specific funding even in the pipeline yet
  - on offer: in discussion with one or more specific donors to provide funding for that activity but nothing yet guaranteed
  - committed: commitment obtained from donor to provide funding but not yet received
  - received: income received and thereby available for expenditure as and when activity that meets the terms of any restriction is appropriate to take place.

---

[2] Those costs directly attributable to the activity.

5.4 Sight Savers International's Fund Management Committee – the terms of reference

Aim

- To co-ordinate the raising of restricted funds with their application to programmes
- To ensure that all decisions on fund allocations are optimised corporately

Objectives

- To monitor and co-ordinate the raising and allocation of all restricted funding
- To agree on fund allocations in a corporate context
- To provide fundraisers with information on project activity
- To provide an opportunity for programme staff to publicise projects suitable for fundraising
- To provide fundraisers with an opportunity to communicate fundraising plans and campaigns
- To be a forum for discussion over the impact of these plans on Sight Savers International.

Source: Sight Savers International December 2000

Managing the matching process

To be effective, such a process has to be carefully managed. It is not the free-for-all it might sound. Maintaining accurate, up-to-date information by activity is critical if the charity is not to risk making inappropriate approaches to funders to finance activities that already have other funding or which are inaccurately costed. Given that the future is uncertain, the anticipated cost and timing of activities will change over time. The charity must therefore establish how to handle the funding implications of these changes, both in terms of fund management decisions internally, and with respect to the funder. High quality (although not necessarily technologically sophisticated) information systems are needed with responsibility clearly assigned for their maintenance. A well-designed spreadsheet may be adequate.

Most critical of all, is the decision-making process by which funds and activities are matched. There will inevitably be competing funding demands on the same activities at times and, as and when there are, there needs to be a clear internal process to determine which funding source is to be matched with the activity. The charity must be clear whether a particular activity is to be matched with funder A or funder B, especially if the funding is not yet secure. It must understand the consequences, for example, of reserving the activity for submission to funder A and subsequently being unsuccessful in that bid by which stage income from funder B may no longer be available. Consideration has to be given to the nature of funds that have already been received and are available before determining what future income is sought, since there would be no value in seeking funding that would be restricted to activities for which adequate funding is already available.

A final issue for consideration is that of recognising the benefit of matching expenditure that is likely to be long term and ongoing, with funding sources that are also long term and stable. The alternative is to risk facing a funding shortfall for long-term expenditure that was matched with a short-term funding source that is no longer active.

These issues can cause difficulties for the fundraisers. The same activities often appeal to a range of funders who, for all sorts of reasons, are reluctant to switch their interest to other, equally important activities performed by the charity. There may be considerably less room for negotiation with such funders than at first appears to be the case particularly if they are unwilling to finance core costs.

Key stewardship questions – funds

1 Are the reserves at an appropriate level, given the future intentions of the charity?
2 Are the fund balances (restricted and unrestricted) in an appropriate form?
3 Are restricted fund balances being appropriately matched to expenditure?
4 How does the charity intend to achieve these aims?

---

6 Managing assets for financial health

The assets of a charity describe the form in which the fund balances are held. Many will not be in the form of cash. They will have been converted into other forms such as computers or buildings (tangible fixed assets), or have been invested in equities, bonds and the like (investments). The fund balance may not even have been received yet and still be owing to the charity (debtors). Similarly, the charity may have incurred costs that commit it to paying the funds to another party, but not yet have done so (creditors). It is unlikely, however, that many fund balances will have been converted into stock unless the purpose of the charity is met through the supply of goods.[1]

Whatever form the fund balances are held in, the finance steward must be confident that such a form is appropriate and the key to successful asset management revolves around understanding cash and how it moves. The charity has to reassure itself that sufficient cash is being generated and that the assets of the organisation, its resources, are being appropriately used in pursuit of its purpose. Whilst the finance strategy of a charity will have many features that distinguish it from its commercial counterparts, with regard to cash the two should be very similar. The importance of cash is common to all businesses from every sector. 'Cash is to a business what blood is to a living body. Allow it to drain away and the body becomes weak and sickly and eventually dies. The more cash can be generated … the more healthy the company becomes. So rapid generation, conversion and effective utilisation of cash is the whole foundation on which a business rests' (Warnes, 1984 p.39). So it is with charities.

---

[1] Trading subsidiaries however may hold sizeable stock values.

Assessing the charity's financial health[2]

Liquidity

The quickest way to understand the immediate financial health of a charity is to determine how easily the organisation could meet its short-term liabilities. This is done by assessing the liquidity of its assets, reflecting the ease with which assets in a non-cash form could be converted into cash. The *current ratio*, the ratio of current assets to current liabilities should, as a rule of thumb, exceed one (there should be more current assets than liabilities). A very high ratio on the other hand might imply that the charity has excessive liquidity, that assets are being retained in an easily realisable form rather than being spent in furtherance of the charitable purpose.

Solvency

Assessing the longer-term financial health of the organisation requires a somewhat more sophisticated understanding of the structure of the financing of the charity. Essentially the total assets of the charity, its total capital, must be financed from just three sources – fund balances, creditors and borrowings, and the greater the extent to which the financial structure of the charity is dependent on creditors and borrowings the less secure its solvency. Borrowings can be either arranged formally, using financing facilities such as overdrafts and mortgages, or informally, for example by using monies owed to creditors. If there is a net outflow of cash, this has to be financed either by allowing borrowings or creditors to increase or fund balances to reduce. Long-term solvency demands that the charity can generate positive *operational* cash flows (i.e. that it can generate at least as much cash from its daily, operational business as it spends, without the need to rely on cash generated from the sale of assets on the balance sheet). Liquidity ratios will not necessarily highlight this. The short-term liquidity position can be quickly improved, for example, by the sale of fixed assets such as computers or vehicles. However, on the assumption that these assets are required for operational purposes, such action would quickly render the organisation ineffective.

Understanding how much of the organisation's assets are being financed from borrowings, rather than from the charity's own fund balances, can be assessed by comparing the level of borrowings and

---

[2] Herzlinger and Nitterhouse (1994) ch.5 cover this topic fully.

creditors (total liabilities on the balance sheet) with the size of the fund balances. This is the *debt to equity ratio* = total liabilities:fund balances. The larger the borrowings the greater the financial strain on the organisation to generate cash to meet the principal and interest repayments due. A very low ratio on the other hand (fund balances high compared to debt) could lead the financial strategist to conclude that the charity was in a position to expand its level of activity by taking on more debt or by reducing the fund balances. However, in taking on debt with consequent interest obligations when it has healthy fund balances, some of which may be invested in equities, etc., the charity exposes itself to the charge that it is borrowing money to invest. It must be ready to defend its policy of accepting debt, which is likely to command higher interest charges than can be earned by the investment of fund balances.

Cash management

The funds handled by the charity must not only be of the right type, held in the right form, and subsequently used in the right way, but in addition, all this must happen at the right time. Cash management is about understanding the flows of funds into the charity, onto the balance sheet and out through the SOFA (see Figure 6a). Why? Simply because, whilst the SOFA will state how much income has been raised, and may show that there have been 'net inflows of resources' during the period being accounted for, it does not tell its reader whether the income has been received in cash yet. And it is cash, of course, not surpluses, which is needed to pay staff and suppliers, to make grant payments, and so on. There can be a critical difference between surpluses on the SOFA and cash; to understand the cash position, therefore, the charity's financial steward must go to the balance sheet and the cash flow statement. This issue is worth spending time understanding.

Cash requirement

Most charities require cash to cover two types of cost:

- operational expenses such as grants, salaries, rent, supplies, printed materials, fees, etc. – these items appear as expenditure on the SOFA
- capital expenses such as property, computer equipment, fixtures and fittings, vehicles – these costs appear as fixed assets on the balance sheet.

6.1 How cash flows in a charity

The start of the process is the arrival of cash from donors, the shareholders of the charity investing their funds in order to generate a charitable impact. Those funds may arrive immediately in the form of cash or, if committed earlier than paid, may be in the form of debtors until cash is received.

If the funds are not immediately needed, the cash can be converted into investments in order to generate investment income or additional cash if sold at a higher value than when purchased. There is of course the risk that cash will disappear in realised investment losses if the investments are sold at a lower price than when purchased. These cash losses would be recognised as expenditure.

Some cash will have to be used to purchase fixed assets in order to provide the infrastructure to run the organisation. Only the cash generated from any sale of these fixed assets will re-enter the cash flow. In the case of most assets the resale proceeds will be considerably less than the original purchase price. Cash spent on fixed assets is unlikely to be recovered and will eventually be recognised as expenditure by being charged as depreciation. As well as fixed assets being bought with cash, credit can be used, the value of creditors representing the value of cash to be paid out at some time in the future.

With fixed assets in place, and funds not yet needed suitably invested the remaining cash sums are spent in one of three directions running the organisation. Some payments of cash will be invested in further income generation activities, such fundraising investment thereby feeding back into donor funds. At least some cash will have to be used to pay for essential management and administration costs such as fees associated with regulating the organisation as a legal entity (e.g. audit fees). As much cash as possible, however, should be devoted to financing the charitable services by which the organisation aims to further its objects. As with fixed assets, in all of these cases, the payment of cash out of the business can be delayed by financing the transactions through creditors.

At its simplest, there are only three options as to what to do with cash received from donors. It can be kept in the form of cash, converted into another asset form in order to protect it to provide future value to the charity, or spent (on fundraising, management and administration or on furthering the charity's objects). There are no other choices.

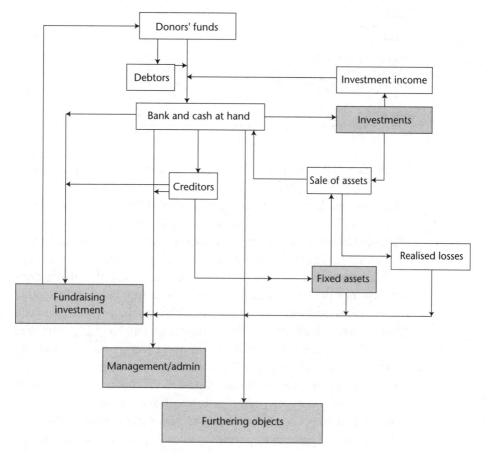

Source: Adapted from St John Price (1979) p.75

Figure 6a Cash flow in a charity

The operational and capital expenses are the items for which cash will flow out of the charity. Cash will flow in to the charity as as a result of generating income, which is also shown on the SOFA. Reference to the SOFA only however will disguise the cash position of the charity, potentially leading to a false sense of security. The simple example below should illustrate the key principles.[3]

Illustration of the key principles of cash flow

The charity's SOFA and balance sheet show that during the period it raised £1,000 in income, incurred £950 on operating expenditure, and spent £200 on fixed assets such as computers:

---

[3] This example is based on material presented in Warnes (1984).

SOFA	£
Income	1,000
Operating expenditure	950
Net incoming resources	**50**

BALANCE SHEET	£
Fixed assets	200

On the face of it all would appear to be well. The SOFA shows a surplus, and the charity has £200 of new capital assets. However, the real picture is less positive. Even on the assumption that all the figures above were represented by cash, the charity would be showing a cash outflow of £150. Not all the income however will have been received in the form of cash. Some funders will not yet have met their liability and, as a result, the charity will have some debtors. On the other hand, the charity similarly will not yet have met all its liabilities to suppliers for items that appear as either expenditure or capital. Although the circumstances will differ between charities, it is likely that many will have larger debtors than creditors. This is simply as a result of the fact that the funders will be relatively powerful compared to charities and have greater influence over the timing of when the funds are paid to the charity than the charity does over the timing of payments to creditors. Assume in the above example, that 20 per cent of income is in the form of a debtor rather than cash, and that 10 per cent of payments are still showing as creditors. The primary statements would now look as follows.

SOFA	£
Income	1,000
Operating expenditure	950
Net incoming resources	**50**

BALANCE SHEET	£
Fixed assets	200
Debtors (20% × income)	200
Creditors (10% × operating expenditure and capital)	(115)
Total net assets	**285**

The total net assets of £285 have to be financed with money from somewhere, with only £50 generated from the surplus of income over expenditure, leaving a £235 shortfall. That is perhaps more obvious if the above results are reflected in terms of what has happened to cash.

The *cash* results of the charity look like this:

CASH FLOW	£
Income received in cash (80% × £1,000)	800
Cash inflow	**800**
Operating expenditure incurred in cash (90% × £950)	(855)
Fixed assets bought with cash (90% × £200)	(180)
Cash outflow	**(1,035)**
Net cash outflow	**(235)**

The performance has, in fact, resulted in a cash *outflow* of £235 that has to be found from somewhere. Study of the figures on the SOFA and balance sheet will show that this has been caused by the increases in fixed assets (£200) and net current assets (debtors − creditors = £85) exceeding the surplus generated on the SOFA (£50). The total cash paid out (£855+£180) is £235 greater than the cash received in (£800).

Where can the charity find the £235 that it needs to close this funding gap? The answer is from three sources. It could pay fewer of its creditors; it could borrow funds from a third party, such as a bank overdraft; or it could reduce its own fund balances. All three have obvious dangers. The greater the creditors the greater the strain on the charity's resources, since the creditors will use increasingly punative measures to recover their debt. Borrowing money incurs costs such as interest payments that further increase the expenditure payments needed, as well as accumulating potentially major cash flow problems when the principal sum has to be repaid. Reducing fund balances, as has been discussed, results in a permanent depletion of the charity's capital base, which is fine if fund balances are healthy, but a problem if they are not.

It is important to note from the above example that the effect of the charity's business over the period on cash is much greater than the SOFA surplus, hence the need to track cash movements so carefully. Note too that trying to resolve the cash problem by expanding the operations to generate more income is likely to have precisely the opposite effect. Gearing the organisation up to raise twice the income would leave the primary statements showing a funding gap of £470:

SOFA	£
Income	2,000
Operating expenditure	1,900
Net incoming resources	**100**

BALANCE SHEET	£
Fixed assets	400
Debtors (20% × income)	400
Creditors (10% × operating expenditure and capital)	(230)
Total net assets	**570**

CASH FLOW	£
Net cash outflow	**(470)**

What emerges from the above example is that cash *flow*, the change in cash during a period, is influenced by just three factors.

1 The surplus or deficit incurred on the statement of financial activities.[4]
2 The change in a charity's net current asset requirement, where this is measured by debtors less creditors.[5]
3 The level of capital expenditure on fixed assets such as computer equipment, fixtures and fittings and vehicles.

All three have to be monitored assiduously and before action that will have cash implications is taken, those implications have to be understood and covered. If the charity wishes to expand, for example, that will place cash demands on the organisation (at least temporarily in terms of net current assets and fixed assets) and the charity must be clear where the cash will be found to finance those demands. What is crucial is that action is taken continuously to prevent the cash requirement stimulated by the above three factors from spiralling out of control. The cash flow statement, the third primary statement, which is so rarely used (or understood) can play a key role. It is structured precisely to show what has happened to cash with respect to the three factors, and helpfully shows the reader how the cash movements are derived from the SOFA and balance sheet. For cash-starved charities it deserves far more attention than it gets.

---

[4] This should be calculated after removing non-cash items such as depreciation charges.

[5] If the charity has stock this should be added to debtors to calculate the net current asset requirement.

Cash flow monitoring and forecasting

The tighter the cash situation the more important the need to engage in good monitoring of historic cash movements and forecasting of anticipated ones. Tracking historic cash movements should not be difficult, particularly with the help of computerised bank facilities that monitor movements in and out of the account of automated and cleared items on a daily basis. This can also greatly help with very short-term cash flow forecasting. The bank should be able to identify those transactions that are already in the system and due to be charged or credited to the account over the next three working days. To the extent that the charity's business in the future will be similar to its recent past, tracking cash history should help the charity build up a good picture of the nature of its transactions, and the cash demands that are likely to be imposed. Within any month, for example, there are likely to be cash outflow peaks, coinciding with the timing of the cheque runs, the payroll, or grant payments.

Comparing the historic cash flow with the expenditure pattern could also prove informative. Great care must be taken to ensure that cash is not confused with income or expenditure. A charity's income and expenditure plan/budget is not the same as its cash flow forecast, and it could have disastrous consequences if decisions are made, for example, in the mistaken belief that the phasing of anticipated income on the SOFA identifies when cash will be available. For accuracy, a cash flow forecast has to be derived from the income and expenditure forecasts, with assumptions built in as to when cash will be received in or be paid out.

Asset management

Identifying the demands that drive a charity's cash requirements highlights the importance of tight management of all the assets and liabilities on the balance sheet. Some key trends have to be tracked. It is most important that the financial steward of the charity understands why each asset and liability exists and what is an appropriate size of each, in relation to the financial position and performance of the organisation. Monitoring a set of key ratios that define the relationships between certain assets, liabilities, income and expenditure will promote such understanding. In all cases, there is no ratio that by definition represents an absolute measure of success. The charity must make its own judgements on, for example, how much it should be investing in fixed assets taking into account its level of activity, past record, financial position, and industry benchmarks if available. Analysis of ratio trends over time will give a clear indication of whether asset management is improving or deteriorating.

Asset turnover

Are the assets of the charity working hard enough? If they are not, funds invested in the assets could otherwise be released for charitable expenditure, or the productivity of the assets should be increased. Asset productivity, or turnover, is measured by the *asset turnover ratio = total income or total expenditure in the period:average total assets in the period.* Assessing whether the level of investment in capital (i.e. fixed assets), which has been identified as one of the three determinants of cash requirement is appropriate (see page 86), can be done by using average total fixed assets in the ratio, in place of average total assets. The usual aim is to see a high measure of output (income or expenditure) in relation to assets held. This would suggest that the assets are being productive. Too high a ratio, however, could be a sign of old assets with low balance sheet values, and thus a signal of the imminence of significant asset replacement costs. A very low ratio would suggest that the assets are insufficiently productive and might be better converted into another form, such as cash, to be used on charitable expenditure. The choice of an appropriate asset turnover ratio will be heavily dependent on the business of the charity: some will require significant investment in assets in order to function effectively, others much less so.

Debtor control

Is the charity collecting funds owed to it at an appropriate speed? This is measured by tracking over time the relationship between income and debtors, the aim being to reduce the proportion of income that is in the form of debtors. At its simplest, debtor control is measured by *total debtors:total income* although sometimes the relationship between the two is expressed in terms of the number of days income that the debtors represent. Good debtor management will see the charity chasing the funder to meet the terms of the funding contract or, at the very least, being aware of how outstanding the debt is. As income grows, whilst the absolute value of debtors will also grow, it is essential for cash flow purposes that the level of debtors in relation to income at least remains constant. That is equally true of creditors so that, whatever the level of income, the ratio of net current assets to income should remain constant. A deteriorating *debtor control ratio* will indicate that the charity is taking longer to collect funds owed to it than previously and this should be investigated.

Creditor control

Is the charity settling its liabilities with third parties at an appropriate speed? Good creditor control means ensuring that the charity takes advantage of any payment terms that are offered by suppliers or that it negotiates favourable terms where there is scope to do so. However, this should not extend as far as unreasonable withholding of legitimate payments, even if many charities lack the muscle to prevent some funders from behaving similarly. Nevertheless, at times when cash is very tight, delaying making payments to creditors is an obvious tactic, albeit a potentially dangerous one. Focusing on net current assets, where creditors are *deducted* from debtors, can deflect attention away from a worrying level of creditors, since the higher the creditors the lower the level of net current assets. As Warnes (1984) advises, a very good indicator of the cash flow strain in the organisation is to measure the 'creditor strain', the value of creditor payments that are overdue. It should be possible to use most accounting systems to identify the creditors (and debtors) aged by month, according to when the liability was incurred.

Investment management

This book is not the place to discuss how to manage investments. Nevertheless there are a number of key issues that need to be carefully considered by the financial strategist before any funds of the charity are invested. The first of these is to determine whether the charity has any fund balances that are appropriate for investment. Although investments such as equities and fixed interest securities can be realised into cash very quickly, making them a relatively liquid asset, they are only an appropriate form for fund balances if certain conditions prevail:

- the funds must not be required by the charity for other purposes in the short term, arguably at least 12 months
- it must be possible to anticipate the need for them to be realised with a reasonable lead-time.

The overriding aim of investing funds must be one of protecting the real value of the asset. If either of the two conditions above do not exist, the charity exposes the investments to the risk that they will have to be realised suddenly, and at a point when the investment markets are depressed. In such circumstances the fund balances may have lost value. The ideal scenario would see investments being realised in a managed way for use in financing charitable expenditure after they have exhibited real growth in value. It follows that it is crucial for the objectives of investing fund balances to be determined and documented before the investments are made. Do the investments need to generate short-term income that will be used to finance operating activity, for example?

The charity also needs to reassure itself that it is within the terms of any restriction imposed by donors for their funds to be invested, and to be clear what investment powers it has as an organisation. Professional advice has to be taken in order to ensure that any decisions about investments are appropriate for the charity. This will centre on understanding and managing the tensions between risk and return. The trustees of the charity have an obligation both to protect funds placed in their trust, and to generate an adequate return on balances not required for operational purposes. Consideration must also be given as to how the investments will be managed, and how their performance will be clearly and accurately measured. Professional investment managers should expect the charity to require their performance to be compared to one of several published industry benchmarks, and for them to be set objectives in relation to those benchmarks. The most useful objectives are expressed in relative terms (for example, the performance should be in the top quartile of charity portfolios) rather than absolute ones (for example, the portfolio should deliver total growth of at least 10 per cent per annum). These objectives must be set in recognition of the long-term nature of such investments. Short-term investment performance can be very volatile.

Key stewardship questions – assets

1 Are the assets of the charity sufficiently liquid?
2 Is the debt/fund balances funding structure of the charity appropriate?
3 Is the charity's cash flow being well managed?
4 Are the assets sufficiently productive?
5 Is debtor and creditor control adequate?
6 Is the charity managing its investments properly?
7 How does the charity intend to achieve these aims?

7 The level, distribution and effectiveness of expenditure

Expenditure may be discussed here as the last element of finance strategy but it is just as important as the other three, income, funds and assets. All these four perspectives of strategy must be attended to if the charity is to demonstrate good stewardship of its financial resources. Rather, expenditure is discussed last because it is the ultimate destination of the flow of funds through the charity. Funders donate income to the charity in order to see their financial contribution have charitable impact to the benefit of those that the organisation was established to serve; the charity delivers this impact through the expenditure of its funds on charitable services. Reference to the financial stewardship map on page 3 will remind the reader of this cause and effect. Expenditure refers to the costs incurred by the charity that are recognised on the SOFA as *resources expended*.

For the purposes of determining the finance strategy, the charity's financial steward must address three issues relating to expenditure:

- its size or level
- its direction
- its effectiveness.

In doing so, finance strategy recognises the three-way link that exists between the organisation's intended impact, its funds and its expenditure (see Figure 7a). The funds provide the resources (the inputs) enabling the organisation to incur expenditure on activities (the outputs) through which it has impact (the objectives). Understanding this triangular relationship, represented as a value for money diagram, is promoted as one technique to measure charity performance, as in Wise (1998 ch.12). In such models the relationship of objectives to inputs defines the *economy* of resource consumption, inputs to outputs measures its *efficiency*, and outputs to objectives determines its *effectiveness*.

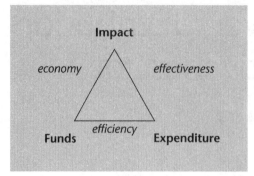

Figure 7a The value for money triangle

The level of expenditure

The first strategic question to ask about expenditure relates to its total. Is the *level* of expenditure appropriate given the resources available to it? There are potentially three sources of funds to finance expenditure: income, fund balances and creditors (including borrowings). The structure of the SOFA, which places expenditure underneath income generated over the same period, can mislead its inexperienced reader into believing that the expenditure has been financed solely from that income. That would be rare, and opening fund balances in particular provide a valuable supplement to new income.

The task of determining those resources that are available to be spent must be undertaken in the context of the dual responsibility of charity trustees and management to maximise impact today and maintain the organisation as a going concern. Unless the purpose of the charity has been met, maintaining it as a going concern must have first call on the resources. In practice this means addressing the balance sheet issues discussed in the previous two chapters, principally ensuring that the level of reserves is sufficient, that the fund balances are in an appropriately liquid form and that borrowings and creditors are not excessive. Income generated may be needed to increase reserves. Alternatively, the level of fund balances may be greater than is needed thereby enabling them to be depleted and added to the income generated. Arguably, some of the wealthier charities are far more prudent in terms of the funds that are made available for expenditure than is appropriate. Whatever the case, it is only once these issues have been addressed and the balance sheet is appropriately healthy that the level of resources that are *really* available for expenditure purposes can be identified.

Once this is clear, a second question arises. Are those financial resources adequate to fulfil the operational plans of the charity, or indeed are they more than adequate? This is a question of the closeness of the match between the available resources and the activities that would be funded by those resources. A judgement needs to be made as to whether the ambitions of the charity seem reasonable in terms of the impact that the expenditure could have (Herzlinger and Nitterhouse, 1994 pp.133–4).

The distribution of expenditure

The SOFA profile

The textbook model of charity management would suggest that determining which financial resources will be used to finance expenditure *follows* the determination of what activities the organisation will undertake, and which ones therefore need funding. The chronology of matching funding and activity is activity-led; activity (the cause) defining the funding requirement (the effect). Ideally, of course, trustees and management would wish to be needs-driven. In reality however many charities have found themselves having to consider whether to alter their proposed activities in order to make them more acceptable to potential funders. In these cases the cause and effect is reversed: activities follow funding. The dangers of being funding-led are obvious and yet it is easy to be seduced into spending resources on activities that do not best fulfil the charity's mission as a result of the charms or demands of funders. Once more the value of generating unrestricted funds that enable the trustees of the charity to spend resources as *they* see fit, so that they can be truly needs-driven, are clear.

Whether needs-driven or funding-led, the financial strategist must picture what expenditure *profile* the charity should have. That presupposes that the organisation knows how it wishes to categorise the areas of expenditure (activity), both for presentational and management purposes. Usually the expenditure classification reflects the structure of the organisation, which in turn reflects the distribution of work internally. It should identify the main ways in which the charity meets its purpose. SORP 2000 calls it a functional classification, defined as the 'aggregation of costs incurred in pursuit of a defined purpose (e.g. provision of services to elderly people or counselling)'.[1] Most charities will pursue a whole host of activities in furtherance of one or more purposes. Many medical charities established to support those suffering

---

[1] SORP 2000 appendix 1.10.

from a particular medical condition, for example, will offer services to individuals suffering from the condition today, and at the same time fund research into finding the cure for tomorrow.

Expenditure distribution

Supporting multiple purposes or services is not unusual. Reference back to Figure 2a under 'Purpose' (see page 26) shows The Refugee Council with four defined strategies for achieving its objectives – providing direct services, supporting other agencies, providing information and influencing the policies of government and other organisations. Sight Savers International has three core strategies for delivering its mission – delivery of eye care services, advocacy, and partner capacity building, all of which are essential if eye care work is to be sustainable and replicable. Similarly, The Ramblers' Association defines four charitable objectives (see Box 7.1) and one of the tasks of governance must be to determine the relative importance of each. The trustees and senior managers of The Ramblers' Association, for example, must determine how much of the organisation's available resources they devote to promoting walking rather than, say, to protecting the countryside.

It is worth noting that the relative importance of activities within the organisation in terms of meeting purpose, of having impact, may not be well reflected by expenditure. Crucial activities of the charity may be very cheap or vice versa and expenditure may not be the most appropriate way to measure the degree to which the organisation's resources are invested in them. International charities, for example, can find that comparable activities in different parts of the world incur very different costs. One programme could have much lower expenditure than the other does although both have similar impact. For true comparability, non-financial measures need to be used or more sophisticated financial techniques applied, such as adjusting to reflect purchasing power parity.

7.1 The Ramblers' Association charitable objectives

- Promoting walking
- Opening up footpaths
- Protecting the countryside
- Securing a legal freedom to roam

Source: The Ramblers' Association Annual Report 1999

Accepting that point, the financial steward must determine what relative proportions of the financial 'pie' different activities of the organisation ought to consume. They should also be assured that there is a strategy in place to enable the 'pie' to be cut in this manner.

It may be useful to consider what profile would be desirable on the SOFA in terms of the three-way classification of costs as defined by the SORP (see Box 7.2). How much of the charity's expenditure should *not* be in furtherance of the organisation's objects, for example? Once this top-level profile between the three main categories of expenditure is determined, discussion of the extent to which activities within each category should be supported can begin, for example how much is to be allocated to direct services, advocacy work and research under the category 'furthering the charity's objects'.

7.2 SORP classification of resources expended

■ Costs of generating funds
■ Costs in furtherance of the charity's objects (split between grants payable, costs of activities and support costs)
■ Costs of management and administration of the charity

Source: Adapted from SORP 2000, paragraph 60

Comparisons with other charities may give some guidance as to the expenditure distribution to aim for, but such comparisons need to be approached with care, even when using information such as that provided in statutory accounts. Although the SORP has brought consistency to the format of charity accounting, there is still considerable discretion available to charities as to how costs are charged between the various expenditure headings. What one charity recognises as management and administration costs, another might treat as expenditure in furtherance of the charity's objects. There is a danger of comparing apples and pears. Differing operating efficiencies apart, even if identical accounting policies are used there are good reasons why charities' ratios may differ. The costs of generating income, for example, will be heavily determined by the nature of the fundraising being undertaken and the degree to which the charity is investing in growing its support base. Charities that receive a large proportion of their income as investment income, grants or legacies are likely to have a lower cost:income ratio than charities that rely on direct marketing. Similarly charities that are in a phase of investing for income growth, rather than simply investing to maintain current levels of support, will incur relatively heavy costs and have a correspondingly high cost:income ratio in the short term.

Achieving the desired expenditure profile

If the desired profile of expenditure differs significantly from the current profile this raises some key strategic questions.

- Are the funds equally available for the desired profile as for the current one, i.e. do the terms of any restriction prevent the funds being applied in the way that the charity now wishes?
- Is the charity going to *reduce* actual expenditure in some areas, or is its strategy to hold expenditure constant (or at least restrict the level of increase) in order to divert more funds elsewhere?
- What is the lead-time needed, operationally, to change the expenditure profile of the organisation?
- How long will it take to set up new projects/services, or to conclude existing commitments? How far into the future is it sensible to commit funds now?

The issue of dispersal of funds becomes particularly pertinent when resources are tight, when the funds available from income and from fund balances are stretched and it is difficult to cover the expenditure. In these circumstances the financial stewards of the charity must guard against making expenditure decisions that solve a short-term problem (a funding gap) at the cost of long-term damage to the capacity of the organisation to continue to have impact. It can be characterised as the expenditure strategy of 'the have-nots' (see Figure 7b).

Perspective	Short term not long term
Language	'Cuts' not 'growth' or 'change'
Priority	Urgent not important
Sacrifices	New not lowest priority; investment not short-term impact

Figure 7b Characteristics of the 'have not' organisation

A preoccupation with reducing expenditure, or at least avoiding new commitments, means that the 'have-not' strategists focus on the urgent costs, not the important ones. Activities sacrificed are those that lack quick impact, even though in the long term they are crucial. These are typically the investment activities of staff training, fundraising development, building membership and so on. The 'have-not' charity shys away from shutting down current activities of declining priority, to the detriment of new, higher priority activities. The vocabulary internally (and possibly externally) is of cuts not growth or change. Such an organisation might have to choose between stopping one activity to release funds for another or continuing both by drawing down on fund balances or increasing borrowings. It has to understand the implications of each option, the possible risks, and the consequences if those risks materialise.

The effectiveness of expenditure

Measuring the level and destination of expenditure does not measure its impact. Measurement of effectiveness takes the reader back to the top of the financial stewardship map (see page 3) to 'impact'. To assess impact the steward needs non-financial information about the activities and outcomes resulting from those activities to set alongside the financial results. Most charities are now ready and able to provide good information about the activities they have financed. Output statistics indicating, for example, the level of uptake of the services provided by the charity are commonly tracked and published. Measuring impact, however, has proved much more difficult. Argenti (1993) has been amongst the most vociferous in demanding that organisations such as charities stop defining their performance in terms of what they do but instead measure it from the point of view of the beneficiary, in terms of impact (see Box 7.3).

7.3 Measuring impact

If you are proposing a project, or founding an organisation, you *must* say what effect you expect it to have on your individual intended beneficiaries, people with faces and names. You *must* say it with figures. You *must* then check up to see if it had that effect. You *must* calculate the return to the beneficiaries. Otherwise all your efforts are just vanity.

Source: Argenti (1993) p.131

Measuring impact from the point of view of the beneficiary implies undertaking a much more thorough assessment of the impact of a charity's work than normally results from monitoring performance against specific objectives through regular reporting or project visits, as important as these latter evaluations are. It involves measuring the impact of the organisation in terms of its overall *raison d'être* – has the charity had the impact it intended on the beneficiaries that it exists to serve? The nature of this impact can often only be assessed over the long term and of course measuring cause and effect is often not easy: many factors influence impact. Nevertheless, informed thinking now accepts that impact can be attributed where a 'plausible causal relationship' can be demonstrated.

In line with the cause-and-effect approach of Kaplan and Norton's strategy map (see Box 2.5 and Figure 2d on pages 35 and 37), and more formal planning and evaluation tools such as Logical Frameworks, the explicit link between activities and overall purpose has to be established. This can be illustrated with reference to one of Sight Savers International's key strategic initiatives, that of integrated education (see Figure 7c). Whilst the programme can be rationalised within the overall *raison d'être* of the charity, the real challenge for its financial stewards is

Corporate goal

No one is needlessly blind and everyone who is blind or severely visually impaired enjoys the same rights and responsibilities as people with normal vision.

Programme goal

Inclusive education for all blind and low vision children.

Programme purpose

Improved opportunities for inclusive education, in SSI target countries for a greater number of children, especially those in least-served communities.

Outputs

1 SSI is a successful advocate of inclusive education.

2 SSI successfully builds the capacity of key players in-country to provide inclusive education.

3 Improved service-delivery, especially to the least-served.

Source: Sight Savers International (2001b) appendix C

Figure 7c Sight Savers International's Integrated Education Programme framework idea

to confirm that its support for the education of blind and low vision children is appropriately targeted, cost-effective and sustainable. This requires a sizeable input of resources to finance a more participatory approach to assessment, with greater emphasis on qualitative rather than quantitative data, such as anecdotal evidence of improved quality of life of beneficiaries. The charity's recent review of its integrated education work summarises the distinction in the kind of indicators that need to be monitored, recognising the importance of tracking changes over time (see Figure 7d). The difficulty for all charities of adequately measuring impact simply adds to the pertinance of the need to try. Drucker (1990), Argenti (1993), Hind (1995), Wise (1998), and Hudson (1999) all devote space to this crucial issue.

Quantitative	Qualitative
■ Number of training sessions held	■ Extent of female participation in Parent Teacher Associations
■ Staffing numbers	■ Change in communities' attitudes towards blindness as a disability
■ Numbers of children screened	■ Perceptions of integrated education (IE) students on how they have benefited
■ Number of children identified for integrated education	■ Achievements of ex-IE students measured against their expectations
■ Number of awareness raising initiatives held	■ Extent of enabling home environment to support a child in IE
■ Details of equipment and materials distributed	■ Increase in confidence of IE student
	■ Increase in independence of IE student
	■ Increase in communication skills of IE student

Source: Sight Savers International (2001b) pp. 28–9

Figure 7d Example impact assessment indicators – Sight Savers International's integrated education

Key stewardship questions – expenditure

1 Is the level of expenditure appropriate given the resources available to the charity?
2 Is there an optimal distribution of expenditure between activities relating to generating funds, furthering the charity objects, and management and administration?
3 Are funds being spent on the right activities within each of these three categories?
4 Is the expenditure cost-effective?
5 How does the charity intend to achieve these aims?

PART 3

FINANCIAL MANAGEMENT

8 Day-to-day financial management

Several observations have significantly shaped my views on day-to-day financial management.

1 Most organisations engage in very detailed financial planning despite the fact that many factors with a critical influence over their future are entirely unpredictable. Whether planned or not they have to react to the circumstances in which they find themselves operating. Most find themselves in the position of having to respond quickly to unforeseen circumstances: income streams are uncertain; unplanned opportunities arise; social, political or economic situations change unexpectedly; stock markets move unpredictably; key suppliers' viability disappears. You name it. It is probably safe to say that any charity at any time in the year is not where it expected to be, or if it is, it is the result of luck rather than judgement. As Bryson (1995 p.9) states 'strategic planning is likely to result in a statement of organizational *intentions,* but what is *realized* in practice will be some combination of what is intended and what emerges along the way.'

2 Most performance management systems continue to compare performance to a fixed plan even though the plan is acknowledged to be out of date and no longer defines the best way forward. Success and failure are defined in terms of the plan rather than in relation to the actual circumstances in which the performance was achieved.

3 Many organisations experience a surge in expenditure in the first month or two of the new financial year or in its last few weeks. More often than not this profile has nothing to do with the demands of the charity's beneficiaries for the services provided. The reason? Annual budgets, based on negotiated targets and resources, which encourage a 'spend it or lose it' mentality in their holders. Cost centre managers find something to spend any spare budget on rather than lose it. The expenditure profile reflects the timing of the distribution of new allocations of money (budgets) at the start of the financial year or the imminence of their withdrawal at the end. Sub-optimal cash management and resource allocation decisions result.

4 Most management teams rely on financial information that does not extend beyond the end of the current financial year even if that year ends in a matter of weeks. There is a brick wall built at the end of the final accounting period of the year over which the manager or trustee cannot see. Typically, management accounts for period 10 of the year, for example, will not tell the reader anything beyond period 12 even though by the time the information is available period 12 probably ends in about six or seven weeks' time. Why, as a charity progresses through a financial year, does it make sense to shorten the forward perspective of management accounts until, by the final quarter, it extends no further than several weeks ahead? Predictably, obstacles and/or opportunities are, as a result, seen later than they could be and potentially too late.

5 Most management information is presented in relation to 12-month 'chunks' of time irrespective of the duration of the discrete activities by which the charity delivers its mission. Service provision may need to be planned, and commitments made, over a significantly longer time-frame; fundraisers may legitimately argue that they cannot forecast with any degree of accuracy beyond the next six months. There may be no element of the charity's work that fits a 12-month timeframe.

6 The traditional budgeting process is typically drawn out over several months and detailed, involving literally thousands of numbers. Many a finance team finds itself moving straight from the year end audit work relating to the previous year onto the budget preparation work relating to the following year. What gets squeezed is any attention to what is happening now.

The tools of financial management

The observations above suggest that the tools and techniques that most organisations are using to help in matters of day-to-day financial management are flawed. They fail to provide the appropriate information that decision-makers need and, consequently, inappropriate decisions about what to do with the resources at their discretion are likely to be made.

As has been described in Part 2 on finance strategy, the financial resources held by the charity are all shown on the balance sheet. The only decision to be made is how best to protect and use these resources. There are no decisions to be made with regard to the information presented on the SOFA. The SOFA provides only a historical record of expenditure or income performance that can no longer be influenced, however satisfactory or otherwise that performance may have been. But how well the financial assets or liabilities on the balance sheet are managed *will* influence future financial performance. To that extent financial stewardship is exclusively a matter of balance sheet resource allocation. That is the only financial *decision* to be made: what should the charity do with the financial resources under its management for which the trustees and senior management are responsible (i.e. the ones on the balance sheet)? Should it spend them on charitable activity or on the administration of the charity? Should it invest them in activities to generate future income? Or should it retain them in order to maintain the organisation as a going concern? Seemingly infinite demands are placed on finite resources by these choices. Some tools are needed to help plan such decisions, and to understand their consequences (see Box 8.1).

8.1 Tools of financial management

- An overall financial picture of the results to be achieved from a proposed operational plan.
- Forecasts of what results are expected.
- A target, for example, of income to be raised, or expenditure to be incurred in a particular area of activity.
- A measure of performance against which actual results are compared.
- Controls to ensure that the financial position does not unravel.

The role of budgets and their limitations

Traditionally 'the annual budget' has played the major role in providing the essential financial planning tools where 'a *budget* is a plan expressed in a financial terms against which performance will be measured. It is a tool for allocating scarce resources and for committing managers to a pre-determined financial outcome – usually on an annual basis. It also acts as a constraint on spending and a basis for evaluating management performance and rewards. A budget also defines authority levels and influences how managers behave' (Hope and Fraser, 1999 p.7).

The budget as financial management tool

An assessment of the traditional budget against the required tools listed in Box 8.1 indicates why the use of budgets has acquired such wide acceptance.

- In its consolidated form the budget does provide an overall financial picture of future expected results as at the snapshot in time at which it is prepared. To that extent it provides a forecast.
- It can be used as a target of, for example, income to be raised, and thereby becomes a measure of performance. It defines what, at the time the budget is prepared and as a result of the assumptions on which it is based, would represent a satisfactory outcome. The budget becomes the benchmark against which actual results are compared. Typically, if the budget is achieved that is regarded as a good performance; if it is exceeded (expenditure) or not reached (income) that is regarded as requiring explanation, the implication being 'poor performance'.
- It can be used to guide resource allocation, the budget outlining how the resources are to be allocated between the operating units and activities.
- These allocations become entitlements to spend, and simultaneously constraints on spending. The budget becomes a ceiling on spend for managers.
- It can also provide a marketing tool with which to appeal to donors, especially statutory, corporate, and institutional donors, to provide funding to support particular activities. It says to them 'this is what your funds would be used for'. It then becomes the key 'comparator' (control) against which actual results are reported.

The budget therefore can meet a number of the crucial demands of financial planning. And yet the frustrations of working with traditional budgets are deeply felt and regularly experienced by managers in organisations in every sector.

Criticisms of the budget as management tool

The opening observations of this chapter will have rung bells with many readers, prompting the common criticisms levelled at the principles and processes associated with budgeting.

- The budget can be out of date before the year even starts, let alone when it finishes. How often do managers find themselves having to explain large variances in the very first month of the year? It is not surprising. Much time has usually elapsed since the budget was put together, and its construction will have been reliant on a whole variety of assumptions any one of which may prove to be fallacious.

- The budget can be very time consuming to prepare stretching over several months; a major distraction from looking after the charity's current activities. It can become a voluminous entity. A budget of 20 cost centres each with, say, 20 budget lines phased monthly for the financial year, results in a total of almost 5,000 numbers. Is it really necessary to have 5,000 numbers to steward the finances of a 20-cost centre organisation? Common sense would suggest not and would challenge the value of such an exercise.
- The budget becomes a single annual event, much like completing the year-end accounts, even though the responsibilities of allocating resources and achieving good performance are continuous. It becomes the one time that the spenders can get commitment from the organisation for resources.
- It creates a mind-set that says it is appropriate to think in terms of 12-month periods whatever the natural activity cycle of the charity's work. This is one of those sacred cows ('we've always done it that way') that deserve challenging. Why is it necessarily appropriate to plan in 12-month lumps?

These limitations of budgets are significant. However sophisticated the budget preparation it cannot predict the future with 100 per cent accuracy and the greater the uncertainty about the future the greater the possibility that what subsequently happens will not have been anticipated by, or caused by, implementation of the plan. As Haeckel (1999 p.3) says, 'traditional planning is useless in the face of great uncertainty'.

It is these sorts of frustrations that have led to attempts to find a more effective financial planning tool that provides the key stewardship tools without the drawbacks of budgets:

> 'In its simplest form, a budget is an estimate of income and expenditure and has few behavioural implications. This is neither our meaning nor our problem. When we refer to budgeting, we mean an annual process that sets the performance agenda for the year ahead. This has wide behavioural implications because it is a performance contract. The purpose is to commit people to achieving a certain result. Terms are likely to include a fixed target, time period, resources, limits of authority, reporting intervals, and rewards. The problems caused by the budget-based performance contract are obvious in most large organisations. Budgets lead to undesirable results. Over 90% of medium to large companies use the budget model. Most are dissatisfied and want to consider alternatives.'[1]

---

[1] Hope, Jeremy and Robin Fraser, Letter to *Financial Management* magazine, CIMA, September 2001.

A new financial management methodology

If good financial stewardship demands that organisations make crucial decisions about how the financial resources at their disposal are used, then three prerequisites have to be accepted to enable such stewardship. The organisation must:

1 be able to identify (a) where it is trying to get to, and (b) where it is now
2 have as good a sense as possible about (c) what is ahead of it
3 accept that where it is now, and what is ahead of it, are continually changing even if where it is trying to get to is not. Therefore it must be prepared to reconsider what resource allocation decisions it should make as it goes. That necessarily means that what it should consider to be satisfactory performance might also change as it progresses.

Reacting to circumstance

Good financial stewardship should be based on the use of up-to-date information about the current financial position and latest thinking about the future in the context of defined targets or goals. This information will be continually changing. The crucial task is not, therefore, to predict where the organisation will be at some point in the future; that is a near impossibility and financial stewards have to accept the fact. Instead the crucial task becomes one of understanding where the charity *might* be, given how it intends to get where it *wants* it to be, and of being confident that the organisation could *afford* to be, and could *manage* being, in that circumstance. That last sentence is worth digesting carefully. The game is to develop an ability to react to the actual circumstances the charity finds itself facing, rather than trying to predict accurately where that will be. It is about developing an 'ability to rapidly implement whatever strategy [is] necessary, rather than determin[ing] *the* strategy in advance' (Haeckel, 1999 p.11). If that is accepted the whole basis of financial (and operational) planning changes and the methodology of financial management based on a detailed, fixed budget is likely to be too cumbersome, unwieldy, and inflexible an approach at best. At worst, it will be a dangerous one, sending decision-makers inappropriate signals about how resources should best be allocated.

To provide the flexibility and adaptability needed the design of the methodology by which a charity should steward its finances must be underpinned by four principles (see Box 8.2).

8.2 The principles of planning

1 The charity must have key performance measures that between them are sufficient and necessary to show whether the financial performance and financial state of the charity are satisfactory or not. The organisation should be stewarded using these critical measures of performance (i.e. on what it is really important to get right) not a mass of detail.

2 Information about the charity's current financial performance and state of play that is accurate, appropriate and right up to date must be available at all times.

3 Planning and forecasting must be a continuous, participatory activity not an annual event. The possible impact of opportunities and problems must be assessed when they arise.

4 The perspective and timeframe looking forward should reflect the nature of what the organisation does, not the requirements of accounting statute (see Box 8.3 for example).

8.3 The planning perspective of Sight Savers International

In Sight Savers International's case the key operational 'unit' is a project that is run in partnership with a local organisation. Such projects are formalised in a Memorandum of Understanding committing both parties to an agreement over a three- to five-year timeframe. This is the natural planning and resource management timeframe for Sight Savers International: once a Memorandum has been signed the charity has a moral commitment to complete the project. The financial year has no relevance to Sight Savers International's business other than representing milestones at which statutory accounts that are in the public domain are published. Quite rightly, attention is paid to what those accounts will say and, ultimately, the importance of the public message might influence either the timing or distribution of resources in an effort to present the best possible picture to the public. But managing the finances to be able to present a particular picture at 12-month milestones has become very much subsidiary in importance to managing the finances to deliver effective charitable services.

Using the five-step financial management methodology

The four principles listed in Box 8.2 translate into a five-step financial management methodology that is entirely logical and built on common sense, not rocket science. It is a very straightforward approach to enable the organisation's decision-makers to manage its finances as they go, taking on board circumstances and issues that present themselves on the way. At its simplest it is no more than an adaptation of how a human brain behaves as an individual moves from A to B. The five steps are as follows.

1 Understand where the charity is now. Deciding how and where to move forward must be determined in the context of where it is now.
2 Look ahead to see what is in front of it. Before starting to move forward the charity has to check whether there is an obstacle in its path that is going to impede progress.
3 Decide where it wants to go. Armed with the intelligence collected in steps one and two the charity's financial stewards are now able to make a sensible decision about the organisation's intentions: where it wants to get to, by when, etc.
4 Decide how it intends to get there. The decision-makers must identify the alternative ways of reaching the charity's destination and choose between them, using criteria such as weighing up the relative importance of speed and cost.
5 Set off towards the intended destination.

Moving from step to step

This is a very logical series of steps that works as well for managing the forward movement of an organisation as that of an individual. The steps are sequential, each step building on the previous one, and together creating a continuous performance management model. In practice it is a continuous cycle of information gathering and decision-making in reaction to that information: a cycle of MONITOR–AIM–PLAN–ACT … MONITOR–AIM and so on (see Figure 8a).

Following the cycle shown in Figure 8a, each step requires information to be collected to inform the charity on how to proceed to the next step. A number of key questions need to be answered in order to provide this information. In terms of financial stewardship these would be the kind of questions shown in Figure 8b.

Step one
First, the organisation needs to understand its current financial position: critically important is to assess the resources it has available now, and its recent financial performance.

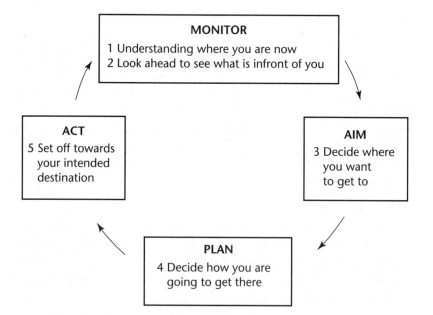

Figure 8a The five-step management cycle

Step	Questions/actions	
1 *Understand where you are now*	● What is my current financial position? ● What resources do I have? ● What is my recent financial performance?	MONITOR
2 *Look ahead to see what's in front of you*	● What additional resources do I anticipate generating and when? ● What commitments have I already made to new initiatives? ● What will they cost and when will the cost be incurred? ● What ongoing costs will I have to incur? ● What spare resources will I therefore have available?	
3 *Decide where you want to go*	● What financial outcomes am I looking to achieve? ● What would success look like in financial terms?	AIM
4 *Decide how you intend to get there*	● What 'available' resources can I commit now, either from reserves or from future income? ● What else would I like to do? ● What's the priority? ● What additional commitments is it appropriate to make now? ● What existing commitments is it appropriate to stop making now?	PLAN
5 *Set off*	● Make or stop commitments: incur expenditure, liabilities, etc.	ACT

Figure 8b The five-step management cycle: questions and actions

Step two

As part of the information gathering before it moves forward, the organisation also needs to assess what is in front of it financially, in terms of the commitments it has already made, and especially in terms of future income generation, and ongoing costs it is likely to have to bear. This will enable it to assess the financial room to manoevre by identifying those resources it anticipates having available to apply where there is still some discretion over how these are applied. Only then can its financial stewards sensibly assess where it is realistic to aim to get to (step three).

Step three

The risk of taking step three before the monitoring stage (steps one and two) is that the aim may be unrealistic given the resources available to the organisation. The sequence of monitor before aim helps ensure that the ambitions of the charity are realistic given its starting point, and what it anticipates is in front of it.

Step three is where the charity defines what success would look like in financial terms. Then the organisation can worry about how it is going to get there (step four).

Step four

In particular step four must enable the charity's financial stewards to understand what resources they are able to commit now, and to what. A process for deciding where to allocate these resources has to be in place, including a way of prioritising those activities and initiatives that do not yet have funds committed to them. This may include deciding to stop some activities that are currently being funded.

Step five

The final step, step five, then simply requires the decisions made in step four to be implemented. Resources are committed, new activities and initiatives are brought on stream, and current activities discontinued, immediately shifting the position of the organisation. 'Where you are now' has changed from what it was prior to step five. The monitoring steps, steps one and two – understanding the current financial position of the charity and what is ahead – therefore need to be repeated, and the cycle continues.

Key attributes of the new financial management methodology

The approach described above has three key attributes that differentiate it from traditional financial management methodologies using budgets.

First, the process of MONITOR–AIM–PLAN–ACT is a continuous cycle not a single event undertaken once a year. In particular, the planning stage, step 4 when resource allocation decisions are made, takes place when it is needed, whenever that is in the year, not when a budget timetable pre-determines that it should happen. The annual event called 'the budget' disappears.

Secondly, the methodology does not assume that the appropriate time-frame over which to plan and look ahead is a 12-month one. It may be but equally it may not be. The forward perspective is determined by the nature of the activities undertaken by the charity and the timeframe over which funds have to be committed. Again, this may or may not be 12-months.

Thirdly, the key controls in the methodology, the checks and balances that prevent expenditure in particular spiraling out of control, are provided by a few key indicators defined in step 3, not by detailed budgets and variance analyses prepared line by line, period by period.

The following Chapters 9 to 13 explain how each step should be completed in practice. The methodology makes no presumptions about the characteristics of the charity that could use it, the nature of its work, the state of its finances, etc. What all charities have in common is the need to steward finite resources through an uncertain future so that they maximise impact over time.

Key stewardship questions – financial management

1 How satisfied is the charity with its budgeting process or other financial planning?
2 What objectives are the charity's financial process designed to meet?
3 What behaviour does it encourage?
4 What principles should underpin the charity's financial planning?
5 Is the charity's financial management methodology effective at informing the resource allocation decision-makers?
6 How able is the charity to react appropriately to circumstance?

9 Step one – understanding the current position

The purpose of step one is simply to make sure that the charity knows where it is and where it has come from. Where should a charity's financial steward look to get an understanding of the current financial position of the organisation?

At this stage what is relevant is history and the obvious place to start is the statutory accounts. These offer income and expenditure history over a 24-month period (the last financial year and its prior year comparative), the balance sheet as at the end of the last two financial years and a cash flow summary over the same period. To understand the financial state of any charity start with the balance sheet, not the SOFA. It is the balance sheet that will show, crucially, what assets and liabilities the organisation has as it moves into the future from the date at which the balance sheet is prepared. Not that many lay readers of statutory accounts find them easy to read. That is important to note; one of the key roles for senior finance professionals involved in a charity is to help users of the published accounts understand what they say.

As time progresses, of course, the statutory accounts at the end of the previous financial year-end will be increasingly uninformative to the reader searching for an understanding of where the organisation is now. Other information is required and it is normally produced under the label of 'management accounts'. As its name implies such information is prepared solely for the benefit of internal management and trustees: it is not required statutorily, nor is it accessible outside the organisation. The information contained in the primary financial statements of the statutory accounts must, nevertheless, be kept in mind throughout the year if only to be aware of how the public would interpret the organisation's performance and state of play.

The role and characteristics of management accounting

Management accounting refers to any information about the financial performance and state of play of the organisation that is prepared for its decision-makers (see Box 9.1).

9.1 Chartered Institute of Management Accountants (CIMA) definition of management accounting

The application of the principles of accounting and financial management to create, protect, preserve and increase value so as to deliver that value to stakeholders of profit and not-for-profit enterprises, both public and private. Management accounting is an integral part of management requiring the identification, generation, presentation, interpretation and use of information relevant to:

- Formulating business strategy
- Planning and controlling activities
- Decision-making
- Efficient resource usage
- Performance improvement and value enhancement
- Safeguarding tangible and intangible assets
- Corporate governance and internal control

Source: Chartered Institute of Management Accountants (2000) pp.15–16

Such information, and those who provide it, have a particular role to play in contributing to the financial stewardship of any organisation. As the example in Box 9.2 below acknowledges, the role of management accounting extends far beyond simply generating numbers. It is about supporting good financial stewardship, which is one of the key tools needed to maximise charitable impact.

9.2 The role of the management accounting team at Imperial Cancer Research Fund

To provide financial information and guidance to enable decision-makers to generate, manage and distribute financial resources more effectively.

Source: Imperial Cancer Research Fund management accounting workshop, February 2000, facilitated by the author

---

What should a financial steward be looking for to make the management accounts successful? The information contained in management accounts and the advisory service that should accompany that information must demonstrate eight characteristics (see Box 9.3). Each of these is considered in turn.

9.3 The eight characteristics of successful management accounts

- relevant
- up-to-date
- accurate
- intelligible
- accessible
- informative
- in context
- dynamic

Relevant

Management accounts must actually refer to whatever financial information the reader needs to plan and control the financial resources for which they are accountable. That may mean a cost centre report, but the management accounting team had better make sure that this is the most appropriate information for the decision-maker. They need to ask 'Who am I doing this for and what information can I provide that will make a crucial difference to the quality of the decisions they have to make?'

The issues raised in Part 2 on funds and assets may require most attention: understanding and managing cash flow may be a much more serious issue for the charity than income and expenditure. Is the balance sheet position satisfactory? Is there adequate debtor or creditor control? What impact have changes in the market value of the investment portfolio have had on the reserves position? Has each restricted fund been used in accordance with the wishes of the donor? If these are the critical questions, the key financial information tool – the management accounts – must provide the answers.

Up-to-date

How quickly can the decision-makers in the charity see the management accounts? Very typically it can be 10 to 20 days after the end of the month. Anecdotal evidence would suggest that many organisations put up with management accounting deadlines that result in them making decisions using information that is six weeks out of date.[1] If it is the

---

[1] Confirmed by an audience of 150 at a presentation on management accounting given by the author at the Charity Accountants' Conference in September 1997.

middle of the month, and the management accounts are published monthly, and have not yet been published for the previous month in your charity, that is you. How many well-run organisations rely on six-week-old information in order to make decisions? It is not necessary. Any competent finance team should be able to produce information within three to five working days, and their readers must be dissuaded from believing that somehow the circumstances of their particular organisation make this standard impossible. The production of fast actuals is a crucial component of the methodology: they provide the best indicator of where the charity is now. Tight reporting deadlines can be achieved, even for international organisations. Worldwide multi-currency organisations should be aiming for management accounts deadlines of five working days at most, national and single-site operations less. The development of electronic communication facilities should reduce this further to the point where management accounts are available real-time on line.

Achieving deadlines

Achieving such tight deadlines requires discipline, and a clear sense of what information is important and what information isn't. Excellent information systems both to generate and communicate information are required (see Chapter 17). At Sight Savers International management accounts have been consistently produced to these sorts of deadlines month after month. How? There are some key points to note.

■ Most important of all is getting the culture of the organisation right. 'Buy-in' is needed from the top on the importance of getting fast, accurate management accounting information published. The more valuable the management accounts prove to be the more the operational management will *demand* the information they provide.

■ Restrict the management accounts to key data only. Operating units should get the key information to the place where it is consolidated quickly – detail and hard copy can follow later.

■ Reconcile the balance sheet *after* the income and expenditure information is published if it cannot be done before. There is a risk that the key summary data published is inaccurate, containing errors that would be picked up when the detailed reconciliation work is done. But the relevant question is whether the error is likely to be of a magnitude that would change the decisions made in its ignorance. Trade 100 per cent accuracy of detail for speed.

■ Keep on top of the trial balance by dealing with queries and reconciliations as quickly as possible and certainly before a further month's data obscures it.

- Ensure commitment to getting the accounts information processed on time throughout the organisation.
- Get the finance team committed to delivering a high quality service to the organisation and recognise their achievement when they do it.

Do not underestimate the importance of understanding quickly where the charity is now. It is difficult to steward the organisation forward in an appropriate direction if information is not available to identify where it currently is. There is definitely an accuracy/timeliness trade off. The more accurate the recipient wants the information to be, the longer they are going to have to wait to get it. Delaying the publication of management accounts in order to get greater accuracy can only be justified if that greater accuracy would affect the decisions that will be made using those accounts. That trade-off needs to be understood well enough to determine at what point further accuracy no longer affects the decision to be made.

Accurate

Arguably, to produce inaccurate information is worse than not producing any information at all. Accuracy in this context means not only minimising the data handling errors – miscodings, data entry errors, incorrect totalling or transfer of figures – but also eliminating errors of omission.

Intelligible

Irrespective of how timely and accurate the accounts are, if they don't inform the reader they are not useful. Too many management accounts contain too many numbers presented in a layout which discourages the reader. It must be clear who the audiences are and what information they need to make the decisions expected of them. Trustees need different information from a cost centre manager, and it is usually appropriate to present financial information (actual results, and/or future plans/forecasts) to trustees, for example, on only one or two pages like the format of a SOFA and a balance sheet. If nothing else, that absence of detail forces the trustees to focus on the big picture.

It is worth understanding why many recipients of management accounts struggle to use them effectively. In many cases it is because the accounts obscure the key messages in unintelligible language or presentation. Do not accept the word of the accountant who insists that the finances are complicated to understand. Demand simplicity.

Accessible

The user of the accounts should be able to access this management tool at the time when they need the information, not when the system is designed to prepare it. That is unlikely to coincide with the pre-set monthly management accounting reporting deadlines. At the very least 'on tap' must mean being able to request a standard report when it is needed. But it should mean much more than that. If the accounts are computerised staff should be able to have read-only access to relevant parts of the accounting system from the computers on their desks, which would allow them to make ledger enquiries or request standard reports. There is no reason why this kind of 'self-service' should not extend into data entry or report design, providing appropriate controls are in place.

Informative

The accounts must tell the reader what is actually going on. For example, what do the users of the information understand 'actual' to mean? Expenditure and payments are not the same thing, but do readers realise that (see example on pages 83–85)?

In context

Management accounts that report that X has been spent on legal costs explain very little. The information begins to be interesting and useful once the reader is able compare that figure to a benchmark. It is not possible to reach a judgement about whether expenditure of X on legal costs was satisfactory without a context. Even with a good financial context, it is not possible to have a thorough understanding of the financial performance of the organisation without understanding the operational performance as well. Not only is it inadequate to know only that X has been spent on legal costs, it is also inadequate to know that expenditure of Y on legal costs was planned. An explanation as to *why* X has been spent on legal costs is needed. What impact has this expenditure had? Chapter 7 has already explored some of the challenges that this creates at a strategic level.

At a more operational level it may, equally, be very difficult to identify what impact a particular activity has had on the charity's beneficiaries – but at the very least there should be a clear sense of the outputs from that activity. That might mean, for example, knowing how many delegates attended a conference, how many people are subscribing to a charity publication, how many calls have been taken by the helpline, how many blind children have received mobility training and so on. In each case these measures of output should be accompanied by context. How many were expected? How many were achieved last year/month? How many do the best in the business have? Why not compare the fundraising performance of the charity against the best in the business? It may not be possible to match that performance but it is an informative exercise to ask why another organisation can achieve a higher level of excellence, to understand the answer and to see what can be done to close the gap. The performance of athletes is always compared to their personal best or to the relevant record performance for the event. Why not management accounts? Paucity of benchmark data may be one answer.

Dynamic

The accounts and the advice must be alive, forward-looking, taking into account the inevitability that unexpected events will affect performance. This philosophy is explored in detail in the following chapters.

The format and structure of management accounts

Fundamental to generating useful management accounts for the reader is being clear on what information they want. The data must then be put into the accounting system in a way that enables it to be extracted in the format they want. As already acknowledged, trustees require different management accounts from cost centre managers with a different level of detail. It may be helpful to think of a hierarchy with the accounts becoming more and more summarised at each level until, ultimately, expenditure can be quoted as a single figure for the whole charity or group (see Figure 9a).

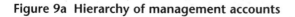

Level 6	■ Total group including subsidiaries		
Level 5	■ Total charity		
Level 4	■ Cost centre groupings e.g. regions, divisions	■ Activity centre groupings e.g. by charitable objective	■ Fund groupings e.g. total restricted funds
Level 3	■ Cost centres	■ Activity centres	■ Funds
Level 2	■ Account codes		
Level 1	■ Individual transactions		

Figure 9a Hierarchy of management accounts

The base level (level 1) is that of the *individual transaction*. All the accounts rely on the base level of data entry: from it all the summary information must be generated. At its simplest the accounts could be a list of the individual transactions entered. The first level of summary (level 2) is to group transactions by *account code*. This is the conventional nominal account code giving a traditional classification of expenditure. It tells us what the money has been spent *on* (for example, salaries or rent). The third level is to group account codes into some form of classification, which reflects units that can be managed discretely. There are three types of classification typically needed at this level. Most typically this means categorising expenditure into *cost centres* which reflect the operational structure of the organisation. However, these days it can also mean *activity centre*. In line with the SORP this classification groups costs into the activities by which the charity meets its objectives to beneficiaries. It tells the reader what money has been spent *for* rather than on. The third classification of costs at this level could be by fund. In complying with the requirements of fund accounting, again an integral part of the SORP, this classification groups costs (and income) into the funds by which the charity must account to donors. Level four groups cost centre or activity centre totals into broader categories, such as *regions* or *divisions* in the case of cost centres, or perhaps into the *charitable objectives* in the case of activity centres (for example, education and support for beneficiaries). Level five combines these category totals into a single *organisation* figure, and level six adds in any subsidiary figures to give a *group* total.

Creating the right coding structure is absolutely critical to the success of producing such a hierarchy of management accounts. If a changed coding structure is needed it is much easier to do the hard thinking up front before going 'live' on the system than to do it piecemeal later. Nevertheless, users of the system and codes inevitably learn as they go. Adopting an activity-based costing system, for example, with each transaction coded to one of a number of pre-determined activities may not be easy. It may be difficult to reach a sensible classification of activities. Some activities are easy to define (such as one-off fundraising events) but others are not (such as general parliamentary activity undertaken to influence and inform policy-makers). Ideally each level 4 activity would have a unique link to one charitable objective but how should the charity account for activities that straddle more than one objective? Some sensible bases for allocating costs by activity will be needed.

The internal SOFA

Recognising that readers of management accounts and statutory accounts may be different audiences, many organisations produce information for them in significantly different formats. This makes sense if the statutory accounts do not categorise income or expenditure in the most useful way for management use. But it would be worth checking that that is true before devoting time and energy to generating management accounts formats that differ from the statutory ones, and then being obliged to reconcile the two.

Sight Savers International concluded that the top-level management accounts should be almost identical to the statutory format. At a corporate level, for the senior managers charged with the overall performance of the charity, the SOFA format is a very valuable tool. It summarises, for example, the financial results in a cost classification that reflects the three core internal functions – work in furtherance of the charity's objects, fundraising and publicity, and management and administration, which in Sight Savers International's case mirrors the organisation's structure, a director heading up each of these areas.

Managers and trustees must have a continual understanding of the effect that the resource allocation decisions they take would have on the statutory accounts. It is highly desirable that the top-level management accounts are presented in a very similar format to those of the statutory accounts for two reasons.

1 It minimises the risk of misunderstanding, which can occur when the statutory and management accounts look very different. Much time can be taken up trying to reconcile management accounts and statutory accounts.
2 It forces the readers to focus on few numbers, the numbers that will make the crucial difference.

The SOFA classification however is unlikely to reflect precisely how responsibility for expenditure is assigned to management. It will spread the costs of some cost centres to more than one expenditure line on the SOFA, support costs being a case in point. It is usually not possible therefore to read the SOFA and see, for example, what costs one unit of the organisation is incurring. To the extent that the management accounts should enable expenditure decision-makers to monitor the expenditure for which they are accountable, it is important to provide financial information that focuses entirely on those costs that they can control. At Sight Savers International an *internal* SOFA has been developed that presents expenditure according to the statutory accounts

SOFA format but without the allocations of cost centre costs to categories such as support costs (see Figure 9b).

The internal SOFA report forms the apex of the management accounts reporting pyramid on expenditure within the charity. On a single page it provides information at levels 4, 5 and 6 of the hierarchy described in Figure 9a. For the directors it has unquestionably become the key income and expenditure report for resource management purposes, and is the first port of call in the monthly financial review. Below that report are a sequence of more detailed reports each breaking down the totals on the higher report into greater detail. The single line on the SOFA called central services cost centres' expenditure, for example (row 4), is broken down into individual cost centre totals. Each cost centre total can then be analysed on a further tier of reporting, broken down by cost type.

Rows

- **Fundraising cost centres' expenditure** (row 2) is shown without any allocations to support costs. The costs represent the expenditure for which the director of fundraising is accountable (even if some of the costs end up being shown in the statutory accounts under direct charitable expenditure). Using this 'raw' expenditure figure, attention can continue to be paid to the total cost of the fundraising and publicity activities.
- **Total contribution** (row 3) shows the funds raised in the year that can be added to the opening balances to finance the service delivery of the organisation or its administration. Showing contribution is designed to encourage the reader to note how much of the resources available to the charity (whether from opening fund balances or income) are invested in fundraising and publicity activities.
- **Central services cost centres' expenditure** (row 4) shows the management and administration costs of running the charity. These are subtracted from the total contribution, to leave the **net contribution** available for either work to further the charity's objects or adding to reserves (row 5). The order reflects the reality that there are unavoidable and important management and administration costs that have to be incurred, irrespective of the marginal level of charitable activity. Management and administration costs are likely to be semi-fixed in relation to charitable activity. There will be step movements in such costs as charitable activity reaches critical levels beyond which the existing management capacity is exhausted
- **Service delivery cost centres' expenditure** (row 6) is then shown. This line consolidates the expenditure of all cost centres responsible for the provision of the services by which the charity furthers its objects.

Line ref.	History – actual results				
	Previous year Y^{-2} £	Last year Y^{-1} £	Current year (Y^0)		Latest 12 months £
			Latest month £	Year to date £	
1 Fundraising income					
2 Fundraising cost centres' expenditure					
3 **Total contribution**					
4 Central services cost centres' expenditure					
5 **Net contribution**					
6 Service delivery cost centres' expenditure					
7 **Net incoming/ (outgoing) resources**					
8 Gains/(losses) on investments					
9 **Net movement in funds**					
Opening fund balances					
10 General funds					
11 Other funds					
Closing fund balances					
12 General funds					
13 Other funds					
14 **Total closing fund balances**					
Key performance indicators (examples)					
15 Fundraising cost/ income ratio					
16 Service delivery expenditure as % of total					
17 General funds as % of future expenditure					
18 General funds – excess/(shortfall)					

Figure 9b Sight Savers International internal SOFA (historic perspective only)

- As per the external SOFA the **net incoming/(outgoing) resources**, (row 7) gains or losses on investments (row 8), and net movements in funds (row 9) are then shown.
- On the **funds** position (rows 10–13), attention concentrates on understanding the level of free reserves, in absolute money terms, but also in terms of future expenditure intentions. Funds balances show only general funds and other funds.
- **Key performance indicators** are then shown (rows 15–18). At a glance, the impact of the result on the critical key performance indicators is clear. Crucially for understanding the financial position of the charity, those general funds are compared to future expenditure plans, and the excess or shortfall in relation to the agreed reserves policy is shown (row 18). This excess or shortfall shows very clearly how much 'spare' room the charity anticipates having given its current thinking about the future, or flags to management by how much it need to replenish reserves in order to comply with its reserves policy.

Columns

- Reading from the left, the columns start with the results of the last two completed financial years, Y^{-2} and Y^{-1}. This gives context, and crucially an indication of trend. It tells the charity in relation to the current results where it has come from, whether it has a recent history of growth, contraction or status quo.
- The **latest month**'s results are then shown, in isolation and then in aggregate as part of longer timeframes – the final two columns.
- A conventional **actuals year to date** column shows the impact of the latest month's results on the cumulative position since the start of the financial year.
- The latest month's results are then added to the previous 11 months actuals to give the results for the most recent 12 months. This is an extremely useful perspective, indicating the very **latest 12-month position** which can be compared, for example, to the last statutory financial year. It is much more useful to management than any year to date picture. By showing 12-month results any seasonality, which might skew the results year to date, is removed. The impact of latest decisions and activities can be very easily assessed using a trend of 12 months' results.

Accounting by fund and activity

The importance of understanding how the various activities in the organisation are being funded has already been recognised in Chapter 4.

'What is paying for what' must be understood, as demonstrated by the format of the SOFA which requires columnar analysis of income and expenditure by type of fund. In similar fashion, one way of ensuring that the question of 'what is paying for what' is understood is to present the income and expenditure results in the form of a two-dimensional matrix: funds will appear on one axis and either cost type (e.g. salaries) or activity on the other (see Figure 9c). This approach would enable the reader to see whether restricted funds are fully covering the costs of the activities for which they are earmarked, and how those precious unrestricted funds are being used. However it may not be possible or appropriate to identify which funds are being used at the time expenditure is incurred (see page 75).

	Fund 1	**Fund 2**	**Fund 3**	**Fund 4**
Activity 1				
Activity 2				
Activity 3				
Activity 4				

Figure 9c Expenditure by fund matrix

Communicating management accounts

Presentation of the management accounts is critical if the reader is to feel enthusiastic about the information they receive. A typical set of management accounts is communicated in a written report format, showing actual results versus budget for both the latest month and cumulatively, the annual budget and perhaps the projected full year actual. But the philosophy of dynamic adaptation required by the methodology encourages rather more imaginative thinking about how best to communicate the key financial information with which decisions will be made. Alternative ways of presenting the results, using trends, graphs and face-to-face presentations should be experimented with.

Trend analyses

As indicated above, the use of trend data to review performance can be a powerful management tool whether looking at the total corporate picture as described in a SOFA or a balance sheet, or at the financial results of one cost centre, activity or fund. Using rolling 12-month results (i.e. results for the latest 12 months, rolled forward by one month each month) will indicate very clearly whether action being taken is having the desired impact. This could be done either showing rolling 12-month totals or simply the last 12 individual months' results. The advantage of monthly data is that monthly trends become obvious much more quickly than annual ones. The advantage of the rolling annual totals is that it provides a very clear picture of performance since the last statutory year end, and highlights exactly what still needs to be done if any forward-looking data such as year end forecasts or annual budgets is available for comparison. Trend data of course lends itself to graphical representation.

In Sight Savers International the internal SOFA described above is also presented in a rolling trend format. The same rows appear, but the columns are devoted to showing actual results history for the last 12 months. Each month the report drops the earliest month in favour of the latest month and the 12-month trend is maintained. An example of the format, presented as at the end of May in the current year (Y^0) for two lines on the report, would be as follows:

£'000	Jun Y^{-1}	Jul Y^{-1}	Aug Y^{-1}	Sep Y^{-1}	Oct Y^{-1}	Nov Y^{-1}	Dec Y^{-1}	Jan Y^0	Feb Y^0	Mar Y^0	Apr Y^0	May Y^0
A	587	619	598	655	677	689	668	635	716	765	782	742
B	755	734	682	705	670	572	520	536	509	431	569	755

Both lines demonstrate some volatility as the impact of replacing one month's data with another is felt but whereas the trend in line A is definitely up, in line B it is far less clear. After a steady fall over the first ten months to March Y^0 a dramatic upturn in the final two months leave the cumulative 12-month position at the end of May Y^0 as it was 12 months earlier in June Y^{-1}. The statutory year-end position (December Y^{-1}, shown shaded) simply becomes one month in the trend of annualised totals.

What can be powerful is to present this trend alongside a target or planned result. It would illustrate very starkly what work is still to be done to reach that target or planned result. Imagine that the two lines shown above were income lines. The addition of the December Y^0 column as shown below would concentrate minds. The performance of line A over a 12-month period must increase from 742 in the 12 months to May to 800 by the end of December.

£'000	Nov Y-1	Dec Y-1	Jan Y0	Feb Y0	Mar Y0	Apr Y0	May Y0	....	Dec Y0
	←——————— Actual ———————→							....	Target
A	689	668	635	716	765	782	742	....	800
B	572	520	536	509	431	569	755	....	600

A variation on the above table is to show figures for individual months in successive columns, and to use the table to compare the actual results with the planned results for the latest month. At the start of the year, for example, the 12 monthly forecasts might be shown. As the year progresses the first month's forecast is replaced by the second month's actuals. Actual performance is built up from the left and the forecast runs off to the right. At the interface the actual and the forecast for the latest month are shown side by side[2] (see table below). Arguably, presenting monthly trends rather than annual ones offers greater precision: a significant problem will be shown more quickly than its effect on the cumulative average.

£'000	Nov Y-1	Dec Y-1	Jan Y0	Feb Y0	Mar Y0	Apr Y0	May Y0	May Y0	Jun Y0	Jul Y0	Aug Y0	Sep Y0
	←——————— Actual ———————→							←——— Forecast ———→				
A	689	668	635	716	765	782	742	750	760	770	780	790
B	572	520	536	509	431	569	755	500	550	600	650	700

Using graphics

Pictures often give a clearer message than numbers or words, particularly to the less confident financial reader. If used selectively, for the critical information only, graphic representation of financial information can be a very useful addition to the management accounts portfolio. Figure 9d on the next page communicates the same information about the cash flow for an organisation over a six-month period in graphic and numeric formats. Many would argue that the graph communicates more effectively than the table the extent of the cash outflow over the period.

---

[2] For a detailed exposition of this see Warnes (1984).

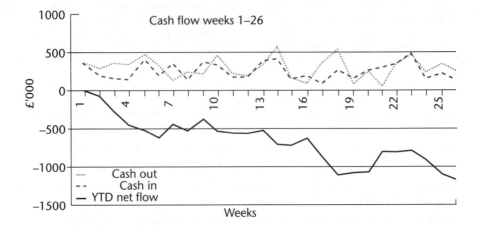

Week No.	Cash out	Cash in	YTD net flow	Week No.	Cash out	Cash in	YTD net flow
	£'000	£'000	£'000		£'000	£'000	£'000
1	355	355	0	14	588	399	−726
2	270	185	−85	15	164	142	−748
3	349	154	−280	16	96	188	−656
4	322	141	−461	17	336	83	−909
5	465	396	−530	18	529	252	−1186
6	305	192	−643	19	81	151	−1116
7	121	330	−434	20	233	237	−1112
8	233	133	−534	21	55	293	−874
9	204	358	−380	22	323	321	−876
10	464	313	−531	23	468	470	−874
11	214	173	−572	24	227	146	−955
12	189	175	−586	25	420	204	−1171
13	320	369	−537	26	243	124	−1290

Figure 9d Cash flow in graphic and tabular formats

Face-to-face presentations

As far as possible, information should be seen as a resource for all and made openly accessible without compromising individual privacy. That extends to provision of news. The methodology requires staff to have an excellent understanding of the financial position of the charity. If there is bad news they need to hear it. One option is to communicate orally, in the form, say, of a monthly 20-minute management accounts surgery to which staff are invited. At the surgery a headline-only overview of the income and expenditure results can be given and the balance sheet talked through slowly and simply. Any key financial decisions taken by the trustees and the impact of these results and decisions on the overall financial position of the charity such as reserves levels can be outlined. It is also an opportunity for staff to quiz the relevant management on issues affecting the financial performance and state of play of the organisation, or to obtain clarification on how to use the management accounts reports that they receive as a manager. Sophisticated electronic presentation tools are not necessary for such an approach: a flip chart will do.

Access to management accounts

The more the user of the management accounts 'owns' the accounts the more they will value the information they provide as an aid to decision-making. Increasingly the supplier/customer relationship between the finance team and the decision-maker can be modified in an effort to make the user as self-sufficient as possible. This might be demonstrated by expecting the user to be involved in, or even lead, the following sorts of tasks:

- designing reports or coding structures
- inputting data
- generating hardcopy reports
- interrogating the accounting system to make enquiries about individual transactions.

There is no reason these days, with the security features that are available, not to give the users appropriate access to a computerised accounting system so that they can access information whenever they wish to, rather than according to a pre-determined management accounts publication timetable. The importance of information systems is discussed in Chapter 17.

Understanding the presentation of information as actuals

It is worth stressing the importance of being clear about what information is presented as actual results. Are the readers of the charity's financial information clear what is meant when they see a column headed 'actual'? Part 2 of the book should have confirmed the distinction that must be made between income and expenditure that appear on the SOFA and cash transactions. Under an accrual accounting policy (see below) expenditure will include non-cash transactions such as depreciation and accruals, but not include cash transactions such as purchasing property and equipment and other fixed assets.

Accounting for transactions

Good financial control means knowing what funds have been received and what has happened to them. The earlier it is known that some of those funds received have been spent, or at least earmarked, the less likely it is that the charity's decision-makers will believe that those funds are still available at their discretion. Throughout the period between making the commitment and meeting the liability there is the risk of overestimating the size of the funds available. The longer the gap, the greater the risk. What the reader of the management accounts sees in the actual column will depend on the method of accounting for transactions that is adopted (see Figure 9e). If the reader does not clearly understand what transactions are included, there could be a serious misinterpretation of the true financial position.

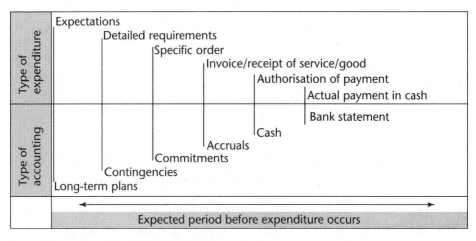

Source: Adapted from Lynch (1994) p.131

Figure 9e The monitoring of money

Cash accounting

Using a *cash accounting* policy an amount will appear in the actuals column as expenditure only once a payment has been made, for example once a cheque has been written. This may be some time after the legal liability has been incurred and well after a commitment has been made to spend the funds. If management accounts only reflect the commitment once the liability has been met, the risk of overstating the 'free' funds is considerable.

Accruals accounting

The first step in rectifying this is to move to *accruals accounting* by accruing liabilities when they are incurred rather than recognising them only when they are met. This means, for example, charging invoice values as expenditure and coding payments to creditor balances. It is worth looking at the flow of documentation through the organisation to support this. Often invoices are routed first to the recipient of the goods or services and may end up halfway down a bulging in-tray. However it may be sensible to route them via the finance team first, so that they can be logged.

Commitment accounting

The earlier the invoice details can be entered on the accounting system the earlier they can be included in the management accounting information. This does not mean that payments need to be made any earlier. Whilst invoices provide the ready paperwork to enable creditor liabilities to be recognised relatively easily, at least with a computerised accounting system, accounting for accruals (those liabilities for which an invoice has not yet been received) is more difficult. This would require a switch to *commitment accounting* where 'actuals' include commitments made (for example by the placing of an order) even though the good or service has not yet been provided and therefore no liability for payment has yet been incurred. Some form of ordering system is required in order to adopt commitment accounting. Typically, copies of orders made are entered into the accounting system to be matched against invoices once received. As well as enabling the management accounts to inform the reader at the point of commitment that funds have been earmarked and therefore are not 'free' for other purposes, using orders minimises the risk of payment for a good or service being processed twice. Even if a full-blown ordering system is not introduced it can help financial controls if larger commitments are accounted for in this way (for example, all orders over a certain value). The 80/20 rule is likely to apply: 80 per cent of an organisation's costs will be tied up in 20 per cent of its transactions. Start with those.

Just from this brief resumé of the alternative ways of accounting for individual transactions it should be apparent how easily the figures shown as 'actual' can be misunderstood. That can have serious repercussions. Managers and finance staff could work at cross purposes for months and months, comparing actual results against plans or forecasts unaware that actual results were being prepared by the finance team on one accounting basis and forecasts by the managers on another. If forecasts are prepared on an accruals basis and actuals on a cash basis, for example, it is not surprising if there are frequently significant differences between the two to explain. An important rule of thumb therefore is that actuals and forecasts/plans must be prepared on the same accounting basis if the latter are to be of any value in informing the decision-maker. Many readers of financial information simply aren't aware of the different methods of accounting that could be used and have conceptual difficulties in grasping how, for example, depreciation of assets is accounted for. It is crucial that the reader is guided and supported in interpreting the accounting information they receive and yet most finance professionals allow themselves little time to carry out this role. What effect would it have on the quality of decision-making if the time currently spent on generating information was instead devoted to interpreting it?

Key stewardship questions – understanding the position

1 Do the management accounts of the charity have the eight required characteristics?
2 Are both the format and structure of the management accounts the most appropriate for their audience(s)?
3 Is the communication of management accounting information in the organisation as effective as it could be?
4 Are actual transactions recorded using an appropriate accounting policy that is understood by the charity's decision-makers?
5 How does the charity intend to achieve these aims?

---

10 Step two – looking forward

Step two changes the perspective on financial management and looks forward. Its purpose is to collect as much relevant information as possible about what is ahead, so that coupled with the understanding about where the organisation has come from and where it is now (step 1) it can decide on an appropriate way forward (steps 3–5). Two questions need to be answered to continue with this step.

1 What financial resources can the charity reasonably anticipate having available in the future?
2 What expenditure commitments has the charity already made that will use some of these resources?

This step is about forming a view of the future, an assessment that needs to be made continually. The continual re-assessment of the future is incorporated into updated forecasts of the future income, expenditure and cash results (and any other important financial information) that can be reasonably expected. Crucially, what must be included in the forecast is what the forecaster *expects* to happen, not what they expect the recipient of the forecast to *want* to happen. It is an important difference. Honesty must replace the political gamesmanship that accompanies most budgeting processes; this poses some tough challenges as it will be necessary to develop an internal culture which discourages the playing of such games. Hope and Fraser (1999 p.7) define forecasting as 'a financial view of the future derived from a manager's best opinion of the "most likely outcome" given the known information at the time it is prepared. Thus it should be unbiased, reflect all known events (good and bad), and be realistic.' It is a good definition, highlighting the importance of basing the forecast on known information, however unpalatable that information might be.

The purpose of forecasting

The purpose of forecasting needs to be clear in all participants'minds. Chapter 8 showed (see page 106) that the role of the conventional budget was multifarious, including performance measurement and control. In this methodology the forecast plays no such role. Its only rationale is to help guide resource allocation decision-making. Forecasts help an organisation understand what resources it can reasonably anticipate having available in the future. At any time this sum will be a composite of fund balances that are available now, and future income that it can reasonably anticipate generating. Decisions can then be made about how much of these resources it can responsibly afford to commit now.

Although the only resources that can be *spent* now are the existing fund balances, the decisions about what future income to *commit* now obviously need to be informed by expectations about future resource availability. If the charity's financial stewards knew that on the horizon the organisation had some sizeable financial liabilities to meet, and that income streams would dry up, they would probably be far more cautious over the decision as to how much of the current piggy bank to raid, and rightly so. The methodology therefore requires judgements to be made about future income streams and a clear understanding the commitments already made to be arrived at. Armed with these pieces of information it is possible to determine how big a pot the charity is likely to have to spend in the future, and therefore how much of that pot it is appropriate to commit now. But it is not about crystal ball gazing. The forecaster can only take account of *known* events and accept that there will be some *unknown* circumstances that will affect future results. The greater the future uncertainty, the greater the argument for building in prudence to estimates of future resource availability.

Forecasting characteristics

Before considering how to make judgements about future resources and current commitments it is important to think about three characteristics of the forecasting process:

- how far forward to look (the forecasting timeframes)
- how often changes in the outlook should be reflected in judgements (updating forecasts)
- the level of detail required.

Forecasting timeframes

How far forward to forecast must be determined by four factors.

1 How far into the future the charity intends or needs to commit resources that are currently available now. Sight Savers International recognised that it is making commitments on projects lasting, typically, three years. In order to avoid the risk of giving stop-go

messages to the project managers mid-project it needed to be clear about whether it could underwrite the costs of the whole project before it started. i.e. whether the costs could be financed from the estimated future resources. The Sight Savers International methodology, as a result, now demands rolling three-year forecasts. If the charity had to make five-year commitments that is the timeframe over which it would need to understand what resource availability it could reasonably anticipate before making those commitments.

2 The investment lead-time the organisation needs to establish new projects, activities and/or services. Sight Savers International needs to make resource-availability guarantees to those within the charity directly responsible for service provision with 12 to 18 months lead-time, the time required to set up new projects. The forecasts enable senior managers to give messages about the likely future resource availability so that the programme management can determine what level of activity to cultivate within their area. Without committing any funds the charity is able to inform the programme staff that overall programme growth of, say, 10 per cent per annum in expenditure terms is realistic over the following three years. This enables the programme staff to be quite active in the development of new partners and sow the seeds of new projects that can be brought on stream within two years.

3 The lead-time the charity needs to make critical changes to the way it operates. Having, say, a four-year forecast of income does enable the organisation's decision-makers to ask a critical question. If that is the size (financially) that the organisation is likely to be in four years' time what buttons need to be pressed now to enable it to manage that size most effectively? Research and development activities to grow a new income stream, create a new membership profile, or develop a new cadre of management, for example, will take several years to achieve.

4 How far forward the charity's donors want to look, or want the charity to look. If long-term funding agreements are being negotiated the donor will want a long-term picture of how their funds will be used.

Within the overall forecasting timeframe of, say, three years, consideration will need to be given to what time periods the forecasts should be broken into. Should it be months, quarters, operating years, or what? Three thoughts may help here.

Decisions on resource allocation

Resource allocation decisions of course must be made not only with regard to *how much* resource there is to allocate, but also to *when* it is available to be allocated. The timing of cash flows is an important factor for all but the cash-richest of charities, and the tighter the cash position the more important the understanding of future cash movements. Very short-term forecasts of receipts and payments (note, not income and expenditure) for treasury purposes can therefore be crucial if the charity's financial stewards are to ensure that funds are in the right place at the right time. Tight treasury management will prevent cash from sitting idle, ensuring that it is working (i.e. generating interest) until it is needed. These forecasts could have a timeframe of just days or weeks and require daily updating.

In terms of the costs relating to individual projects, overall *expenditure control* may not require forecasts to be broken down into shorter timeframes than the total project life. As long as the overall estimated project cost is acceptable there may be no expenditure control issue. However, cash flow management will almost certainly demand some breakdown into shorter time periods. To the extent that the project is being financed from future income streams it is critical that the timing of receipt of that income and of its expenditure is understood. The charity cannot spend the income if it hasn't been received yet. The tighter the cash position, the shorter the forecasting timeframes will need to be.

The requirements of public relations

Whilst the activities of the charity may not be run neatly in the timeframes of the organisation's statutory accounting year (resource management will need to reflect the nature of charity activities not the accounting calendar – see specific projects below), the public relations aspect of the statutory accounts cannot be ignored. The results in this timeframe will be published in the public domain and what such public accounts say does matter. To the extent that the charity wants or needs to steward the organisation towards delivering a particular SOFA or balance sheet in the statutory accounts, the decision-makers will need to be conscious of what the forecast results in that timeframe would say.

The adoption of rolling forecasting

If the charity is trying to break mindsets that automatically think in statutory accounting years, requiring managers to forecast in alternative timeframes may be worth doing for just that reason regardless of the needs of expenditure control or cash flow management. For example, forcing managers to think in rolling 12-month timeframes that inevitably extend beyond the end of the current financial year can be an important contributor to changing the culture. It breaks the mindset, whilst allowing the spenders and fundraisers to continue to think in 12-month blocks. It may help to think about forecasts by quarter. Just as 12-month rolling histories give an incredibly useful comparator against the last financial year's results, so four quarter forecasts force the managers to think about the trend that they believe will occur in the future not just the end result. A comparison of the forecast for the next four quarters against the forecast to the end of the current financial year will highlight what is expected to happen in the quarter(s) beyond the end of the current financial year. The split of this forecast by quarter does provide useful milestones against which to assess actual performance as the quarter dates pass.

When Sight Savers International first moved onto the rolling forecasting methodology we did not attempt to think in timeframes that straddled the financial years. Rather, forecasts were restricted to the current and following two financial year-end positions. With hindsight it proved a valuable interim step towards fully rolling forecasting, allowing managers to ease themselves away from the previous current-year-only thinking.

Updating forecasts

Ideally forecasts would be updated as soon as they have changed, rather than in response to a pre-determined timetable. Certainly it would be regrettable to continue to base decisions on one assessment of the future if a more appropriate assessment had been made and could be used. This does not mean asking for repeated submissions of largely unchanged figures; only the forecasts that have changed need be revised. The forecasts could be updated continuously as soon as new information affecting the latest forecast is known. However, it will probably be sufficient for forecasts to be updated at regular pre-defined intervals. The natural frequency for Sight Savers International, where the charitable activity is long-term, sustainable development work rather than emergency response, is quarterly. Initially the expectation was that forecasting would be rolled monthly but trying to get managers to think about 12-month periods that straddle quarters (for example, May–April) proved to be confusing and unnecessarily precise. The degree of predictability required to be able to forecast what would happen in a four-week period, say, 11 months ahead does not exist in the charity's world and such an exercise is therefore unprofitable. Thinking ahead and revising forecasts once each quarter has proved adequate.

Broad-brush forecasting – the level of detail required

A traditional budget would typically break down the total allocation of an operational unit (or cost centre) into detailed income or cost types, such as salaries, consumables, etc. The real danger of adopting a rolling forecasting methodology is that what used to be an annual exercise of planning in great detail what would happen becomes instead a much more frequent exercise of similar effort. So how does the charity avoid producing four or more detailed budgets each year? The key to success is to make forecasting broad-brush and intuitive, rather than detailed and 'scientific'. Short-term forecasting for cash management purposes does require careful consideration by operational staff (if cash is very tight, potentially thinking payment by payment). However forecasting for any timeframe beyond that ought to be, and can be, a quick, top level exercise completed by a very few number of people.

At Sight Savers International the forecasting detail discussed at senior level does not extend beyond the detail included on the one page internal SOFA. A director responsible for spending, say, £1m a year should have a good intuitive feel as to how much is needed in their areas of accountability given the current expectations of future activity. A detailed forecast to be produced function by function, cost centre by cost centre, account code by account code simply isn't necessary for the purposes of determining how to allocate resources. If there is any detailed forecasting to be undertaken it is in the area of income genera-tion. Sight Savers International's approach demands an assessment of future resource availability, not a forecast about how those available resources will be spent. Once a judgement about future resource avail-ability is made the expenditure 'forecast' is simply a top-level assessment of how those resources are likely to be distributed between the SOFA categories. It is about saying, for example, that the charity expects to have £X million to spend on charitable activity, rather than forecasting how that allocation would be spent.

Encouraging managers to move from a tradition of preparing detailed, static budgets to one of submitting intuitive, broad-brush, rolling fore-casts is not easy. Mindsets are deep rooted and the managing the pace of change is important if staff are to be engaged emotionally. Managers need to learn to trust their intuition. Many initially at least need the comfort of preparing the top number from detail. In Sight Savers International managers did initially prepare line by line forecasts but on a rolling basis, the prime interest initially being to get them to get out of the financial year mind-set. Only the evidence of time, which alone can demonstrate that intuitive feel is good enough, will give the manager confidence to let go of the detail. They need to be sure that it is understood that they cannot forecast the future with 100 per cent accuracy and that it doesn't matter if they don't. It is in fact crucial to be able to dissociate accurate forecasting from performance measurement. Performance cannot be measured by the accuracy of a forecast, only in relation to the circumstances in which it was achieved.

Forecasting future resource availability

The format of the SOFA misleads the reader by implying that expenditure in the year is necessarily funded from the income received in the year. The requirement to show the balance of income less expenditure (operating inflow/[outflow]) encourages the reader to believe this. As has been discussed in Part 2 the reality of course is that there are also other crucial sources of funding – opening fund balances, and if necessary borrowings. In assessing likely future resource availability it is important to consider not only future income streams but also how much, if any, of the fund balances held by the trustees could be expended.

Making reasonable assumptions

The aim is to identify how much resource the charity is prepared to release for future expenditure *now*, recognising that some of those resources are secure (fund balances are already 'in the hand', some future income may be contractually guaranteed) but that some, maybe the majority, is not. This is about risk management. The charity cannot commit more than it can guarantee to finance without the risk of having to renege on some of those commitments. Not that minimising risk in this case is appropriate. If an organisation were to commit to spend only when income was 'safely in the bag' or at least guaranteed to arrive (a risk-minimisation policy), it is more likely that it would end up with unspent income than having to exercise the opt-out clause on expenditure commitments previously made. Why? Simply that, for most charities, to assume no future income at all is unreasonably pessimistic.

The general advice to be given here must be to ensure that assumptions about future funding availability are reasonable rather than over-optimistic or pessimistic, and to understand the risk/return trade-off for the charity. At what point does the risk of over-committing funds that are not yet secure outweigh the returns in the form of additional charitable activity that could be offered if those funds were, in fact, to be generated? Prudence will serve the financial steward well. Much better to find the organisation with more funds than expected to play with than to deal with all the problems associated with over-stretching the charity. Most charities will find it relatively easy to increase the level of expenditure as a result of having cash in the bank (albeit perhaps over a long period of time if they are to use it wisely) than to reduce raised expectations or possibly withdraw from existing commitments.

The philosophy of the methodology is to allow future resources to be committed up to a level that could be underwritten in the event that the future income forecasts on which those commitments were predicated do not materialise. If insufficient income were generated, the charity's only other sources of funding to cover its expenditure commitments would be reserves and borrowings. The greater the charity's ability to underwrite expenditure in the event of income not being generated, the more liberal it can be in determining the level of future resources that can be committed now. But the winning approach is undoubtedly to have unrestricted, general reserves to call on. With the confidence of those funds as contingency, the charity can vigorously market itself to potential donors in an effort to secure the income that will render accessing the reserves unnecessary.

Forecasting income

Reliable income streams
Ask a fundraiser how far into the future they can accurately estimate income streams and they will most likely say, and with some legitimacy, that the horizon quickly becomes hazy. Six months ahead may be as far as they can see. On the other hand, there may be particular income streams that are very reliable and completely predictable. Typically, the more committed the form of income, the greater the predictability. Take direct marketing for example. Charities that are successful in fundraising through direct marketing, such as Sight Savers International, are able to persuade an increasingly large proportion of their individual donors to support the organisation in a committed way, contributing a regular sum of money by, for example, direct debit. The payment continues indefinitely, until the donor cancels the instruction. Very quickly, the charity can build up a picture of the speed with which donors do cancel their payments, known as the *attrition rate*, and thereby make accurate forecasts forward of income from that source. Sensitivity testing of the key variables – the number of donors, the mean value of donation and the attrition rate – can be used to assess the volatility of the forecast to

changed assumptions. Increasingly sophisticated techniques, such as Future Expected Lifetime Value (FELTV)[1], are being used in this field of fundraising to infer the future performance of charity donors[2].

Other sources of income

Forecasting other sources of income may have to be less analytical. Restricted income, often agreed contractually, especially with the statutory funders, is predictable only until the end of the existing agreement(s). Beyond that the charity may be required to tender competitively for future contracts and grants, a process that is by no means assured of success.

Legacy income is notoriously difficult to predict and no wise charity would plan on the assumption that a sizeable legacy will appear in the future. Such an event would have to be treated as a bonus and the sum handled in a manner that was appropriate at the time it happened. Two sources of information can help in forecasting legacy income. First, past legacy income trends, and the question to ask is whether it is reasonable to expect the historic legacy income stream to continue into the future. Is there any reason why it would not? There may be. A large individual bequest may have distorted the overall picture; the size of the supporter base may have changed markedly; the level of legacy promotion undertaken may have altered significantly. Secondly, there are the current notifications from solicitors of legacies that are yet to be received, although the size of the legacy (in the case of residual legacies) and the date at which it will be received can be very difficult to ascertain with any confidence.

Future investment income crucially relies on the size of the capital sum to be invested, and the future rates of return that the investments might attract.

Forecasting expendable reserves

To estimate how much of future reserves a charity can afford to expend requires a judgement to be made as to how large those reserves will be and how large they *should* be given the purpose for which they are held. This need not be complicated to do and is only an issue if the current level of reserves is higher than the charity would like. If they are not, there are no expendable reserves. Given that reserves policies are typically expressed in relation to percentage of expenditure, broad estimates of future expenditure levels can be made simply from an understanding

---

[1] FELTV = the net contribution by each donor each year × the expected duration of the relationship in years × the discount rate.

[2] See for example Aldrich (1999).

of likely future income streams and current reserves levels. A simple spreadsheet model would enable an estimate to be made of how much of the reserves level at any point is in excess of the stated policy.

Understanding expenditure commitments

What is meant by a commitment? The methodology requires the financial steward to identify what costs the charity is already obliged to incur at some point in the future. But this is not a watertight definition and some judgement is required. There may be some future costs towards which the organisation has a clear legal and/or moral obligation. Those commitments are relatively easy to identify. Less straightforward are all those costs for there is *no* such obligation but which it would be reasonable to assume the charity will have to bear: its intentions. What needs to be clear is what the charity is *already* committed to spending, not what it anticipates it *will* spend in a particular period.

Thinking in terms of commitments tends to lead in turn towards an activity-based approach to costing. In practice, a distinction needs to be made between individual initiatives or projects with discrete costs that directly result from undertaking the work of the project, and general activity that cannot be attributed neatly to any one project. Individual initiatives will typically have a finite life with specific objectives and direct costs. Support activity tends to be ongoing and within individual cost centres there is almost certainly a mix of the two types of activity, whether the cost centre's role is one of service delivery, fundraising or administration/support. Identifying the costs to which the charity is already committed is a task that will need to be addressed differently depending on whether the reference is to specific projects or general activity.

Specific projects

The organisation should not have embarked on any initiative without some understanding (however broad) of its purpose, intended outcomes, expected length of life and cost implications. A project proposal should outline these areas. The perspective that needs to be adopted is that of the project life not the accounting calendar, recognising that funding arrangements or the project's activities may require thinking about over a period of time concurrent with the accounting calendar. In determining whether to begin a proposed project, consideration needs to be given through to the completion of the project not just to the end of the next accounting period.

In Sight Savers International's case the charitable work of the organisation is almost entirely project based, each project lasting three to five years with an agreement between the charity and the local partner, through whom the charitable services will be provided, in place before it begins. This Memorandum of Understanding places moral commitments on both parties to deliver the objectives of the project over its lifetime. Whilst there are get-out clauses relating to funding and *force majeur* circumstances that would enable the agreement to be terminated earlier than planned, these are very much seen as a last resort and exercised very infrequently. No project agreement is signed without a firm expectation that the project will be funded through to its completion assuming satisfactory delivery of the project objectives. The agreement does include indicative top-level costings giving an overall project cost and it is this project cost that is recognised as the charity's financial commitment and the baseline against which any future changes in expected cost is assessed. These projects are not designed with the charity's statutory accounting requirements in mind: the majority of the project agreements do not start in line with the beginning of the accounting year, and the project life never fits neatly within one statutory accounting year. The driving forces in project design and management are, rightly, the needs of the beneficiaries of the project and the capacity of the partner organisation to meet those needs.

Specific projects in fundraising and in the general management functions of the charity must be considered in a similar vein and managed in relation to the overall project life and its objectives. The total costs of a particular fundraising appeal, or event, or of a major IT development must be considered and compared to the proposed benefits of the initiative before the button is pressed. There is no point thinking only as far, say, as the end of the current financial year. Once the initiative has the go-ahead the methodology requires the charity to recognise the full costs of the project right through to completion as already committed.

General activity and support service functions

As at today, what financial commitment has the organisation already made with regard to running, say, the chief executive's office or the human resources department? There will be no one, straightforward, answer. Conceptually it is far easier to identify commitments already made in relation to specific projects, with firm start and end dates, than it is to identify the general activities that underpin such projects. Yet in all units of an organisation, and particularly the support or central service functions, much of the activity will be ongoing and general in nature. Identifying the current cost commitments of general activity cannot, therefore, be carried out in the same way as specific projects. One of several possible different approaches must be used instead.

1 Estimate the level of general activity (running costs) needed to support the specific projects already committed to i.e. showing the change in running costs in relation to the decrease in current commitments over time.
2 Assume the current *absolute* levels of running costs will continue over a defined future period.
3 Impose a cost target, reflecting the level of running costs that the charity believes it will allow over a defined period. This target could be determined in absolute terms or relative to total expenditure, for example.

In Sight Savers International the expenditure forecast for the total costs of the support service functions is set in the context of the cost target imposed (in the form of a key performance indicator – see step 3, Chapter 11) which places a percentage ceiling on these costs in relation to overall expenditure. A best estimate forecast that exceeded the ceiling would raise questions about the level of proposed expenditure and the importance and urgency of the proposed activities.

Determining which approach to adopt to value the current commitments of general activity has an important influence later in the methodology in step four. Step four will assume the costs identified in this step are committed and not the subject of further negotiation. A useful rule of thumb when considering whether running costs are already committed or not therefore is to question the extent to which they are eligible for future negotiation. If they are, it is more helpful *not* to regard them as among the current commitments.

Mapping future available resources and expenditure commitments

Ideally, the level of future resources will increase, reflecting growing income streams. And, usually, the level of existing commitments will be falling the further into the future the charity looks until, at some future date, there are no specific projects and therefore no general activity needed to support them. An example of what these two trends might look like if they were to be plotted is shown in Figure 10a. Looking forwards from the present (Y^0) shows that resources available and existing commitments diverge. The gap between the two represents those future resources that are expected to be available and have not yet been committed. Note this picture is a snapshot in time: an earlier or later picture would look different, reflecting different levels of knowledge and perhaps expectations at the time.

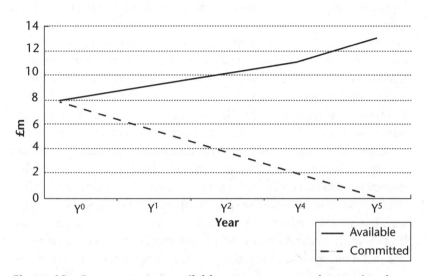

Figure 10a Resource map: available resources exceed committed resources

But what if the future resource availability was very uncertain, very insecure? It is very likely in this circumstance that the charity would, nevertheless, have ongoing expenditure commitments such as employee salary costs, rent and other general activity that would need to be financed. Any activity currently undertaken has to be financed and if current commitments exceed current resources something has to give immediately. That is a relatively straightforward, if uncomfortable, decision. More difficult is deciding how to move forward when the anticipated future resource availability raises questions about how the existing future commitments are going to be financed.

The key question is whether to start up or continue an activity that can be financed today but which may not be affordable tomorrow. The financial stewards have a choice. They could continue with the activity drawing on whatever funding they already have in the hope that they will be successful in raising further funds; this approach must make sense if the funding is heavily restricted so that it cannot be used for an alternative purpose. Or they could discontinue the activity as quickly as possible in order to free up those resources that they were intending to spend on it. Such an option becomes particularly relevant where the funds being used are unrestricted, and could, therefore, be diverted to another purpose.

Figure 10b illustrates the point. During the current year (Y^0) and the next year (Y^1) available resources are equal to commitments: the activities can be financed. Beyond that, however, the level of available resources currently expected falls off faster than the commitments. Unless the level of available resources rises above the level of existing commitments some activity or activities will have to be stopped. Commitments will have to fall. In such circumstances should an organisation seek to reduce the commitments immediately to release the resources or continue until it *has* to reduce the commitment? The more important the activity to the charity the more likely it is to conclude that the activity should continue, the decision to stop only being made when it has to be. You never know what resources might come the charity's way. If a priority activity is stopped earlier than it has to be there must be a clear understanding of why. In determining a priority activity, do not make the mistake of assuming that the urgent activities are necessarily the priority ones. It rarely makes sense to turn off the tap on activities that are of an investment nature such as future income growth, membership growth or staff development – and yet these are the easiest to chop if short-termism takes over (see Figure 7b on page 96).

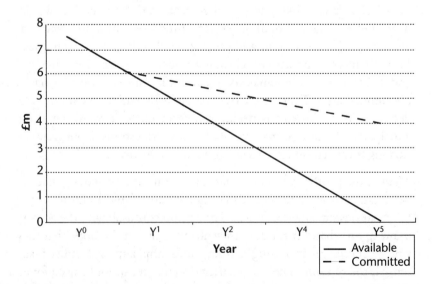

Figure 10b Resource map: Committed resources exceed available resources

Completing step two

At the completion of this second step in the methodology the information that should have been collected in relation to the future will indicate what resources the charity expects to have available (which is an income forecast) and what expenditure commitments have already been made. At this stage the financial steward does not know what expenditure the organisation expects to incur, other than knowing what ceiling it has, as defined by the anticipated level of resources available. That comes later in the process once the expenditure profile that is sought – step three – has been determined and – step four – once it is clear which of the activities that the charity has not yet committed to it would like to finance.

Key stewardship questions – looking forward

1 What financial resources can the charity reasonably anticipate having available in the future?
2 Are the forecasts being prepared for the right timeframe and to an appropriate level of detail, and are they updated with the appropriate frequency?
3 What expenditure commitments has the charity already made that will use some of these resources?
4 What is the relationship between the future available resources and expenditure commitments already made?
5 What is the charity's attitude to funding risks?

---

11 Step three – deciding where to go

Steps one and two of the methodology were concerned with monitoring the current financial position of the charity, and the financial commitments already made and extending into the future. Those steps are the crucial forerunners to the remaining three stages which, looking ahead, determine a destination and a plan of how to get there and then set off towards that destination. Step two ultimately provides the financial steward with an understanding of resources currently available that the charity can afford to commit, given the level of resources that it can reasonably anticipate having available in the future. This step, step three, guides the decision-maker in determining how best to commit these resources by establishing explicitly the kind of financial performance and position required. It does this by translating the organisation's finance strategy into key performance indicators (KPIs).

Step three therefore defines the charity's financial targets, as derived from its finance strategy. As Part 2 has detailed, it is the role of finance strategy to define the intended financial performance and position and to detail how the charity aims to achieve these aspirations. The act of writing a finance strategy will have defined those areas of the charity's finances to which strategic attention must be paid. These are the areas for which KPIs are now needed. In this way, the KPIs provide a long-term financial performance framework within which shorter-term, and more operational, targets can be set and decisions made. By the end of this third step, the decision-maker should have all the information needed to determine in which direction resources should be allocated. The following information should be clear:

- what funds are currently available
- what funds are expected to become available
- what financial targets the charity aims to meet.

The role of key performance indicators (KPIs)

As their very name (and the two definitions in Box 11.1 above) imply, KPIs are typically regarded as being measures by which performance can be judged. Target levels of performance can be set by defining the standards that should be reached in relation to each KPI within a defined time period. Led by performance management models such as the Balanced Scorecard, KPIs are now being used to measure organisational performance from many perspectives, of which finance is just one. And it is through comparison of the actual and forecast results with the KPIs that corrective or reinforcing action is stimulated, with the aim of ensuring that, at all times, the organisational objectives are achieved.

However, conditions of uncertainty raise questions about the value of using targets as performance measures, whether expressed in relation to KPIs or in more traditional forms such as budgets. The more uncertain the future the less easily an organisation can pre-determine what success will look like, and therefore the less validity any such pre-determined definitions of success have when analysing actual results. The theme of divorcing targets from performance measurement is returned to at the end of this chapter.

Setting KPIs

You will recall (see Box 8.2, page 109) that one of the principles by which a charity should conduct its financial stewardship is to use critical measures of performance. These key performance indicators must, between them, be sufficient and necessary to inform the charity's financial stewards about whether the financial performance and financial state of the charity are satisfactory or not. It is these KPIs that replace the target setting and control roles of budgets. Actual performance is expressed in terms of the KPIs, not in comparison to a budget, and the KPIs guide the reader's judgement as to the satisfactoriness of the results. If well defined, the KPIs will reassure when all is well and raise a flag when corrective action is needed. Used as targets, the KPIs reflect the financial aspirations of the charity; as parameters they identify the boundaries within which performance is expected.

In creating a finance strategy, the charity's financial stewards will have identified those aspects of the organisation's financial performance that are key: they are by definition the key indicators of performance that must be tracked. The KPIs therefore naturally arise from the finance strategy. Step three now requires each selected KPI to have an aspiration or target attributed to it. Consider the key stewardship questions summarised at the end of each chapter in Part 2 for example. Each of these could be an area of the charity's financial activity for which a KPI is established. For each indicator there could be a target performance level or a parameter within which performance could be agreed, and against which actual results would be tracked, as in Figure 11a. Deadlines for reaching each required standard, as measured by the target or parameter, would also be established.

Lead and lag indicators

Since the KPIs will be used to guide future decision-making they must not only inform the charity retrospectively whether satisfactory performance has been achieved, but also act as early-warning systems to alert management to the fact that the organisation is going off course in sufficient time to enable corrective action to be taken. Effective financial stewardship therefore requires two kinds of KPIs. It needs *lag* indicators to record with hindsight what performance was like i.e. to measure outcomes. But it also needs *lead* indicators to highlight what future performance can be expected in light of events occuring now that will influence those outcomes (performance drivers).

To set appropriate lead indicators it is necessary to identify what information would give reassurance that the future outcome, as defined by the lag indicators, was on course to be achieved. For example, in Sight Savers International, given the importance of growth in direct marketing income (a lag indicator) it is essential that the charity can anticipate whether income from this source will be generated. It therefore tracks closely those activities that will contribute to determining whether the direct marketing income sought will be achieved. These lead indicators

Perspective	Performance indicator	Target/parameter
Income	Sufficiency of costs covered	X% of funding agreements funding core costs
	Growth in fundraising contribution	X% above last 12 months, +/or in X percentile of comparable charities
	Cost/income ratio	Between X% and Y%
	Break-even level of income	No greater than £X
	Degree of income restrictions	X% of income unrestricted
	Diversity of income sources	Income from any source at least X% and/or no more than Y% of total income
Funds	Reserves	± 3 months expected expenditure
	Form of funds	X% of funds realisable within Y weeks
	Fund/activities match	No greater than X% of activities subject to competing funding bids
Assets	Liquidity	Ratio of current assets to current liabilities at least X:1
	Funding structure	Ratio of debt to fund balances no greater than X:1
	Cash flow	£X cash inflow or outflow required
	Asset productivity	Ratio of total expenditure to average total assets no less than X:1
	Debtor control	Ratio of debtors to income no greater than X:1
	Creditor control	Ratio of overdue creditors to total creditors no greater than X:1
Expenditure	Level of expenditure	X% of available resources to be spent
	Distribution of expenditure	Costs of generating income as % of total expenditure to be at least X% and no greater than Y%
	Prioritisation of activities	At least X% of costs in furtherance of objects spent on activity A
	Cost effectiveness	Qualititative impact assessment indicator (see Figure 7d on page 99)

Figure 11a Illustrative KPIs from the finance strategy perspectives

include the numbers of individual donors recruited, and the average donor yield. If these lead indicators give poor results, the charity has early warning of disappointing income figures to come and can act accordingly.

Be careful however, of setting too many KPIs. Each added indicator distracts attention from those already set and may ultimately result in the 'not seeing the wood for the trees' syndrome. It is worth being ruthless about identifying those indicators that can truly be regarded as key. As a guideline, Kaplan and Norton (2001 p.375) expect, from experience, to see between 20 and 25 measures on a strategy scorecard, of which typically five will be financial. And bear in mind that they are referring to that number to track the implementation of a corporate strategy, not just a financial one. Arguably, in terms of a charity's financial stewardship map (see Figure A, page 3), each of the four perspectives of finance strategy could ultimately be measured by just one KPI:

- income – growth in contribution
- funds – reserves levels
- assets – liquidity of assets
- expenditure – percentage of total costs on activities in furtherance of objects.

If all of these four KPIs were achieved, the charity would be enjoying increasing expenditure on activities in furtherance of its objects financed by growing income, underpinned by an appropriate level of reserves held in a relatively liquid form. Achieve good performance against these four KPIs and the organisation will be demonstrating good financial stewardship. It is of course possible to set KPIs not only at a corporate level by which to steward the organisation, but within particular operating units of the organisation in order to steward performance more locally.

In setting KPI targets/parameters three points arising from Sight Savers International's experience may help.

1 It is important to have a good sense of what is 'out of bounds', that is, what *un*acceptable performance looks like. KPIs can be set to define where this is, so that once the boundary has been reached steps are taken to ensure it is not crossed. These boundaries could be regarded either as strictly out of bounds (i.e under no circumstances would it be acceptable to end up here) or as trigger points at which enquiry into whether corrective action is needed would be stimulated. Example boundaries could be:

- cost/income ratio in any year to be a *minimum* of 1:3. The concern here would be to ensure that investment in further income-generating activities is not forgotten
- expenditure on activities in furtherance of the charity's objects as a percentage of expenditure to be a minimum of, say, 60 per cent – this would in effect place a ceiling on other activities' costs
- free reserves not to exceed six months' worth of future expenditure plans.

Again it is important to note that the steward needs to develop *lead* indicators that informs them in advance that they are likely to cross out of bounds in time for them to take some corrective action. It is not satisfactory to rely on a *lag* indicator that would simply tell them that they had already gone out of bounds.

2 Within the extremities of the boundaries, in most cases it is not helpful to be overly prescriptive about the KPI target. Sight Savers International has begun to develop target *ranges* for its KPIs, rather than precise outcomes, in recognition of the impossibility of forecasting with 100 per cent accuracy. In effect this approach sets a minimum and maximum for each KPI. It is simply an extension of defining out of bounds, allowing the charity to acknowledge the imprecision of the exercise by saying 'we want to see this indicator somewhere in this sort of range' without being overly prescriptive.

3 Sight Savers International has accepted in principle that it might be necessary or desirable to change the KPI goal in the light of actual circumstances. There is nothing sacrosant about the KPIs, although changing them must not become a means of 'shifting the goalposts' in order to dress up an unacceptable performance.

KPIs and performance measurement

In using KPIs to define what financial performance is sought there is a risk of believing it is possible to predict accurately what is going to happen, in which case the charity will be subject to the same problems and constraints as are created by budgets. The scenario of negotiating budgets – income or expenditure – from a budget-holder perspective where the aim is to minimise the risk of failure by padding expenditure and keeping income budgets low will be a familiar one to most readers. The exercise becomes one of self-protection – maximise one's chances of 'success'. Most readers will have played these games or been the accountant in the middle, reviewing budget submissions and looking to find the fat. Everyone knows it is there but just can't find it. Conceptually this approach is flawed because it probably leads to sub-optimal resource allocations and probably also to sub-optimal performance. Budgets become the floor or the ceiling – no need to question exceeding the ceiling or dropping below the floor.

Imagine instead, setting targets solely for the purpose of inspiring the staff to obtain results that they previously felt were unachievable. That can only be possible if the targets are divorced from performance measurement, in other words staff are not held to account if they do not achieve the target. Instead they should be held to account for the actual performance in the light of the circumstances which it was delivered, and in relation to comparatives such as the previous year or to competitor performance. This is a key concept in the Beyond Budgeting Round Table (BBRT) model and that spirit underpins this step. The KPIs, set with the purpose of the charity in mind, provide the targets, the goals, the aspirations.

As Hope and Fraser (1999) argue, it must make sense to decide what is acceptable performance *retrospectively*. The level of performance can be judged once the actual circumstances in which the performance was delivered can be considered, and once it has been possible to compare against others in a similar position. What is the sense in deciding now what will be an acceptable performance in, say, 12 months' time? What is now expected to be an excellent or poor performance may, in hindsight, prove to have been quite the reverse. Ten per cent income growth may sound fine until it is compared with what everyone else has achieved. Five per cent growth might actually have been fantastic performance given the conditions under which it was achieved. The more this argument is accepted the more KPI targets need to be regarded not as pre-determined measures of performance but as intended outcomes made at a certain point in time and which can change over time. Human nature responds very positively to targets, to setting and reaching goals. Ask any fundraiser. The BBRT model strongly advocates setting relative rather than absolute measures of performance. Good performance, it persuasively argues, is reflected by doing better than others rather than bypassing absolute milestones. This ensures that targets provide continual stretch thereby driving incremental, continuous improvement (see Box 11.2).

The way in which the KPIs are used needs to be carefully thought through, understood and communicated.

1 They can be a pre-determined measure of performance, which, at the extreme, represents the absolute definition of the boundary between acceptable and unacceptable performance.

11.2 Adaptive performance management

Specific targets are constantly reset at a level that, if reached, will improve the relative position of the organisation unit (or whole company) against some relative benchmark. This can be an external or internal competitor, last quarter or year, or simply a self-imposed stretch target based, perhaps, on some world-class benchmark or group aspiration.

Source: Hope and Fraser (personal communication)

2 They can represent a target that defines an intended outcome to encourage certain behaviour, but which does not represent a (pre-determined) measure of performance, which will be determined retrospectively.

Completing step three

The power of setting KPI goals is, hopefully, obvious. KPIs will guide the financial steward in managing resources and, between them, can indicate if the charity is being successful in financial terms if they are defined properly. Performance can be properly tracked through as few as half-a-dozen indicators. Equally crucially, all resource allocation decisions can be guided by the impact that those decisions would have on the KPIs. Such is the influence of the KPIs on the whole issue of resource allocation (and thereby on the performance of the charity) that the trustees must be involved in their establishment, setting and monitoring. The trustees must not allow themselves to be by-passed, and they cannot abdicate responsibility either for determining where out of bounds is, or for what KPI goals the organisation should set.

Key stewardship questions – deciding where to go

1 What should be the charity's KPIs (i.e. which elements of the finance strategy is it *critical* that the charity gets right?)
2 What target or parameter is it appropriate to set in relation to each KPI?
3 What lead indicators will tell the charity whether the strategy is being implemented successfully or not?
4 How is the charity determining what good performance looks like: in advance or with hindsight?

12 Step four – deciding how to get there

Step four is the decision-making step of the methodology, the stage at which resource allocation decisions are made. Crucially, it assumes that in step two the charity has determined how much resource it is willing and able to commit now for future expenditure, recognising that some of that resource will be future income that has not yet been generated. The logic of the methodology is that prior to determining the available resources that the organisation is willing to commit now, it has addressed its need to maintain an appropriate level of reserves as contingency, in the event of future income not materialising. By this stage therefore, the charity should be confident that it has access to contingency funds (reserves, or as a last resort, borrowings) in the event of anticipated income not materialising.

The aim of step four is to determine what commitments to make now with regard to currently available fund balances and future expected income. This involves making decisions about the gap between future resources and current commitments as determined in step two (see Figures 10a and 10b on pages 147 and 148) and using the KPIs set in step three to guide those decisions. If current commitments exceed future resources the decisions relate to how to reduce the former and/or increase the latter. If future resources exceed current commitments they are about determining the additional activities to take on. It is this latter scenario to which the remainder of the chapter is devoted.

There are two distinct phases to the step. The first is to determine the top-level allocations that are needed at a corporate level in order to achieve the financial profile described by the KPIs in step three (i.e. the SOFA and balance sheet profile). The second is to determine how to use the resources within each of the SOFA expenditure categories.

Top-level allocations

12.1 Calculating the resources available

Available resources = current spare fund balances + future income – existing commitments not yet met

There are four ways to use the resources available to the decision-maker, and the question here is which to adopt.

1 How much of the organisation's available funds should be devoted to activities in furtherance of the charity's objects?
2 How much should be reinvested in income-generating activities?
3 How much should be spent on the management and administration of the charity?
4 How much should be retained in reserves for future contingency purposes?

Such decisions are made on the basis of which allocation will best serve the objectives of the charity as guided by the organisation's KPIs. Appropriate and quick decisions can be made about top-level resource allocation decisions if the decision-maker knows:

- what the current financial position of the charity is (step one)
- what financial commitments it has already made that still have to be met (step two)
- what resources the charity is able to commit now (step two)
- what KPI targets have been set (step three).

These decisions about resource allocation can be made as and when the need to make them arises – whenever that is – rather than at a pre-determined time when an event called 'writing the budget or the plan' occurs. Traditionally resources would be allocated on the basis of a budget. Spending units would submit detailed financial plans that would be consolidated into a total budget. Once the overall budget was agreed, the components that made it up would become allocations. This approach, in contrast, enables and expects allocations to be made continuously in the light of the current situation and the latest expectations of the future.

At its simplest level, choosing how to allocate available resources between the four options above can be determined by KPIs that set targets for the proportion of expenditure that should be committed to each – that is it simply becomes a matter of slicing the pie according to the KPIs. However, the KPIs, which reflect finance strategy, are likely to be long-term aspirations that will take time to achieve. Decision-making will need to be more carefully thought through than simply allocating, say, 75 per cent of the funds in the direction of activities that further the charity's objects in line with a KPI target. In the short term there may be good reason why the charity cannot sensibly spend funds in those proportions. It may need to build the capacity of staff managing the service delivery, for example, to handle growth before it can achieve the KPI target. Whatever allocations are determined the decision-makers must be confident that they move the organisation towards the KPI targets at an appropriate pace and stay at all times within the boundaries defined by those KPIs. The ultimate test is to be confident that the chosen allocations represent the optimal distribution of resources at the time the decision is made. No alternative distribution should offer greater progress towards successful implementation of the finance strategy.

There is a natural order to determining the four-way split of allocating available funds, as follows.

1　How much does the charity need to retain as reserves to maintain its financial stability?
2　How much does the charity need to re-invest in income-generating activities if it is to have the funds to enable it to have impact in the future?
3　How much does it have to spend on managing and administering the organisation, like it or not?
4　How much is left for activities that further the charity's objects?

Note the obligatory tone of these first three questions. There is no choice but to commit precious funds to these activities if the charity is to maintain itself as a going concern. The art is to maximise cost-effectiveness, keeping these allocations as low as possible without sacrificing effectiveness. As suggested by the questions above, the allocation for activities that further the charity's objects becomes a balancing number. In practice, the process of allocation is likely to be reiterative. There will be negotiation at the margin, or at least there should be. The managers responsible for service delivery should always be finding scope to press for additional funds, and endeavouring to persuade the fundraisers that they can improve their return on investment, in other words generate the same or higher levels of income with fewer resources. Both fundraisers and service deliverers are likely to be eagle-eyed over costs incurred on the charity's management and administration.

There are three essential ground rules to note however. First, at this stage the allocation of total resources available is simply into four – there is no detailed allocation whatsoever. To avoid the risk of stop-go management the allocations have to be regarded as secure, as minimum funds available. Once made allocations cannot be retracted. Secondly, the allocations are reviewed frequently, at least quarterly, and may be increased in the light of new information about current state of play or future outlook. Thirdly, the allocations are indicative targets of the expenditure profile required, but not spending contracts against which performance will be measured.

Allocations to reserves

The charity cannot expect to have long-term impact unless it is run on a sound financial footing. The issue of reserves must therefore come first in the competing demands for the charity's available funds. Not that this means prioritising it at the total expense of the other three competing demands. Diverting significant funds to reserves in order to reach a desired level of reserves quickly rather than allowing the funds to be used for expenditure purposes may not be practical without serious detrimental impact on the continuity of activities. More realistically, if the current reserves are substantially less than the level required as identified in the finance strategy, the charity's stewards will need to build the reserves up over time, making modest allocations to reserves year by year.

Allocations for income-generating activities

With regard to allocations for fundraising purposes, the key constraint probably should not be an absolute sum of money but a relative one. Fundraising must be judged according to return on investment, on long-term return and, to a lesser extent, short-term return. Allocations to fundraising can therefore be set with reference to the return on investment ratios. There will be a natural constraint on how much the charity can raise in a defined period of time, be that an internal one (such as management capacity) or an external one (such as the fundraising environment). Cash flow will probably be relevant given the time lag in the receipt of income following fundraising activity. Even if the long-term return on investment (ROI) looks excellent, if the short-term cash resources would be excessively depleted further investment in fundraising would have to be delayed. In the process of determining the level of investment to make in fundraising, it would certainly be profitable to understand fully the sensitivity of income to alternative levels of investments. What would be the short- and long-term impact of spending an additional £0.25m on fundraising activity in the next six months? It would be worth knowing and understanding the impact on the rest of the charity's performance. What would happen to the percentage of expenditure devoted to charitable activity? Would that percentage still be defendable publicly? Any one of these resource allocation questions requires an understanding of the whole, such is the interdependency of each area of operation on the others. What is clear is that the concept of ROI however it is measured or interpreted does provide an inherent self-regulating tool – how much is invested in fundraising activity is judged in relation to how much that activity raises to pay for itself and more.

Allocations for management and administration

With the exception of the fundraisers, none of the units within a charity are directly responsible for income generation. They are genuinely cost centres, rather than profit centres, relying on funding given to them from elsewhere to finance their activities. It is not possible to identify at individual budget line what expenditure will be required 12 months away, but doing this is not necessary. What *is* necessary is to give the managers of these units some parameters to work within. They must know, without having to go continually cap-in-hand to a higher authority, what resources they can rely on. Determining the corporate allocation for management and administration activities can usefully be set at a strategic level in one of two ways.

1 Set an *absolute* sum of money. This is probably best done in relation to historic expenditure levels, and provides a means of setting tight expenditure targets, for example a 2 per cent reduction on last year.

2 Set a *relative* allocation in relation to overall expenditure for example, only 7 per cent maximum of the total charity expenditure in a particular period to be on administration. This approach requires corporate co-operation since all units in the organisation affect the achievement or otherwise of a relative target through their own expenditure behaviour, not just that part of the charity responsible for management and administration. It is a zero-sum game. The higher the spend in one area, the lower the proportion of total spend represented by another area. In reality the ability of the management and administration units to react to lower than anticipated expenditure elsewhere, with consequent upward pressure on the relative percentage spent, will be limited. Many of the management and administration costs are fixed in the short term – the charity is

committed to incurring them whether the charitable or fundraising activities take place or not. Nevertheless, setting some constraint on funds spent on management and administration to be met over the long term, or over a rolling basis, is extremely valuable.

Such a strategic level parameter can be quickly set, based on broad assessments of the likely level of activity given the operational plans of the organisation. No detailed numbers consolidated bottom-up are necessary. Once allocations are made, those responsible for managing the sums allocated must be allowed to get on with it and their success in doing so will be evident from the actual results and the consequent impact on KPIs.

Allocations for activities in furtherance of the charity's objects

Once the financial stewards are clear about how much of the charity's funds they wish to reinvest in fundraising, devote to management and administration activities or retain, establishing how much to commit to activities in furtherance of the charity's objects falls out automatically. It is the balancing figure; the funds that remain after the other demands have been met. As described in step two, determining how far ahead to commit funds for these activities is driven by the fourth principle of the methodology (see Box 8.2, page 109). The perspective and timeframe looking forward should reflect the nature of what the organisation does, not the requirements of accounting statute. In practice this means making commitments that reflect the length of the activities the charity is undertaking or supporting, and the lead-time involved in developing them. Time-limited project-type activities have a timeframe by definition; for ongoing activities a reasonable timeframe has to be assumed for the purpose of determining the future level of resource consumption. The timing of the allocation must be determined by the lead-time needed to bring new activities to a point of ready to go (see Box 12.2). If it takes, say, two years to develop a new activity, notice (confirming that funds will be available) of at least that length must be given in order to ensure that the activities are ready when the funding is available. The tap cannot be turned on instantaneously.

The importance of having free reserves to act as contingency in the event of income not materialising to cover the costs of commitments cannot be over stressed. A charity can only commit resources that it hasn't yet raised to the spenders if it has spare funds available that it is willing and able to use, should underwriting of the expenditure

> ### 12.2 Resource allocation lead-times
>
> Like all other charities working in long-term overseas development, for Sight Savers International determining how far in advance to commit funds is a major issue. The overseas programme staff operate to a 12–18 month lead time to set up new programmes, and therefore require that sort of notice period about funding availability if they are to proceed with confidence. It would not be acceptable to operate programmes, which are all about long-term sustainable development, on the basis of short-term stop-go decisions in light of income ebbs and flows. The charity therefore needs to provide a sufficiently long-term context about resource availability to enable the programme staff to plan programme development and growth in line with these lead times. In effect this means being willing to underwrite the costs of any commitment signed by the charity, even though the future funding of the charity is not certain. In other words, the level of funding is guaranteed so that the senior management responsible for overseas programmes can promote programme growth without the fear of funding shortfalls once the projects are ready to be implemented.

commitment be necessary. The only source of those funds (without establishing obligations to third parties through any form of borrowing) is the charity's own reserves. At the risk of stating the obvious, it is not possible to underwrite expenditure without guaranteed funds to draw on should that be necessary.

Committing the allocated resources

The next decision to be made is how to *use* the funds allocated to furthering the charity's objects, or to fundraising, or to the management and administration of the organisation. Once such decisions have been made about how much of the available funds to allocate to each of the four options (see page 160), the management responsible for each area of the organisation need a decision-making process by which to determine how the resources at their disposal are used. Ideally this should maximise the discretion with which they can make their decisions, subject to any constraints imposed by the KPIs. These decisions are not made at a corporate level, which concerns itself only with the overall finance strategy of the charity.

Other than at the very top level, resources are committed as the need to spend arises. The methodology allows the decision to be made at the latest possible moment, when the current situation and knowledge about the future is as up-to-date as it can be, and reflected in the latest information available. There is no value in making the decision earlier. Decisions are therefore made at the time of need not at the time of a pre-defined event called the budget. By doing so two risks emerge. The first is that the decide-as-you-go approach paralyses the spenders who end up coming cap-in-hand for every expenditure decision. Secondly, that the approach leads to *first*-come-first-served rather than *best*-come-first-served allocation decisions. Each risk can be managed (see Box 12.3).

12.3 Committing funds at an operating unit level

How does the Head of IT, for example, know whether the department can spend £20,000 on IT equipment?

- A guaranteed allocation of funds for general activity within the IT department over a defined time period (such as the next six months) is agreed. This could be higher, lower or unchanged from the immediate history of expenditure on such costs. The sort of items to be included in such departmental running costs is agreed in advance (e.g. stationery, computer consumables, service agreement fees, etc.). The Head of IT can approve such costs without reference elsewhere subject to a threshold above which higher approval is required.
- Projects or activities that are not part of the defined running costs of the department have to be presented to the relevant director with a funding proposal outlining the objectives, components and costs. Such projects are discrete, specific, time-limited and major activities. If more than one project is proposed, they are prioritised by the Head of IT.
- The relevant director determines which project submissions to approve from within their top-level allocation.
- Total funding of approved IT projects is guaranteed to the Head of IT, who manages the implementation of the project. Costs of the projects as incurred are approved within normal authority limits.

The 'cap-in-hand' risk

The 'cap-in-hand' risk is overcome by (a) recognising that a certain amount of funds need to be spent on general day-to-day activity and (b) classifying such costs as committed. Responsibility for the management of such costs can then be delegated to the spenders, who would thus need funding approval only for new specific projects. Typically, therefore, each operating unit would have access to guaranteed funds to enable them to deal with the routine expenditure incurred in running the unit. In an effort to drive down costs this sum could be set at a lower level than in a previous equivalent period.

The first-come-first-served risk

The 'first-come-first-served' risk has to be managed by those responsible for the application of the funds in the area for which top-level allocations have been made. They must decide whether to approve options on the table now or to postpone a decision in the expectation or hope of finding more attractive options in the future. In effect the question being asked is 'would you prefer what is round the corner to what is on offer now if you only knew about it?'. There is a trade-off between not being able to finance an activity that is added to the shopping list late in the day because all available funds have already been committed, and delaying financing projects currently on the list in the hope of something better being added to it. It is for the relevant management to determine whether all the available funds are distributed in one go, quickly, or released more slowly, drip-fed over the course of a period of time. Either course of action is necessarily subject to any constraints imposed by cash flow requirements, which may dictate the timing of expenditure. It would be useful for decision-makers to be able to see what is on the horizon (see Box 12.4) if they are to help management in making such determinations.

12.4 Expenditure early warning

In Sight Savers International, operational managers are required, not only to compile a prioritised shopping list of activities that are 'ready to go', but also to identify activities that are 'in the pipeline'. Early warning of activities that are under development and likely to appear on a future shopping list helps inform decisions about whether to commit resources now to activities already on the shopping list or to hold them back to finance activities still to come. It also provides an effective means of reviewing whether the Strategic Framework is being translated into the right activities at the operational level in time to influence what gets done.

Ensuring optimal use of resources

So how does the charity ensure that all resources within each SOFA category are used optimally? This is done by following a decision-making process designed to enable competing demands on those resources to be assessed, compared and conclusions reached. With the three SOFA expenditure areas – income generation, management and administration, activities in furtherance of the charity's objects – the methodology requires the management responsible for the distribution of the allocated sums to determine which activities are funded and which are not by answering the following questions.

1 What resources have we been allocated?
2 What financial commitments have we already made that will use up some of those resources?
3 Therefore how much resource do we anticipate having left?
4 What else would we like to do in addition to those commitments already made, i.e. new activities?
5 What are the highest priorities for our resources?
6 What activities should we therefore start or stop?

Each area of the charity in effect maps available resources and expenditure commitments to identify the gap between the two, over which they have discretion. The process is essentially an activity-based one, whereby costs are considered in relation to discrete activities rather than in terms of the cost classification of a typical general ledger. As in step two, the process of understanding the existing expenditure commitments of each area lends itself to an activity-based approach to costing.

Determining priorities: specific projects

Identifying the highest priorities for the charity's resources is best done by comparing activities, and therefore question five above requires the decision-makers to compile a prioritised shopping list of activities that can be continuously updated as new ideas and/or requirements come to light. A priority list for the fundraising allocation, for example, could be built from prioritised lists submitted by the managers of the operating units within fundraising (see Figure 12a).[1] Note though that the implication of question five is that *all* activities, both current commitments and proposed new activities, need to be prioritised. It is only in this way that the question of whether some of the activities currently commanding precious resources should, in fact, be stopped because

---

[1] Binder Hamlyn (1986) describe this process of ranking priorities in their booklet *Economic Resource Management*.

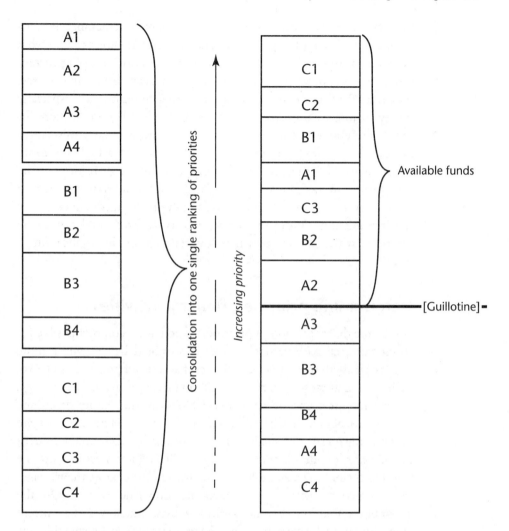

Operating units A, B and C fall within the span of control of one senior manager. Each unit ranks its activities by importance, top down, into one list according to its priorities. The senior manager consolidates the three priority lists into one single listing maintaining the ranking of activities *within* each unit (e.g. A1 remains a higher priority than A2) but now determining the ranking of activities *between* the three units. Activities C1 and C2 are ranked as the highest priorities of the 12 activities. A funding guillotine as defined by the level of available funds determines which activities are funded (C1 to A2)

Figure 12a Prioritising activities

they are no longer a priority can be answered. Remember Porter's comment (see Box 1.1, page 11) that 'strategy renders choices about what not to do as important as choices about what to do.' Stopping current activities does not represent failure and yet that can be a common interpretation of a decision to discontinue existing commitments, especially if they are long established ones, and if the decision has implications for the future employment of staff. It would, however, be a mistake to assume that current activities necessarily represent a higher priority than others. Activities that were appropriate and high priority at the time they were started may not be so now, and must not be assumed to be if resources are to be applied optimally in the furtherance of the charity's mission. This must, of course, be considered in relation to the extent to which the trustees have discretion over the application of funds.

Determining priorities: general activities

Whilst the determination of priorities by activity is comprehensible for specific projects with particular objectives to be delivered within finite lives, what about those general activities that were referred to in step two, such as the central service functions of finance, information technology, human resources and office services? How can the charity determine within this approach what resource to commit to activities that are undertaking all sorts of small-scale activities daily? Such functions exist in all parts of an organisation – the directorates heading up the fundraising and the charitable services arms of the charity, the management functions within each operating unit and so on. On the assumption that the functions already exist, there will be current commitments, which can be identified in step two. Recognising this, any additional resource that is requested for these areas might be required on the 'shopping list' for consideration against specific projects. This is certainly an obvious way of assessing the proposed start-up of such a function where it doesn't already exist. Alternatively, decisions on general activity within any unit could be made prior to the consideration of specific projects. This may be the more realistic approach, recognising as it does that the co-ordination and prioritisation of projects requires some support and general management. Theoretically, the level of general support should be a function of the projects for which the support is provided and therefore determined *after* the latter. In practice, once there is a broad understanding of the level of activity that the function has to support, approximating the size of resource that must be committed to its support is relatively straightforward.

Approving activities

The funding for prioritised activities that are approved is guaranteed for the duration of the activity at time of approval assuming the project is delivering what was intended. This funding security enables the activity's manager to manage the pace of implementation of projects according to the project's circumstances, not according to the corporate accounting calendar. Deciding whether expenditure should occur in period 12 of year one or period 1 of year two becomes a project matter not an accounting one, thereby helping to replace the 'spend it or lose it' culture with a 'spend it when need it' one. The manager has the authority and responsibility to manage the implementation of the project over the course of its life so that it delivers the objectives of the project within the funding submitted in the proposal. Within reason the manager has authority to determine when, over the course of the project life, the funds are spent.

The resource allocation decision-making cycle

The resource allocation decision-making process becomes a continuous cycle (see Figure 12b) in which resources and priorities are assessed and reassessed. The frequency with which the cycle is completed is at the discretion of the organisation, and the determination of that frequency should reflect the rate at which circumstances or expectations are likely to change.

Sight Savers International has established a quarterly cycle. Once a quarter all stages of the cycle are completed, meaning that operating unit managers can propose new activities and/or projects four times a year, as and when it is appropriate from a programme point of view, rather than when it fits into the accounting/planning timetable. This has proved relatively easy to accommodate within the culture of the organisation, dovetailing with existing reporting timeframes. Nevertheless it may not be straightforward to move an organisation towards such a process. It is asking for a significant number of sacred cows to be sacrificed. The pace of change needs to be thought through, balancing the competing merits of the sharp shock associated with rapid change against those that would accompany a slower, more evolutionary development of the new principles. It may be beneficial to develop a trouble-shooting guide to answer the obvious questions that spenders might have. As with any planning process (including traditional budgeting) the system requires proposed activities to have been

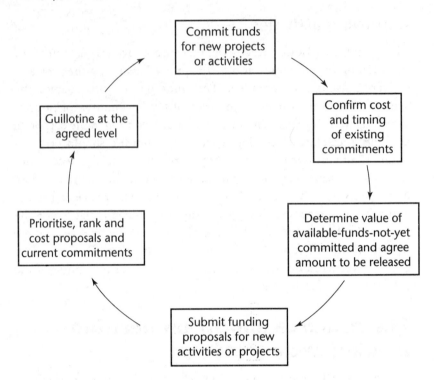

Figure 12b The resource allocation decision-making cycle

properly thought through prior to submission for funding. One risk of being able to propose new ideas frequently is that the discipline of good activity planning can loosen if the culture becomes one in which it doesn't matter if submissions are incomplete, and omitted components can be simply added to the shopping list next time round.

The resource allocation decision-making process in practice

1 Within each of the three top-level expenditure areas (fundraising, management and administration and activities in furtherance of the charity's objectives) the relevant management determine how much of the guaranteed resources to use on general activity in the operating units within their span of control, and thereby how much to make available for specific activities.

2 Operating unit managers within each area submit a prioritised list of activities that they wish to be funded plus lists of activities that are 'in the pipeline' to give early notice of what's on the horizon.

3 Decision-makers within the three expenditure areas decide how much of the allocated funds at their disposal to release. This funding

'guillotine' determines the level to which, within the ranked projects listing, funding approval will be given.

4 Approved projects' funding is guaranteed for the duration of each project, thereby reducing the size of the available funds that are not yet committed.

Key stewardship questions – deciding how to get there

1 How much funding is it appropriate for the charity to commit to expenditure now?

2 How is the allocation *between* the SOFA expenditure categories determined?

3 Is there a satisfactory process for committing funds *within* each SOFA expenditure category?

4 Do the resource allocation decisions reflect relative organisational priorities? Are they the best decisions to support the charity's mission?

---

13 Step five – setting off

The charity's stewards have now decided where they are trying to get the organisation to, and have expressed the charity's financial goals and parameters in terms of KPIs. They have a good understanding of where the charity is now (with reference to actual income and expenditure results, balance sheet, cash flow reports, etc.) and have compiled their best collective sense of what is ahead of them (from top-level income forecasts and expenditure commitments). Using all three sets of information, they have now decided on the allocation of those resources over which they have discretion. Within each of the four directions for resources discussed in Chapter 12 (see page 160), decisions have been made about what levels of general activity and which specific projects to finance. The charity can now act on these decisions, and press the buttons that actually commit funds as agreed so that activities are undertaken that contribute to the delivery of the mission.

The internal SOFA and forecasts

This is the point in the cycle when it would help to express all the decisions that have been made as an overall financial forecast. At no previous stage in the methodology has an expenditure forecast been put together. Income was forecast in step two in order to determine the likely future resource availability, and existing expenditure commitments still to be met were also identified. Step three did consider in what direction to allocate resources and thereby outlined the SOFA profile the organisation would *like* to achieve, but that is not the same as forecasting the *expected* profile. As before, the secret to doing this successfully is to keep the forecasts very broad-brush and indicative. It should be possible for the relevant management to do this based on broad indicators of future activity levels and cost trends without building it bottom-up from detail.

Figure 13a outlines the format of the internal SOFA that is used within Sight Savers International to monitor latest income and expenditure expectations. Note that the rows are identical to those given in Figure 9b (page 125), where consideration was given to the question of *historical* management accounting information and expenditure performance. Particular attention should be paid to the following columnar analysis.

Line ref.		Future – forecast results			
		Current year Y^0 £	Next 12 months £	Next 24 months £	Next 36 months £
1	Fundraising income				
2	Fundraising cost centres' expenditure				
3	**Total contribution**				
4	Central services cost centres' expenditure				
5	**Net contribution**				
6	Service delivery cost centres' expenditure				
7	**Net incoming/ (outgoing) resources**				
8	Gains/(losses) on investments				
9	**Net movement in funds**				
	Opening fund balances				
10	General funds				
11	Other funds				
	Closing fund balances				
12	General funds				
13	Other funds				
14	**Total closing fund balances**				
	Key performance indicators (examples)				
15	Fundraising cost/ income ratio				
16	Service delivery expenditure as % of total				
17	General funds as % of future expenditure				
18	General funds – excess/(shortfall)				

Figure 13a Sight Savers International internal SOFA (future perspective only)

- The columns start with the forecast to the end of the **current (financial) year**. As has been previously argued, financial stewards cannot afford to ignore the expected results at each of the statutory accounting date milestones, however much the organisation operationally works within alternative timeframes.
- **Next 12 months**. In the same way that the review of historic performance over the latest 12 months has proved very informative within Sight Savers International so a similar forward perspective is adopted. This is crucial if the organisation is to avoid the brick wall mentality associated with focusing exclusively on the current year-end.
- **Next 24 months** and **next 36 months**. A medium-term outlook is provided by forecasting both 24 and 36 months ahead, rounding numbers to avoid implying false accuracy. Taken literally, these columns could be updated monthly, rolling forward one month at a time, and straddling the financial year-ends. Alternatively, the charity could update the forecasts, say quarterly, or continue to think in terms of financial years by forecasting to the end of financial years 2 and 3. This could be a useful interim step towards full rolling forecasting.

By joining the two sides of the SOFA together, the history and the forecasts, the charity's financial stewards have all the critical information regarding income and expenditure on one sheet of paper. It offers a very powerful information tool and, together with the balance sheet, can become the single most important financial planning and control tool of the senior management team and the trustee body, neither of which should be concerning itself with detail as a matter of course.

Managing the financial performance of projects

How should the charity react if the financial forecasts relating to a particular project increase above that included in the funding submission in step four? The first relevant point is that the decision-makers need to *know* that the forecast has changed so that they can react. The processes and the culture of the organisation must be such as to enable operating managers to advise when their expectations about future financial performance change.

The process of re-forecasting

The process of re-forecasting at operating unit level is built in to the resource allocation decision-making cycle (Figure 12b on page 172) described in step four. Periodically, unit managers are required to re-confirm the cost and timing of existing commitments. This is replicated at a corporate level within the five-step methodology in step two, when the financial stewards of the charity look forwards and, amongst other things, identify the expected cost of commitments already made but not yet met.

The culture of re-forecasting

The culture of re-forecasting is determined by how the organisation chooses to react to advice that previous expectations about, say, income or expenditure or cash, have changed. That reaction will depend on the extent to which the forecasts are regarded as pre-determined performance contracts. The more they are so regarded, the greater the likelihood that the reaction to news that costs are likely to be higher than previously expected or income lower will be one of criticism. The charity has to understand that a certain culture is required to promote best estimate forecasting rather than desired outcome forecasting: such a culture is almost certainly going to require forecasting to be divorced from performance measurement, with an acceptance that in some circumstances costs may exceed expectations. That is not to imply that managers should not be required to exhibit accurate forecasting skills: what cannot be allowed to develop is a culture in which it does not matter whether the forecast is accurate or not. It does matter because decisions will be made on the back of those forecasts.

Systems that require managers to demonstrate that their funding submissions and subsequent income and expenditure forecasts are reasonable and complete must be in place; simultaneously the charity must be in a position to handle the unexpected financially. Managers should be expected to explain any major changes to forecasts, and distinctions must be drawn between factors that are within the control of the manager and those that are not. However, it is best to avoid the attempt to pre-determine an acceptable level of variation against the last forecast. Such a level simply ends up being interpreted as an acceptable margin of 'error' that is added onto the approved sum; this breeds complacency. And at all costs, the temptation to override a manager's best estimate forecast, imposing the desired outcome instead, must be resisted; the charity needs to understand what its managers really think is going to happen, however undesirable. Instead, there needs to be a continual incentive to maintain tight costs in the pursuit of maximum cost-effectiveness.

Good reporting systems that inform the charity's management of both actual expenditure and forecast costs should prevent a cost-complacent manager from causing the charity undue financial difficulties. If anticipated costs exceed the agreed funding without good reason, the operating manager could be asked to resubmit a funding proposal so that a new understanding of the activity's cost-benefit can be agreed. However, within reason a manager needs to have discretion to allow the costs of an activity to vary from the level of funding approved at the time of the project funding submission (see Box 13.1). Managers need incentives to keep costs tightly under control whilst having discretion to allow costs to be managed (up and down) in line with the demands and impact of the activity or project.

13.1 Understanding changes to activity costs

1 Understand the reasons for the new level of anticipated costs.
2 Understand what impact the activity has had to date and what impact it is expected to have if all the anticipated costs are incurred.
3 Understand what scope there is to reduce the costs and the implications on impact of doing so.

Offering such discretion must be done in the light of the individual manager's competence to handle the responsibility of devolved project financial management. They need to understand the financial context within which they are managing activities, understand the implications to the charity of poor cost control, and appreciate that, ultimately, they are being judged on relative performance against others internally or externally, and on the impact their expenditure has. Managers that consistently deliver high quality activities that further the charity's objects cost-effectively should be rewarded, not necessarily financially, but with further opportunities within the charity. Future funding submissions made by them can be assessed with confidence; professional development opportunities can be awarded, and, of course, they may be well placed for other positions internally.

Using a relative benchmark

Relative benchmarks are the key. The message to the managers needs to be 'you manage the costs within a target of doing better than last time/other units internally/our competitor' or whatever else is the relevant benchmark. The ultimate measure of performance has to be determined retrospectively, based on the extent to which the expenditure of the charity's funds on an activity has had a cost-effective impact.

The five-step cycle in action

The spenders are now getting on with the spending. Time to sit back and relax? Far from it. As mentioned before (see page 108), the answers to the questions of (a) where the organisation is and (b) what is ahead of it will be continually changing. Every day the income and expenditure position, the balance sheet, the cash flow, and the judgements about the future will be changing. Just as the pedestrian reacts to the environment as they move forward, the organisation must react to continually updated financial information about results and expectations. The steps become inextricably linked and completed almost simultaneously. As soon as action is taken (step five) where the charity is now (step one) will have changed. Meanwhile the environment in which the charity is operating will have altered as a result of internal and/or external factors. What is ahead will be continually evolving and changing (step two) and may persuade the financial stewards to adjust their sights (step three), thereby influencing their resource allocation decisions (step four). The speed with which the cycle is completed will depend on the degree of uncertainty and change present in the operating environment of the organisation, but it is unlikely to be evenly paced.

The acid test of the methodology is whether the steps, between them, provide an effective management tool. A key question to be able to answer would be, for example, what happens if the forecasts of the future are wrong, as they may well be? Imagine, for example, that a major investment in fundraising activity fails to deliver, that income does not come in as expected and is, in fact, significantly lower than anticipated. The chronology of steps that would be taken is shown in Box 13.2.

In this way the approach enables decision-makers to react in good time to the information collected and, as a result, steward the organisation forward appropriately. The key to its success is to act judiciously in the management of the financial risks associated with future resourcing uncertainty. Committing the charity to future expenditure of funds (at least some of which will not yet have been generated) must be done with the back up of assurance that the financial consequences of those commitments can be managed. It requires careful judgement to prevent the charity either over- or under-committing itself financially.

Financ◦ ◦e methodology

◦ invest in fundraising activity is made (step 4) following
◦n of a funding proposal from the fundraising department in
◦impact on key performance indicators already set (step 3).
◦ers implement the investment decision which becomes a
◦mitment (step 5).
◦ig expenditure increases, cash levels fall (step 1).
◦ing reports indicate that donors are not being recruited in
◦ponse to the fundraising initiative as expected (step 1).
The future costs of current commitments increase and the size of 'still-available' funds drops correspondingly (step 2).

6 The future income implications of low recruitment are assessed and forecasts of income are reduced (step 2).
7 Forecasts of likely-to-be-available resources are reduced (step 2).
8 KPIs are reviewed in light of this new information but reconfirmed (step 3).
9 The future allocation for service delivery twenty-four months ahead is reduced (step 4) with consequent implications for the level of general activity and/or the number of specific projects that are implemented (step 5).

Key stewardship questions – setting off

1 Does the charity generate and communicate up-to-date forecasts of financial results?
2 Does the charity follow the five-step cycle continuously?
3 How does the charity react to inaccurate forecasts?

14 Establishing an effective controls framework

The responsibilities of financial stewardship during uncertainty that have been discussed so far – the design and implementation of a coherent, rational finance strategy and the use of forward-looking financial management decision-making processes – must be conducted within an effective controls framework. The issue of control at a governance level has risen steadily up the corporate agenda since the early 1990s when the Cadbury Committee published its report on the Financial Aspects of Corporate Governance. Its successor, Corporate Governance: The Combined Code established by the Hampel Committee in 1998, endorsed the need for stewards of all organisations to review the effectiveness of their internal controls regularly.

Internal control

Within the charity sector, the revision to the SORP in 2000 has placed greater onus on trustees to address internal control by way of risk management, and to confirm that this has received their attention by making a statement as part of their Annual Report and Accounts (see Box 14.1). Reviewing the adequacy of internal control is therefore a process that must be managed by the charity and for this reason it is included as a management process in the financial stewardship map. But what does 'internal control' actually mean? The Chartered Institute of Management Accountants (CIMA) use the Cadbury Report definition (see Box 14.2) which places the role of internal control in the context of assuring effectiveness and efficiency: internal control is about assuring that the charity is delivering purpose.

14.1 SORP statement of risk management

The Trustees' Annual Report should include 'a statement confirming that the major risks to which the charity is exposed, as identified by the trustees, have been reviewed and systems have been established to mitigate those risks'.

Source: SORP 2000 paragraph 31(g)

14.2 Definition of internal control

The whole system of controls, financial or otherwise, established in order to provide reasonable assurance of:

(a) effective and efficient operation
(b) internal financial control
(c) compliance with laws and regulations

Source: Chartered Institute of Management Accountants (2000) p.15

The risk management cycle

This book defines a particular stewardship methodology by which those responsible for delivering the charity's purpose use its financial resources to maximise charitable impact. Financial stewards need to ask themselves: how effective is this model? To answer this, there has to be in place an internal control process that can give such an assurance. And essentially this control process should be designed and reviewed from a risk-based perspective. Financial stewards need assurance that the *design* of their policies and procedures is adequate to enable them to maximise the charity's impact over time, and that there is *compliance* by those using them. This assurance can be achieved by following a basic risk management cycle (see Figure 14a), starting with the identification of the financial stewardship risk facing the charity. The job is to identify where there are control gaps (i.e. where the level of risk remains higher than is regarded as acceptable) and to take action to close them.

Risk identification

At its simplest, risk can be defined as 'any event or non-event that could reduce the chances of the organisation achieving its objectives'

Figure 14a The risk management cycle

(Weighell, 2001 p.2). Note this can occur from 'failure to exploit opportunities as well as from threats materialising.'[1] Over-prudence is a risk,
for example, resulting in failure to exploit opportunities. In this vein, it
is important to recognise that the responsibility of the trustees and executive of any charity is not necessarily to minimise risk, but rather to
manage it. The distinction is an important one, acknowledging the
understanding that must be developed within the organisation of the
relationship between risk and return/reward. An event that is low risk
but offers high rewards, for example, should arguably be exploited not
reduced or eliminated (Mainelli, 1999).

So what are the risks associated with financial stewardship? Since such
stewardship has been defined as the responsible use of financial
resources, the risk that must be managed is that the charitable impact
delivered by the organisation is poor, given the resources at its disposal.
In such circumstances the assets of the charity will have been poorly
protected. So what are the events or non-events that could lead to poor
financial stewardship and thereby result in inadequate impact? The
financial stewardship map (Figure A) on page 3 provides the answer.
There is a risk of poor financial stewardship if the charity does not have
a well-defined finance strategy implemented using appropriate financial management processes within a capable financial environment. The
omission, poor design or poor implementation of the following three
components of the financial stewardship map exposes the charity to
risks of poor quality stewardship:

---

[1] BDO Stoy Hayward seminar Charity Risk Management, London, 27 February 2001.

- finance strategy
- financial management processes
- financial environment.

Each block of each component could pose a financial stewardship risk (see Box 14.3, for example). The controls process that the charity needs to have must therefore aim to assure the stewards that the three components above, and all their blocks, are in place and that, between them, they are effective.

14.3 Example financial stewardship risks

- **Strategy**

Income	Insufficient income generated to cover costs
Funds	Inappropriate level of reserves
Assets	Assets insufficiently productive
Expenditure	Sub-optimal distribution of funds between income-generating activities, management and administration and furthering the objects

- **Management**

Actuals	Poor knowledge of current financial state of play
Forecasts	Forecasts out of date
KPIs	Inappropriate targets/parameters
Decisions	Inappropriate funds committed for expenditure
Actions	Inappropriate reaction to unexpected results or forecasts
Controls	Poor/no controls process in place

- **Environment**

Structure	No clear split of financial stewardship responsibilities
Capabilities	Insufficient financial stewardship expertise in-house
Systems	Inadequate information and/or communication systems in place

Determining which stewardship risk controls should receive first review is best done by assessing each risk in terms of likelihood of occurrence and impact, and focusing on those that are high risk in relation to both. This can be done graphically, giving a risk profile, thereby helping to define the nature of the risks (see Figure 14b). Risks that are, for example, highly likely to occur but which would have a low impact, are day-to-day in nature and should be managed accordingly. Most attention should be directed at those risks in the upper right-hand quadrant.

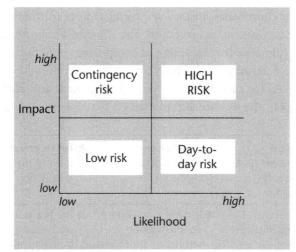

Source: Weighell (2001) p.3

Figure 14b Risk profile

Design, compliance and effectiveness

The assurance needed by the financial stewards is that the components of the methodology described in this book are appropriate (design), being used (compliance) and working effectively (effectiveness). Any review of internal control has to determine therefore firstly whether the design of the strategy, management processes, or environment is satisfactory; secondly, whether, in practice, the organisation complies with that design, and, thirdly, whether by doing so the risk is effectively controlled. In each case management of risk depends both on design and compliance – not only must the design be effective but it must be complied with in practice. This can be demonstrated by the quality of financial stewardship that is exhibited, as evidenced by the answers to the key stewardship questions posed at the end of each chapter.

A risk assessment of each block of finance strategy – income, funds, assets and expenditure – and of the MONITOR–AIM–PLAN–ACT financial management cycle can be carried out using the risk management cycle. Figure 14c illustrates the application of this to one key element of finance strategy, holding appropriate levels of reserves, and to step one of the financial management cycle, understanding the current position. What is the risk associated with these two issues? In both cases the control risk is identified. The reviewer can confirm the system that has been designed to manage the risk, and assess whether the design would be effective in managing this risk if complied with. The reviewer can

185

then test for compliance and reach a conclusion as to whether the risk has been successfully managed. If the conclusion is negative that implies a weakness either in design or compliance, or in both. Solutions can then be determined. A similar process of review could and should be undertaken for each of the strategy, management and environment components of the stewardship model.

Identification What's the risk concern?	**Design** What will give adequate control?	**Compliance** Is the design being complied with?	**Effectiveness** Is the system effective in controlling the risk?
Inappropriate level of reserves	A reserves policy in place setting appropriate level of reserves (Chapter 5)	■ Is there a reserves policy in place setting an appropriate level of reserves? ■ Are resource management decisions made that are consistent with the policy?	■ Are the reserves that are held appropriate in size given the exposure of the charity to uncertain future income and market losses and/or its need to finance expansion or replace existing assets?
Poor knowledge of current financial state of play resulting in poor resource allocation decisions	Financial information that meets the 8 characteristics of successful management accounting (Chapter 9)	■ Is financial information generated that meets the 8 characteristics of successful management accounting?	■ Are resource allocation decisions appropriate given the financial state of play at the time the decision was made?

Figure 14c Risk management by key stewardship area

Internal audit

The importance of having a defined process to enable financial stewards to receive assurance of the adequacy of internal control/risk management cannot be over-estimated. It is only through the review of internal controls that the charity's trustees can ensure that there is a strong control framework within which the funds placed in their trust are managed. As a minimum, it must be a recognised responsibility of those charged with the charity's financial stewardship that, as part of the management function, the internal controls are reviewed. However, more independent assurance can only be given from outside the management structure, most typically from the perspective of internal audit.

Determining when it is appropriate to introduce an internal audit function is a decision governed largely by the question of the organisation's complexity. This could be a function of the size of the charity or of some operational complexity such as geographic spread or funding arrangements. However, it is not necessarily the easiest function to resource in many smaller charities, requiring specialist skills but perhaps justifying only a part-time position. It may be worth considering contracting out internal audit, or even sharing an internal auditor with one or more other organisations.

The respective roles of internal audit and management

The apparently simple dichotomy between the roles of internal audit and management (see for example the Sight Savers International definitions in Box 14.4) can mask how imprecise in practice the distinction can be at the point of interface between the two functions. Internal audit is not an easy role to play. The internal auditor is part of the organisation and yet has to remain one step removed, able to look at the organisation with an objective eye and able to influence change without formal authority over colleagues whose systems have been reviewed. It is difficult to feel welcomed, as the role may generate anxiety, scepticism and even hostility. The internal auditor requires a good understanding of the organisation, be empathetic to how it functions and understand its politics and culture if they are to be able truly to assess the adequacy of the controls that should be in place.

14.4 The respective roles of internal audit and management

1 It is the responsibility of management to establish and maintain the systems of internal control used in the charity
2 It is the role of internal audit to assess whether the controls and systems designed by the management are adequate, being complied with as intended, and operating effectively, and to advise management to those ends.

Source: Sight Savers International

Ultimately it must be for the charity's management to determine what areas of activity are covered by the internal audit function. Internal audit is a tool which managers can use to reassure themselves that the internal controls are effective. But who is 'management' in this context – the trustees or the executive? Internal audit instils discipline into the evaluation element of any performance management system but it definitely 'ups the stakes', given that internal audit reports are likely to end up being read by trustees. No manager wants to find themselves defending a critical internal audit report in front of the trustees. And that highlights the difference between management review and internal audit – *independence*. An internal auditor is independent of those responsible for the establishment and maintenance of the systems and has scope to review systems irrespective of the wishes of managers. But often that is the only difference. There are no reviews within the remit of the internal auditor that management would not wish to be doing for itself. It is simply engaging a specialist to play this role. Tension can arise if the internal audit programme feels imposed on management as a policing function designed to highlight any management shortfalls internally rather than a resource for them to steward. In such circumstances it is very easy for management to get into the habit of running ahead of internal audit to ensure control gaps are closed or unnoticed. Yet if it is working well, there will be genuine collaboration between management and internal audit with the shared goal of designing and maintaining appropriate control systems. To that end there is no substitute for frequent dialogue between the two.

In order to work, any internal review, whether labelled internal audit or not, must meet the following criteria.

- It must be undertaken properly – formally, with terms of reference, a written report and a follow-up action plan. It needs the time that management, with their responsibilities for the organisation day-to-day, can rarely give.
- It must have authority to effect change.
- It must be undertaken with sufficient objectivity to enable the systems' design and maintenance to be seriously reviewed afresh. It can be difficult for managers to stand far enough back from their own systems to do this. But if they can, all well and good.

There is a danger of being over-anxious about separating the function of internal audit from that of day-to-day management. Pragmatism is worth applying. If management can meet the above criteria when completing reviews, it should be of little concern that an internal auditor has not undertaken it. It is the quality of the review that is paramount.

Internal audit etiquette

Early experiences with an internal audit function at Sight Savers International taught the charity many lessons about managing expectations, about being clear who was responsible for doing what and what the internal audit process was. The result was the development of an internal audit etiquette outlining the key steps that should be taken at each stage of the internal audit process (pre-, during and post-audit), defining the authority of the internal auditor, and the format and timetable of audit reports (see Box 14.5). Such etiquette should highlight the critical factors that have to be got right if internal audit is really to add value.

- Expectations. Staff need to appreciate what process is to be followed, what scope the audit has, what their responsibilities are, and what authority the auditor has.
- Ownership. Management must feel and take ownership for getting effective internal controls in place by, for example, being responsible for taking action to close control gaps.
- Communication. Control issues must be identified with evidence, set in appropriate context, and communicated fairly, where possible face-to-face.

14.5 Internal audit etiquette

Preparation pre-audit must include:

- Consultative determination of scope and timetable of the proposed audit within an overall audit plan.
- Written terms of reference, published at least X days before the commencement of the audit.

Conducting the audit must include:

- Face-to-face discussions at the start and end of the audit with relevant management outlining the process and findings respectively.
- Unrestricted access throughout the audit to whatever systems, procedures and information are requested.

The audit report must:

- Be written fairly, identifying where controls are effective in managing risk, or where action has already been taken or planned to address the risks identified, as well as highlighting control gaps.
- Be evidence-based.
- Distinguish between control issues that can be addressed locally, and those that relate to corporate policy or procedures.
- Include timetabled action agreed with management in response to the issues raised.
- Be written and signed off within X working days.

Continued

Audit follow-up must:

- Be timetabled and conducted within a timeframe consistent with the timetabling of action agreed in the audit report.
- Include a first draft progress report written by the management responsible for the controls that were audited, and a final report jointly signed by the auditor and management within an agreed timeframe.

Source: Extract from Sight Savers International internal audit etiquette

Key stewardship questions – controls framework

1 Does the charity have an explicit process for reviewing the adequacy of its internal financial stewardship controls?
2 Is the design of those controls effective and complied with?
3 Are the risks associated with the charity's finance strategy, its management processes and its internal finance environment understood and being appropriately managed?
4 Are the respective roles of audit and management appropriately defined and understood in relation to reviewing internal controls?

PART 4

FINANCIAL ENVIRONMENT

15 Structures: determining the spread of responsibility

If financial stewardship is about the successful execution of finance strategy, who within the charity should be responsible for it? To some extent the answer will depend on the size of the charity. Those without paid employees, for example, will rely more heavily on volunteers, including trustees, to undertake the financial management tasks that are, in larger charities, vested with management. The larger the charity the more scope there is to distinguish between the roles that different positions within the organisation should play. Good financial stewardship assigns discrete responsibilities to the board of trustees, the senior executive and managers.

The role of the board of trustees

There are many sources to guide the reader on the legal role of the trustee in relation to finance. Try, for example, the Charity Commission's leaflet CC3 *Responsibilities of Charity Trustees*, or Kate Kirkland's excellent *Good Trustee Guide* published by NCVO.

15.1 The role of trustees

At its simplest, the role of a charity trustee is to receive assets from donors, safeguard them, and apply them for a charitable purpose according to the wishes of the donor. The board of trustees is ultimately responsible for everything the charity does.

Source: Kirkland (1995) p.7

Trustees are accountable for the solvency and continuing effectiveness of the charity ... they must exercise overall control over its financial affairs.

Source: Charity Commission (1999) paragraph 43

These definitions affirm the central role that trustees must play in financial stewardship. Receiving assets, safeguarding them and applying them are exactly what finance strategy is about. The central tenet of this book aligns with Kirkland's definition (see Box 15.1): to have charitable impact, the organisation must successfully implement a finance strategy that establishes performance criteria in relation to the flow of funds through income, onto the balance sheet and out as expenditure. Part 2 of this book determined the key stewardship questions that have to be addressed in order to achieve such a strategy.

But what, in practice, does this mean that a trustee actually does? In essence it means ensuring that the charity answers the stewardship questions and, by doing so, defines its finance strategy. The trustee body then has responsibility for overseeing the implementation of the strategy so that it has the desired financial consequences and the ultimate charitable impact.

Argenti (1993 p.214) argues that the task of trustees is one of acting as 'internal watchdogs on behalf of the intended beneficiaries'. Translate that into terms of financial stewardship, and the role of trustees becomes one of defining acceptable financial performance for the charity in order to have impact on the beneficiaries. As discussed in Chapter 11, where the finance strategy is translated into KPI targets, it is the trustee body that must sanction the KPIs used, and the targets set in relation to those KPIs (see page 158). Note Argenti's focus on the beneficiary; he rightly promotes the task of trusteeship as being one of acting in the interests of the beneficiary not the charity. In financial stewardship terms this means the trustee body has a duty to ensure that the financial decisions taken within the organisation enable it to maximise its charitable impact over time. This takes the discussion back to one of the themes of this book: how the trustees manage the tension between having impact today and maintaining the charity as a going concern so that it can have impact in the future. Without the focus on charitable impact there is a risk that the trustees, inadvertently or otherwise, see their first duty as being to the charity not the beneficiary; if so they will invest in institutional protection not in beneficiary impact. Arguably the Charity Commission (1999 paragraph 28) clouds this issue with its explicit guidance that trustees 'need always to bear in mind the interests of the charity'.

Distinguishing between executive and trustee roles

In practice, the distinction between the roles of the senior executive and the trustees is rarely as clear-cut as Argenti would encourage it to be. The Association of Chief Executives of Voluntary Organisations (Blackmore *et al.*, 1998) conducted research to try to determine what distinct responsibilities distinguished governance from management. The model of governance/management interface that emerged from the research was that three distinct roles had to be played:

- the trustees have the task of 'ensuring that the organisation is held to account' (governance)
- the executive have the task of 'putting strategic policy and practices into action' (management)
- executives and trustees have a combined role of 'establishing strategic policies and priorities' (leadership) (Blackmore *et al.*, 1998 p.32)

This useful distinction suggests that trustees and senior executives would jointly determine the KPIs to be used, and the financial stewardship targets to be set. Given that the executive is likely to have a greater understanding of the practicalities of delivering the finance strategy this approach is sensible.

Governance role of the trustees

The governance role, however, rests squarely with the trustees. It is for the trustee body to ensure that:

- the financial performance and position of the charity are closely monitored and appropriately managed using the KPIs for guidance
- the organisation is held to account publicly for how the funds placed in its trust for public benefit have been used.

The trustee role becomes threefold, therefore, in relation to financial stewardship (see Box 15.2).

15.2 Financial stewardship role of trustees

1 To determine jointly with the executive what financial KPIs the charity uses and what targets are set in relation to them.
2 To monitor the financial performance and position of the charity over time in terms of the KPIs.
3 To account publicly for the management of funds placed in their trust.

Executing trustee responsibility for financial stewardship

All trustees on the board, not just the treasurer, must assume responsibility for financial stewardship and the latter may need to remind them of that periodically. By focusing the trustees' finance agenda on the three roles defined above it ought to be possible to involve all trustees actively in matters of financial stewardship, and to help them appreciate the contribution they can make in this field. The responsibility demands far more than merely rubber-stamping the approval of a set of statutory accounts once a year, and indeed it may well be the case that trustees other than the treasurer are best placed to recognise what financial issues the board needs to address. Just re-reading all the key stewardship questions at the end of the chapters should make it apparent to any trustee that they can bring value to discussions on financial stewardship. They may be, for example, the ones with their fingers on the pulse of likely funding changes or future areas of risk, and have informed judgements to offer on the adoption of appropriate expenditure profiles.

To execute the three financial stewardship responsibilities, trustee bodies have to include finance on each of their agendas. They must reflect regularly, at least annually and more frequently in conditions of uncertainty and change, on those financial matters the charity has to sort out and on the financial performance and position they wish the charity to reach. But all of these discussions should remain strategic in nature, not operational. To exercise their governance role of holding the executive to account trustees must at each meeting monitor actual and forecast results, and reach judgements on the adequacy of those results. The precise information they need to receive at trustee meetings will depend on what the key stewardship issues are but all of them will relate in some way to the primary financial statements. A useful rule of thumb therefore is that they need to receive actual and forecast results expressed on three pages in terms of the SOFA, balance sheet and cash flow statement as described in Part 3. If the reports also identify what the actual and forecast results mean in terms of the charity's financial KPIs, the trustees have all the financial information they need to steward the organisation's finances from a governance perspective. More information may detract from the quality of governance rather than enhance it, encouraging trustees to worry about detailed figures.

Delegating trustee responsibilities

> **15.3 Delegating trustee responsibilities**
>
> It is important and a general rule that trustees act in person and decisions concerning the charity are taken by the trustees acting together. They can always invite some of their number to look into particular matters connected with the charity and to make recommendations, but the decision whether or not to act on the recommendations is for the trustees to take together.
>
> Source: Charity Commission (1999) paragraph 32

Nothing concentrates the minds of trustees better than to remind them of how much time the board has to conduct its business. Typically it will be under 25 hours a year. It sounds frighteningly inadequate, especially once the obligation to deal with formal duties such as approving the annual accounts within that time is acknowledged. As well as being very disciplined about which issues reach the board agenda in the first place, it is therefore worthwhile considering whether some of the duties of the board can be formally delegated.[1] The governing document of the charity may permit the trustee body to use committees with limited powers to undertake particular tasks on its behalf. In these cases, committees can either be established with terms of reference and with executive authority to take decisions on behalf of the board, or as a non-executive body whose role it is to sift the detail and present the full board with a much more focused agenda. It must be clear which of these two roles any committee is to play if it is to be effective. It is very common for charities to establish a committee to carry out many of its financial stewardship functions. Typical committees that will be responsible for some or all of the stewardship matters discussed in Parts 2 and 3 include the following.

- Finance Committee with a general remit to undertake one of the two governance roles relating to finance discussed above. Typically this committee would advise the full board on setting the financial KPI targets, review financial plans and conduct the thorough monitoring of financial performance with the executive. It would then report back to the full trustee body.
- Audit Committee with terms of reference to define and hold to account an internal audit function. This can also include responsibility for reviewing the statutory accounts on behalf of the full board and

---

[1] For a full discussion on this issue see Hind (1995) ch.3 or Hudson (1999) ch.3.

thereby satisfy itself in more detail that the accounts present a true and fair view. Key points can then be brought to the full board's attention.

- Investment Committee charged with detemining the trustees' investment objectives and its position on issues such as socially responsible investment, and managing the investment managers to ensure performance is satisfactory. Typically such a committee accounts annually to the full board on investment matters.
- Remuneration Committee to represent the trustees on issues relating to the terms and conditions of employment of staff. This might include overseeing the charity's reward principles, the terms and conditions of appointment of the chief executive and acting as the final point of appeal on employment matters.

There are opposing schools of thoughts about the appropriateness of using committees or sub-groups. Opponents of committees argue that they disenfranchise the full trustee body and generate more administration; proponents point to the space they create on the trustee body's agenda to concentrate on other governance matters. What has to be appreciated is that the existence of committees with decision-making authority does not remove the liability of the full trustee body for the actions of that committee. Like it or not, every trustee shares equal liability for the financial stewardship of the charity. In the case of finance, much can be gained from well-defined delegation by the full trustee body to a committee, acknowledging that the key stewardship questions are not easy to answer or even perhaps to define. The quality of discussion, analysis and ultimate decision-making can be significantly enhanced by a small, focused group, whose understanding of the issues can be considerably greater than that of a diverse and larger trustee body. However good the charity's professional development of its trustees, it is unrealistic to believe that all members of the trustee body can bring equal expertise to each function, not least finance.

Two points of caution however. First, ensuring that trustees understand their financial responsibilities and have sufficient grasp of them to discharge them wisely can become more difficult if the function is delegated to a committee. Even with a dedicated finance committee, time has to be devoted on the full trustee body agenda to enabling all trustees to undertake their financial stewardship duties adequately. Secondly, the very existence of a committee can reduce the discipline to focus on matters of governance: with the luxury of more time, the committee can more readily meddle. Again a useful rule of thumb is to insist that trustees, even in committees, concentrate only on the primary statements, whether for setting financial KPI targets or for monitoring performance.

15.4 Criteria for delegating to a finance committee

1 The committee must offer governance rather than management on the matters falling within its remit.
2 The trustees must find a way for the committee to be accountable to the board, and for them to be sufficiently informed on the matters presented to them by the committee to make appropriate judgements.

Using committees to act on behalf of the trustee body, or advisory groups to guide it, does give the charity scope to involve individuals who are happy to offer support without wishing to assume all the responsibilities and liabilities of trusteeship. This can prove particularly helpful with some of the more technical aspects of financial steward-ship, such as investments and pensions.

The role of the honorary treasurer

With or without committees the role of the officers, and the treasurer in particular, is crucial if the board is to undertake good financial steward-ship; it is unrealistic to expect the board of trustees to establish KPIs, monitor performance and carry out the financial stewardship roles expected of them without the committed time of officers.

The extract from Sight Savers International's person specification for the position of honorary treasurer, shown in Box 15.5, indicates the sort of role and behaviour that this job-holder must demonstrate.

- The treasurer is the guardian, above all others, of the financial state of the organisation, and should be expected to guide the trustee body in how to exercise good stewardship.
- Fellow trustees must be able to look to the treasurer for advice on the kinds of stewardship questions that should be asked, and upon which financial issues the trustee body should focus.
- The treasurer must lead the internal debate to determine which financial KPIs should be used and what targets should be set, and direct the process of determining the financial information that will be presented to trustees. He or she must also guide the trustees in interpreting that information, in reaching conclusions and in under-standing the financial implications of their decisions.
- Finally, the treasurer must act on behalf of the whole trustee body in accounting publicly for the financial results of the charity, in published documents and at events such as AGMs.

15.5 Sight Savers International's Honorary Treasurer person specification

Skills:

- good strategic and financial governance skills
- able to analyse and assess the long-term financial consequences of decisions
- able to communicate orally and in writing complex concepts in a clear and concise way to lay audiences.

Attributes:

- empathy with Sight Savers International´s objectives, values and mission
- willing and able to network in the charity finance sector and within the accounting profession
- willing and able to make unpopular recommendations to fellow trustees
- capacity to engage in issues relating to charity finance, fundraising, investment management and pension schemes.

To play this role effectively, the treasurer is likely to have to spend time outside the formal board meetings, working with fellow officers and senior management to understand the financial position of the charity properly, and to debate finance strategy. As has been acknowledged throughout this book, there will be competing demands on the resources of the charity, not least as a result of the 'impact today versus impact tomorrow' tension. The treasurer must be able to guide the debate as to how the resources are applied, if necessary encouraging the charity to take unpopular decisions. Urging financial prudence in the cause of long-term financial stability can seem widely at odds with the agenda of those internally whose concern is primarily one of service delivery.

Building key relationships

Such is the importance of the finance strategy to the organisation that key relationships – between the officers and between the treasurer and finance director for example – have to be built to enable disagreements to be dealt with constructively away from the full board. It generates little confidence amongst trustees, and no guidance, if these players are openly disagreeing with each other on finance strategy. The key relationships on finance, as in other fields, therefore have to be robust, founded on trust and respect; this requires the investment of time and energy on the part of all the participants. They need to meet regularly, understand each other's point of view, hold frank discussions and agree a party line, if necessary using external advice (for example, from the charity's auditors) to reach consensus. There is no substitute for spending time together. At the board meeting, an agreed approach needs to be presented by these parties in the form either of a firm recommendation as to what should be done, or as two or more options for the board to consider.

There is however a fine line between guiding the trustees on financial stewardship and presenting them with *fait accompli* decisions that cannot be reversed. There must therefore be genuine opportunity, either at the board meeting, or outside it, for trustees to challenge and understand fully what is presented to them. The degree to which that will happen depends ultimately on the culture that has been developed amongst the trustee body, and one of the chair's particular responsibilities is to nurture an appropriate culture. There are many ways in which the treasurer and other officers can develop a culture that encourages involvement, ownership, and understanding of the key financial issues of the charity (see Box 15.6). Some of these techniques may be particularly helpful in the task of approving the statutory accounts.

15.6 Ways to build a culture of inclusive financial stewardship

- Include financial stewardship in trustee induction programmes.
- Use plain words in place of jargon wherever possible.
- Present financial reports in consistent, easy-to-read formats.
- Distribute information on stewardship issues (such as financial reports, analyses, and strategies) in writing in advance of meetings, in order to free up the latter for discussion about the information.
- Hold pre-meeting briefings and surgeries for trustees at which they can be walked through the key issues at a relaxed pace.
- Invite external advisers, such as auditors, to speak to trustees directly.

Trustee accountability

If the trustees have a key role to play in holding the executive to account on behalf of the beneficiaries and the donors, to whom do the trustees account? Who governs the governors?

Trustees' Report

The trustees exhibit public accountability through the preparation of the statutory Annual Report and Accounts, which includes a Trustees' Report. The revision of the SORP in 2000 has placed greater emphasis on the need for trustees to explain how the charity has gone about meeting its objects, and the Trustees' Report is the place to do this. It is in this report that the essence of the trustees' third financial stewardship responsibility – to account publicly for how the funds placed in its trust have been managed – is articulated (see Box 15.7). The report should highlight the key messages that can be drawn from the financial statements and notes, focusing both on the performance during the year and on the financial position at the end of it. It should also alert the reader to any key financial stewardship issues that will affect future performance and position. This will give confidence that the trustees really are stewarding the organisation's funds, not just monitoring them.

15.7 Trustees' financial accountability responsibilities

The law applicable to charities in England and Wales requires the trustees to prepare financial statements for each financial year which give a true and fair view of the charity's financial activities during the year and of its financial position at the end of the year.

The trustees are responsible for keeping proper accounting records, which disclose with reasonable accuracy the financial position of the charity, and enable them both to acertain the financial position of the charity and to ensure that the financial statements comply with applicable law, regulations and the Royal Charter.

Source: Extract from the Report of the Council of Trustees, Sight Savers International, Report and Accounts 2000

Annual Review

However, as SORP 2000 (paragraph 3) states 'trustees should consider providing such additional information as to give donors, beneficiaries, and the general public a greater insight into the charity's activities and achievements'. Very typically charities will produce an Annual Review in addition to the Annual Report and Accounts in which the organisation outlines in an eye catching, emotive way what impact it has had over the previous year, and which includes a summary of the financial statements. While relevant legislation and best practice such as SORP 2000 largely prescribe the format of the statutory accounts the trustees have no such constraints about how they choose to account publicly in an Annual Review. Save for a statement from the charity's auditors confirming that any financial information included in the document represents a fair extract from the statutory accounts, trustees are able to present the financial information as they wish.

Typically this is done in an easy-to-read summary form using graphs and pie charts. As a tool of accountability and promotion the focus of the Annual Review is on the activities that further the charity's objects. In line with this the Review provides the opportunity for the financial information to focus on the top of the financial stewardship map (see page 3) – on 'impact' as represented financially by expenditure – whilst also explaining the rationale for other stewardship decisions taken such as in relation to reserves. The extract in Figure 15a (page 204) taken from the Annual Report 1999 for Sight Savers International, encourages the reader to focus primarily on expenditure rather than income. It is, after all, through charitable expenditure that the organisation meets its mandate. The format then outlines where the expenditure has been funded from, identifying three categories – income generated in the year, opening reserves, and gains on investments.

Board of Trustees Report

Less typical than the Annual Review is the sort of accountability introduced by Julia Unwin in 1997 during her tenure as Chair of The Refugee Council. At its AGM in November that year the trustees produced a Board of Trustees Report, the equivalent of a report to the shareholders, but written instead for submission to the members of the charity. The report, which has been presented by the trustees at each AGM since 1997, specifically serves to highlight the work of the board of trustees. It is sent with all other AGM papers in advance of the meeting to enable readers to digest it and, if they wish, to question the trustees in person from the floor of the meeting. As the Chair's Introduction to the 2000 Report states:

> 'The trustees recognise that it is important to account to members for how we have discharged our specific responsibilities since the last AGM. We believe that this helps to make the organisation both transparent and accountable. We also hope that it will provide useful information for potential future trustees.'[2]

The report covers four sides of paper and outlines the key issues that have absorbed the attentions of the board. Five issues are highlighted with a paragraph for each one summarising the issue and what action the

---

[2] An extract from Board of Trustees Report: A report to members at the 2000 AGM on the work of the Refugee Council Board of Trustees in the year to November 2000.

Summary Financial Statements		£'000 1999	£'000 1998
Resources used			
Direct charitable expenditure		8,310	7,104
Fundraising and publicity expenditure		3,088	2,488
Management and administration expenditure		845	991
	[A]	12,243	10,583
Funded from			
Income			
Donations		7,686	6,691
Legacies		3,477	2,745
Co-funding grants and contributions		770	854
Investment income		268	324
Other sources		70	92
		12,271	10,706
Opening reserves		7,635	6,998
Gains on investment		689	514
	[B]	20,595	18,218
Closing reserves			
General funds		4,984	3,294
Designated funds		2,124	2,758
Restricted funds		1,154	1,486
Endowment funds		90	97
	[B–A]	8,352	7,635

Auditors' statement

We have examined the summary financial information set out on this page. In our opinion the information is consistent with the charity's annual accounts for the year ended 31st December 1999, on which we have issued an unqualified audit report.

Horwath Clark Whitehill

Registered Auditors, Chartered Accountants

Figure 15a Example of summary financial statements

trustees had taken in relation to that issue. Other matters that the trustees have tackled are simply listed. The document prefaces this overview with an insightful summary of the role adopted by the trustees:

'The trustees have had two roles in this period. Firstly, we have shaped and monitored The Refugee Council's response to the challenges of this last year. Secondly, we have worked hard to develop the organisation's longer-term strategy which we hope will equip it to meet the even greater challenges that lie ahead'.

Public meetings

In the spirit of accountability and transparency some bodies open their doors so that the proceedings of meetings can be observed. Public sector bodies that are making decisions using the public purse on behalf of the general public are obvious examples of this. The public can observe debate and decision-making from the House of Lords to the local planning committee. This is far less common in the charity sector. Nevertheless there are examples, albeit of a more restrictive nature. The Refugee Council has long had a history of inviting a senior official from the relevant Home Office department to attend meetings of its board of trustees in recognition of the importance of the partnership between the two organisations. This is not straightforward by any means. Whilst the Home Office is one of the major funders of the Refugee Council's work it is of course also the architect of the legislative framework within which charities have to support refugees and asylum seekers. Predictably, it can be the target of the Council's criticism. The advent of the age of contracts, in which the Refugee Council has to compete against other possible service providers for Home Office funds, has brought into focus the potential dilemma of having the funder at the table, particularly in the run up to a re-tendering process. Few would encourage an organisation to be transparent about impending negotiations in front of the other negotiating party.

The role of the senior executive

There is probably not a senior manager or trustee of a charity who has not wondered at some time, perhaps in frustration, whether their respective roles are sufficiently clear. Often it is difficult to see the line in the sand where responsibility passes from one party to the other. The line of accountability from the executive to the trustee body is rarely in dispute; it is the definition of who does what that causes the anxiety. Recent literature and research seem to be united in distinguishing between management and governance in the way the ACEVO research concluded (see page 195). Hudson (1999 p.43), for example, reached very similar conclusions. The consensus therefore is that the role of the senior management of the executive is one of joint leadership with trustees in terms of setting strategy and of sole responsibility for its implementation.

15.8 The role of the executive

Staff are responsible for supporting the process of developing strategy and for implementing it once it is agreed by the board. They are responsible for turning the board's intentions into action and for administering the systems and procedures needed to get results.

Source: Hudson (1999) p.42

In relation to financial stewardship this means that it is for the senior executive to ensure that the financial management processes and the financial environment in which those processes are used combine to deliver the strategy as agreed jointly with the board of trustees (see Box 15.9). The executive therefore has to ensure that the board is sufficiently informed on the key financial issues to be able to reach sensible conclusions jointly on what KPIs should be used, and what targets should be set for those KPIs. It must then manage the financial resources using the continuous financial performance management model described in Part 3: MONITOR-AIM-PLAN-ACT-MONITOR-AIM and so on. It is for the executive to *measure* the charity's financial performance and position so that the board can *monitor* the degree to which the finance strategy is being implemented successfully.

15.9 Financial stewardship role of the senior executive

1 To determine jointly with the board of trustees what financial KPIs the charity uses and what targets are set in relation to them.
2 To develop and implement finance strategies that will enable the financial KPI targets to be met.
3 To design and maintain financial management processes that enable the charity's financial resources to be generated, protected and used optimally.
4 To create the internal environment within which the finance processes can be managed and finance strategies implemented successfully.

The finance director

Just as with the trustee body, decisions have to be made about the staffing structure that will be used to effect the financial stewardship role of the executive defined above. This is an issue at all executive levels in the organisation and as Hudson (1999 p.214) rightly counsels as part of excellent general guidance on management structures:

> 'Organisation design is an art, not a science. There are no right and wrong answers – just more effective and less effective arrangements.'

The executive's financial stewardship responsibilities are of such importance to the overall delivery of the charity's objects (having impact on beneficiaries) that the most senior management team within the organisation must be *directly* responsible for their discharge. No chief executive these days can avoid taking a strong personal interest in financial stewardship; this is often stimulated by anxieties about income generation. However, larger organisations wisely place lead responsibility for it in the hands of a senior manager with the financial skills to ensure that appropriate information is provided, decisions taken, etc. This may be a director-level position with no other areas of responsibility than finance. Much more typically however, the finance director role assumes responsibility for some or all of the other support functions such as information technology, human resources, company secretary and office facilities, as part of a broader grouping of functions under a generic title such as 'resources' or 'support services'.

The choice of either (a) employing a dedicated finance director, or (b) employing a more broadly-defined resources director, involves a trade-off and in determining its organisational design the charity must understand what this is. The range of functions under the support services umbrella means that it is not possible to find an expert in all the fields in one job-holder. The chief executive must be clear therefore about what expertise is required in relation to each function within the senior management team. Some sizeable charities operate without either a dedicated finance director or even a finance specialist in the more generic resources role. Inevitably this places greater reliance on the specialist finance expertise of the board of trustees (especially the treasurer), more junior staff (such as a departmental head of finance) or external sources (such as external auditors). On the other hand a structure with a dedicated finance director position raises questions about how the other support service functions such as human resources and information technology are to be represented within senior management. All potentially are of strategic importance and yet a senior management team in which they all have dedicated representation would either result in an over-emphasis on support services, rather than charitable activities and income generation, or require an excessively large team in order to maintain an appropriate balance.

Some hard choices have to be made. Whatever the design, it is critical for successful financial stewardship that someone at the most senior level within the executive has the explicit lead responsibility for ensuring that it performs the role defined in Box 15.9. Some further advice from Hudson (1999 p.214) may help resolve potential design dilemmas:

'The aspiring structure designer needs to remember that the people are the organization and that the primary purpose of the structure is to create arrangements that enable people to work together effectively to achieve the organization's objectives. Structures that are perfect on paper are of no use if they do not capitalize on the available people.'

The role of the manager

At the manager level within the organisation, further decisions have to be made about who does what in relation to financial stewardship. The financial performance management methodology of Part 3 places responsibility for financial stewardship at an activity level firmly in the hands of the operating units undertaking or supervising those activities. Once resources have been allocated to managers, whether from the corporate centre to the relevant directorship, or within a directorship, it is they who must ensure that the funds have the impact that was intended. Assuming financial stewardship of activities requires operational management to adopt the continuous performance management methodology described in Part 3. Continuous reassessment must be made of what funds have been committed to the activity, what outcomes are intended and expected, and what future events may affect those outcomes. The manager must steward the funds to maximise the impact and keep the organisation informed of the expected outcomes, both financial and operational. To do this, the charity must make relevant information readily accessible to the managers; they must be able, and should be expected, to generate information of results to date, conduct 'what if' sensitivity tests, feed in forecasts, and interpret reports in order to reach conclusions about the activity's performance.

The organisation must be structured to enable operating units to assume responsibility for financial management of their activities. The management accounting function therefore becomes significantly devolved, and the relative headcount between the central finance function and the operating units must reflect that. The need for a large central finance function diminishes. The role of the finance team running the central finance function becomes one of supporting operational managers to undertake their financial management responsibilities competently and of providing those financial and management accounting services that are needed at the corporate level (see Box 15.10). The finance team designs systems, consolidates income and expenditure results, manages the balance sheet and cash flow, undertakes financial KPI measurement and fulfils the charity's statutory accounting and taxation requirements. Equally importantly, members of the team play a key internal role in guiding the development of organisational competence in financial management. In larger organisations, the finance director may be able to delegate many of these responsibilities to a finance manager in order to concentrate instead on leading the executive's financial stewardship role as defined in Box 15.9, page 206. In smaller organisations one individual may well have to assume both roles.

15.10 The role of the central finance function

- To design appropriate accounting procedures and systems to be used throughout the organisation that meet statutory requirements and support internal policy.
- To provide payments and receipts services to the organisation (e.g. cheques, payroll).
- To consolidate operating units' actual financial results and forecasts into a corporate picture (i.e. prepare the primary statements and other financial reports for senior management).
- To measure the results and forecasts in relation to the financial KPIs.
- To highlight key issues evident from the results and forecasts.
- To supervise the management of the charity's financial assets and liabilities (e.g. undertaking the treasury function of managing the organisation's cash flow).
- To prepare statutory accounting and taxation requirements in accordance with relevant legislation, best practice and internal policy.
- To develop the financial awareness and competency of all staff.

Key stewardship questions – structures

1 Do the trustees, senior executive and managers have discrete financial stewardship responsibilities?
2 Is the charity organised to enable each party to exercise its responsibilities appropriately?
3 Does the charity need committees to handle some of the stewardship responsibilities?
4 Are the trustees fulfilling their financial accountability responsibilities?
5 Is there a clear split of financial stewardship responsibilities between functional specialists and operational management?

16 Capabilities: employing the requisite financial skills

Good financial stewardship by trustees, senior executive or managers requires that roles are not only well defined but also filled by individuals with the appropriate financial capabilities. Ensuring that the requisite skills, knowledge and attributes are available in-house demands the continual improvement and development of individuals; this is not about reaching an absolute level and then stopping.

16.1 Definition of capability

Capacity to act resulting from the application of appropriate knowledge, skills and attributes.

Developing and maintaining appropriate financial capability must therefore be considered throughout each individual's association with the charity, whatever stewardship role they play, from the conception of the job to their succession. This is best considered in terms of three key stages – recruitment, performance management and professional development – which together form an engagement cycle between charity and volunteer or employee (see Figure 16a). Consideration of the cycle inevitably leads to discussion of the subject of reward. Much literature is available to guide readers on each element of the cycle in general terms, but they have particular implications in relation to those jobs with financial stewardship responsibilities. The charity must manage the engagement cycle so that appropriate calibre financial stewards are first recruited, and then motivated and retained through well-designed professional development opportunities and high quality performance management.

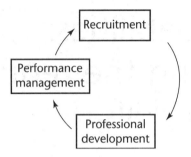

Figure 16a The engagement cycle

Creating a coherent reward strategy

The term reward is used deliberately. While most of the attention directed at reward focuses on pay, it is worth bearing in mind that it is by no means the only component of an effective reward policy. Charities competing against organisations in other sectors in the employment market to retain existing staff and recruit new ones have much to offer actual and prospective employees other than pay (see Box 16.2). This is particularly relevant for financial stewards, the more specialist of whom may be able to command larger pay packages than are typically available in the charity sector.

16.2 Definition of reward

The return for services provided, given in the form of job satisfaction, working conditions, professional development, pay and other financial benefits such as pension contributions.

Those attributes that are required in order to exercise good financial stewardship will be as much in demand in the private and public sectors, as they are in the voluntary sector. Yet like any employer, a charity will only be able to deliver consistently high performance if it has the right calibre of individual working for it whether in a paid or voluntary capacity. People are indeed a charity's greatest asset, and need to be appropriately stimulated, developed and rewarded. But this is not easy for charities whose financial resources are more limited than most, and which, by reason of their typically small size, cannot offer the traditional career ladders that are available in the large commercial and public sector organisations, even in the big charities. The public accountability rightly demanded of charities places arguably undue attention on staff costs, which often represent a very significant proportion of their total expenditure. Charities can often find themselves on the defensive, trying to counter the erroneous conclusion that staff costs equate to 'administration' (which is in some sense 'bad') rather than to the charitable work for which the funds were given (which is 'good').

Of course it is through the staff that services are delivered. It is indisputable, however, that keeping tight control of staff-related costs whilst appropriately rewarding staff is a difficult juggling act. Pay levels are often tied into historic public-sector-originated reward schemes that guarantee not only cost of living adjustments but also increments, with staff rewarded for longevity of service. Staff costs consequently rise faster than the index-linked funding agreements by which they are often financed and which, typically, cater only for *inflationary* increases in costs not *real* ones. Other sources of income have to be found to cover the shortfall.

There are thus the following opposing tensions influencing a charity's position on the reward of those job-holders in whom responsibility for financial stewardship, amongst other things, is vested.

- The external employment market place. Charities compete directly with employers in other sectors for relevant financial skills. This creates upward pressure on reward given the charity sector's tendency to pay lower than the private sector.
- Internal reward values. Very often a charity's pay structure, if not its total reward policy, is related to a ranking of jobs and/or a grading structure. Those jobs on a comparable level internally receive the same or similar pay and/or reward, irrespective of the external market. For many within the sector, this best represents a charity's values, its sense of fairness. This tends to deflate the level of pay of those jobs with higher marketability.
- Donor values. The level of financial rewards can be constrained by the funder, either implicitly or explicitly.

The importance of defensible principles

To attract and retain individuals with the appropriate financial stewardship skills a coherent reward strategy that is underpinned with robust, defensible principles is therefore crucial. These principles enshrine the organisation's attitude to reward, and are important enough to justify trustee attention and approval. These principles must articulate the stance of the charity towards the 'external market versus internal values' tension and outline where the employer intends to position itself within the charity reward range. Does it intend to be in the upper quartile, or to pitch around the median, for example? Two principles above all others are crucial (see Box 16.3).

16.3 Essential reward principles

1 Reward must be set at a level that is sufficient and necessary to attract, develop, motivate and retain the appropriate calibre people.
2 The terms and conditions of employment must be competitive in relation to the recruitment markets from which employees are recruited and replaced.

Any decision about reward must pass the test that it is 'sufficient but no more than necessary'. Note too the explicit acknowledgement in the first principle of the role of reward in retaining appropriate calibre people as well as recruiting them. The second principle articulates more precisely the implications of the first one. Two fundamental points are being made. First, that determination of reward requires the charity to be externally focused. The organisation has to understand that it is competing in the market place against other employers requiring similarly skilled and experienced staff and that the market's values will probably not align to its own. Secondly, that different jobs have different market places.

Accommodating external markets *and* charity values

There is no one single employment market for charity volunteers and staff. The marketplace for fundraisers, overseas development specialists, information technology and finance experts for example are different, each with its own reward norms. The implication of this is a stark one that must be acknowledged. Two jobs within the organisation that might be regarded as being at the same level or of the same worth internally cannot be assumed to command the same reward externally. Competing in the market place may mean that the charity has to offer differing levels of reward to job-holders at the same internal level, which of course risks conflicting with internal values. If so, something has to give. Either the charity holds the reward level of some jobs below their market level in order to retain internal comparabilities cross-functionally, or the internal values have to be re-defined. The former is feasible to the extent that the charity can compete with other sectors on non-pay grounds – on job satisfaction, working conditions or other financial benefits. But if the organisation expects to be able to attract the right calibre staff while offering reward levels below market norms it must understand on what grounds it can do so. What compelling proposition does it offer actual and prospective employees that will persuade them to sacrifice financial reward?

Sight Savers International's experience would suggest that it is possible to orientate a charity's reward policy to the external market place while honouring its internal values, recognising that the employer is a charity established to provide public not private benefit (see Box 16.4 on determining the pay component of reward, for example). In effect, whilst its reward policy sets each job within the context of the *charity* sector employment market, its position within that market (i.e. where it pitches its reward levels within the range offered by charities) is determined, if relevant, by terms and conditions offered outside the charity sector. The charity has to determine therefore what the relevant market place is for each job, what jobs in that market place reflect a fair comparison for benchmarking purposes, and where it will obtain data about the reward offered to those jobs so that it can make comparisons. For some jobs it will be within the charity sector that the employer is competing. Typically, the service delivery jobs and some fundraising jobs will be of this type. Increasingly comprehensive data is available in the form of annual reward surveys for the sector. However, the most accurate benchmarking comes from the exchange of information about jobs and reward packages between human resources peers in comparable organisations. Two market places other than the charity sector may, however, be more relevant for other jobs.

16.4 Determination of pay

1   The charity will aim to be a competitive payer, paying staff sufficient, but no more than is necessary, to retain or recruit them.
2   In all cases, pay will be determined with reference to comparable positions within the charity sector.
3   This judgement will be made, guided by the following factors:
  - the charity's corporate values
  - the charity's own understanding and assessment of each job's nature and worth
  - the terms and conditions being offered by other charities for comparable positions
  - where relevant, the terms and conditions being offered by competing employers outside the charity sector for our existing or potential employees.

Source: Sight Savers International Reward Policy, 2000

- Local market: geographically defined in relation to the location of the charity. Typically administrative jobs are of this type, where the charity is competing with other local employers from all sectors to recruit and retain core administrative skills such as secretarial and data inputting. Local employment agencies and press advertisements can provide very satisfactory benchmark data.
- Functional market: defined in relation to the particular skills and knowledge of a functional discipline such as accountancy, human resources or IT. These markets can be national or at least regional in nature. Benchmark data can be sourced from specialist recruitment agencies or from professional institutes. Developing networks with other similar charities, in which reward data and experience can be exchanged, can also prove very fruitful.

Reward for jobs with high-marketability

By pitching reward for all jobs in terms of the *charity* sector range the employer can ensure that there is some constraint on the pay levels for those jobs with high marketability. By determining the position *within* the range with reference to the relevant market place (whether that is charity market or not) the employer can meet its need to be competitive. The Sight Savers International stance has been to position itself in relation to a particular percentile within the charity sector range (e.g. median) job by job, except for those jobs which have a non-charity market place, when the position within the range is determined by data relating to that market place. In practice this means that some jobs are positioned above the charity's normal reward positioning, whilst others are below it. The sufficient and necessary test applies in all cases.

Benchmarking is not a scientific activity. Crucial judgements have to be made especially when determining what jobs offer a fair comparison for benchmarking purposes. Often data about such jobs is scant, and job titles and even advertisements, can be misleading. Procedures need to be in place internally to prevent jobs being 'talked up' in order to be benchmarked against more senior positions elsewhere. Similarly, the extent to which functional specialisms do truly have cross-sector appeal must be carefully considered. With regard to senior finance positions for example, whilst the charity certainly does have to compete with other sectors to attract individuals with appropriate skills, those who have risen to senior positions from within the sector typically do not have comparable marketability *outside* it. This means that there could be more pressure to increase pay in order to recruit than to retain staff.

Reward is inevitably complex, and charities are always at risk of adopting practice that is at odds with its reward principles or strategy such as in the following circumstances.

■ Reward levels driven by recruitment practices rather than retention ones even though the costs of recruitment (in terms of direct recruitment costs, disruption to continuity, resources devoted to induction, etc.) greatly exceed the costs of retention. This occurs for example where the pay for a vacant position is set at a level higher than received by its previous occupant even though the responsibilities of the job are unchanged.

■ Reward policies that reflect a strategy of cost containment rather than genuine reward. In such circumstances the focus is one of minimising the costs of inputs (i.e. employees) rather than maximising the cost-effectiveness of outcomes (i.e. employee impact).

■ Recruitment practice that seeks to attract 'the best' alongside a reward principle that positions the charity at the median or below within the sector.

16.5 Lessons for determining reward

1   Understand the reward proposition. What is the charity offering that will attract, develop, motivate and retain the appropriate calibre staff?

2   Establish where the charity wishes to position itself on the charity reward range.

3   Identify those market places in which the charity is competing for specialist skills.

4   Obtain good data about the reward commanded by positions in other organisations that are genuinely comparable.

5   Decide whether the charity wishes to determine reward in relation to the job or the job-holder. Two individuals will bring different knowledge, skills and attributes to the same job.

Deciding on recruitment needs and processes

Two elements of recruitment need to be considered. First, the definition of the financial stewardship responsibilities to be undertaken by the job-holder and the attributes they must have to fulfil those responsibilities (i.e. a definition of employer need). Secondly, there is the recruitment process itself.

Definition of employer need

The most useful approach to defining a job is to identify what results the organisation requires that cannot be obtained from the existing resources. In this way, the added value of a job, or its unique contribution, should be made apparent. Documentation such as job descriptions should enable the reader to understand what impact would *not* occur if the job was not undertaken. The focus therefore is on outcomes or results, not processes or tasks, since it is the achievement of outcomes that must stimulate the need for additional resource. The three role definitions (those of trustees, senior executive and managers) included in Chapter 15 all define outcomes without describing tasks. The influence of uncertainty on the roles, skills and attributes needed for financial stewardship cannot be underestimated, and the greater the uncertainty the more this is true. Recall the frames of reference defined by Stacey (1993) as suitable for chaos management (see Figure 1g, page 23). Other observers of organisations such as Haeckel (1999 p.93 and p.112) confirm this:

> 'One effect of operating a business in an environment of discontinuous change is that leaders can no longer know as well as followers how to get things done. A leader's role cannot therefore be one of devising battle plans and issuing orders down a chain of command to co-ordinate their execution... Leadership has responsibility for creating, adapting and governing a viable organizational context, and for populating, with the right talent, the roles defined in it.'

In terms of financial stewardship, this means adopting the roles defined in Chapter 15 (i.e. providing a financial vision, setting the financial parameters and key performance indicators and setting, monitoring and accounting for financial performance in an appropriate financial environment). A useful discipline that can be adopted is for any prospective recruitment for a job to be preceded by a written justification for its creation or continuation. Some straightforward questions can be asked to stimulate careful consideration before the job is approved (see Box 16.6). It may be, on reflection, that the cost-benefit of the job is inadequate, even if just the direct costs are considered. Tools such as job evaluation schemes, whereby a job is assessed against pre-defined factors, can helpful in providing a systematic way of understanding what prospective jobs are really about, as long as they are used properly. Job evaluation is often misunderstood as being a determinant of reward through the attribution of points to factors, thereby enabling each job to be scored, ranked and graded. As has been discussed earlier in this chapter, with internally focused reward policies, pay structures are commonly built around grading structures. However, once it is recognised that different jobs have different market places the link between internal grade and reward is invalidated, thereby raising questions about the need for grading at all. Sight Savers International has operated since 1999 without any grading structure.

16.6 Justifying recruitment to a post

1   What is the purpose of the post?
2   What are the objectives of the post in the first 24 months?
3   What alternative ways of achieving the objectives have been considered other than recruiting to the proposed post?
4   What will be the consequences of not recruiting to this post?
5   What are the direct costs associated with the post (payroll costs, training, equipment etc)?

However, in orientating job definition towards outcomes rather than processes, attention must be paid not only to results but also behaviours. Technical competence has to be accompanied by inter-personal skills and particularly in the more functionally specialist, analytical positions, this can easily be forgotten. Outcomes can therefore usefully be sub-categorised into results and behaviours, the former needing to be achieved and the latter exhibited. The more senior the financial stewardship position the more important it is that the job-holder demonstrates behaviours that promote and influence an appropriate corporate culture, and stimulate competent action in staff and volunteers.

If the job definition (or description) identifies what results and behaviours a job-holder should deliver, the person specification identifies what inputs the job-holder must bring with them to the job in order to discharge their responsibilities effectively. These inputs can best be categorised into three – knowledge, skills and attributes (see Box 16.7). Increasingly, recruitment practice is taking into account that whilst knowledge and skills can be acquired, the personal attributes of job-holders are more difficult to

---

16.7 Person specification – inputs

■   Knowledge – theoretical and/or practical familiarity and understanding of subject (acquired by theory and/or experience)
■   Skills – ability in doing something
■   Attributes – personal qualities or characteristics

Source: The Concise Oxford Dictionary, 1976

---

change or develop. It is of key importance to understand the attributes of good financial stewards. The precise knowledge, skills and attributes that are required obviously depend on the particular role in question (trustee, senior executive, or manager) but, in an uncertain operating environment, they are likely to include many from the shopping list given in Box 16.8.

16.8 Financial stewardship person specification - possible inputs

Knowledge (however gained including education and experience)

- Developing and promoting (financial) visions and strategies
- Designing and implementing solutions to corporate issues
- Resource allocation decision-making
- Costing methods (e.g. activity-based costing, full absorption costing) and drivers
- Fund management
- Developing and using corporate performance management tools
- Understanding of the fundamentals of SOFAs, balance sheets and cash flow statements
- Setting and using key performance indicators

Skills (ability to ...)

- Define and promote a financial vision
- Adopt and maintain a strategic perspective – able to identify what is business critical
- Communicate complex concepts and visions to lay audiences both orally and in writing
- Persuade and inspire individuals at all levels
- Prepare and/or interpret numerical analyses, models and reports
- Assess and manage risk
- Make and explain difficult judgements and decisions

Attributes (must be ...)

- Empathetic with the cause
- Courageous to take difficult decisions
- Adaptable to cope with change
- Comfortable with uncertainty
- Challenging of assumptions, policies and strategies
- Systematic, logical thinker
- Advocate of information sharing
- Committed to professional development of in-house financial stewardship skills
- Committed to devolved management

The recruitment process

The task of defining the job and person specification precede the recruitment process because until they have been written and approved the charity cannot be sure whether there is a process to initiate. From this point the charity needs to follow a well-defined path if a satisfactory outcome – the appointment of an appropriate calibre individual to the job – is to be achieved. Each stage should play its part both in promoting the charity (recruitment is a two-way process after all in which the candidate is as much selecting the charity as vice versa) and in assessing the degree of fit between the candidate and the person specification. The process extends from determining how to advertise the vacancy through to commencement of employment by the chosen candidate. The process must establish *with evidence* whether the candidate has the financial stewardship knowledge, skills and attributes needed: she or he must be able to demonstrate these. Much can be learnt from the use of written exercises or oral presentations on financial stewardship issues (see Box 16.9 for examples).

16.9 Financial stewardship recruitment exercises

Written exercises (30 mins – unprepared) or panel presentations (10 mins – prepared).

1 Write a brief report for the board of trustees outlining what key financial issues they should address in light of the charity's (or another charity's) latest statutory accounts.
2 Outline how a charity should determine what its reserves policy should be.
3 Define what management accounting information you think it is appropriate to present to a board of trustees each quarter/a senior management team each month.
4 Define what you think the respective financial stewardship roles of the board of trustees and the senior executive are (or treasurer/finance director, or finance manager/operational manager).
5 Describe how you would assess the adequacy of a charity's financial health and stewardship.
6 Describe what you would expect a charity's finance strategy to tell you.
7 Discuss the limitations of traditional budgeting and how these might be overcome.
8 Outline how a charity can best plan financially during periods of rapid change or uncertainty.

Continued

---

9   If you could use only five key performance indicators to monitor a charity's financial performance, what would they be, and why?

10 What issues should a charity consider in managing the competing financial demands of maximising charitable impact today and maintaining the charity as a going concern in order to have charitable impact tomorrow?

The importance of professional development

Once appropriate calibre individuals have been appointed to the charity, good financial stewardship demands that they continue to develop their capabilities in line with the changing needs of the organisation. There is a very clear 'win-win' to be enjoyed by both employer and employee if the former can provide stimulating jobs throughout the latter's employment with the charity. Part of this stimulation involves developing the skills and knowledge of each member of staff in line with both the needs of the organisation and the employees' capabilities and interests. The charity needs to demonstrate its clear commitment to professional development and there are many ways in which it can do this (see Box 16.10).

Financial stewardship is so important to the eventual impact of the charity that it must be one of the core tenets of its professional development strategy. It has to define what financial stewardship skills it requires in which jobs and ensure that the relevant job-holders have those competencies. More structured strategies could see the employer defining levels by job ranging from no competence required to expert. For each level methods of acquiring the competency could be defined (see Figure 16b). Competency at the required level can be monitored through the normal line management process.

Level	Competency
1	■ Reading and using cost centre-focused management accounts reports
2	■ Cost centre financial management including forecasting
3	■ Resource allocation decision making using financial key performance indicators
4	■ Design and promotion of finance strategy

Figure 16b Levels of financial stewardship competence

16.10 Signs of organisational commitment to professional development

- An explicit statement from the employer that it encourages staff to spend X days in training and/or development each month/quarter/year.
- An extensive induction programme (including refresher programmes for established staff) during which training and development needs are recognised and assessed.
- Explicit recognition of the responsibility of line managers for supporting staff in professional development.
- Active management of training and development in line with initiatives such as the Investors in People (IIP) standard.
- Provision of an extensive range of training/learning opportunities, such as the following:
  - support from in-house specialists (e.g. 'surgeries' run by the finance staff)
  - development of and coaching from in-house user experts (e.g. more experienced peers)
  - participation in specialist membership bodies, e.g. for chief executives or charity finance directors
  - sharing knowledge and skills within a network of peers in other charities
  - access to relevant finance literature (e.g. journals of the Accounting Institutes)
  - attendance at workshops run by accounting firms and other professional advisers for nominal fees
  - support for staff/volunteers to undertake relevant finance orientated study.
- Commitment to provide support (in the form of funding, coaching, study time, etc.) to enable staff to undertake training for professional qualifications.
- An appraisal process that includes a requirement for each employee to reflect on recent performance and future development needs once or twice a year with their manager and to document that review.
- Committed use of practical techniques of evaluation to assess the effectiveness of learning undertaken.
- A learning culture that encourages good documentation of knowledge (thereby protecting the corporate memory), facility to share it and incentive to do so.

Providing professional development of course has cost implications, both in terms of direct costs that might be incurred by course fees, etc, but also in terms of opportunity costs such as time away from the desk.

Nevertheless the costs to the organisation of not providing professional development will, in the long term, be greater. Even if investment in staff and volunteers does increase their marketability to competing employers it also contributes greatly to improving organisational effectiveness through enhanced productivity and motivation. To that end, professional development can legitimately be included as one component of a reward package. Enhancing knowledge and skills (i.e. learning) can be achieved in many ways, and professional development is much broader than simply training. Not all learning provision need be expensive.

The importance of managing performance

Performance management in relation to financial stewardship has been at the heart of this book, and the basic performance management cycle that was introduced in Chapter 1 (see Figure 1b on page 15) applies as much to individual performance as it does to the corporate entity. Individual targets and plans need to be set in the context of corporate plans (see Figure 16c), with implementation of those plans supported by monitoring and review processes.

A The Strategic Framework outlines the corporate values, strategic themes and parameters within which performance is to be achieved.

B Corporate initiatives and strategies are set with the Framework context.

C Departmental plans are written to develop and implement corporate initiatives.

D Individual plans and targets are agreed that, between them, deliver the departmental plans.

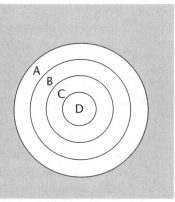

Figure 16c The corporate context for individual workplans

In line with the financial stewardship model propounded in this book, plans for individuals must be expressed in terms of outcomes the individual is expected to achieve in relation to the internal financial environment, financial management processes and/or the finance strategy. Intentions and targets against which the performance of the individual can be assessed must be defined and these must dovetail with and reflect the organisational performance management processes. It must be apparent how the individual staff members and volunteers will between them deliver the corporate plans. In designing an appropriate performance management environment for each individual the model of financial stewardship that has been explored has a number of implications that are relevant.

- Uncertainty means unpredictability: expectations, plans and targets may prove to be inappropriate measures of actual performance.
- Performance must ultimately be measured with hindsight in relation to the circumstances in which it was achieved. Ultimately targets have to be separated from the performance management process.
- Planning must reflect the nature of the charity's activities not the accounting timetable. Plans need to roll forward across financial year-ends.
- Performance targets need to be outcome-orientated, measured by results and behaviours.
- Where available, relative performance targets which are self-regulating can be more effective than absolute ones.

In Sight Savers International individual targets are reflected in workplans determined jointly by manager and job-holder. Where appropriate they are written quarterly, look six months ahead, and focus on outcomes. They describe what should have been achieved by the end of the next six months. Each quarter the workplan is rolled forward another three months so that at any time there is a six-month perspective forward. Progress is monitored with written monthly updates, which are discussed at monthly one-to-one meetings between job-holder and manager. Six-monthly appraisals provide the opportunity for the job-holder formally to document the standard of performance that has been achieved. The targets of the workplan provide the basis for discussion, not a definitive measure of performance.

Key stewardship questions – capabilities

1 What reward proposition is the charity offering its employees and volunteers?
2 What knowledge, skills and attributes do those individuals with various financial stewardship responsibilities require?
3 How does the charity intend to close the gap between the capability requirements of its staff and their current capabilities?
4 Is the performance management and professional development of individuals determined in the corporate context of the charity's mission and strategy?

17 Using information systems

The final piece to place in the financial environment jigsaw is the information system. Competent staff and volunteers operating with well-defined roles within an appropriate structure need excellent information systems if they are to make the financial management decisions on which implementation of the charity's finance strategy depends. Peters (1992 p.110) once described organisations as 'pure information processing machines – nothing less, nothing more: organizational structures, including hierarchies, capture, massage, and channel information. Period.' More recent texts such as Gates (1999 p.3) expound even more fervently on how critical good information management is to organisational success:

'How you gather, manage, and use information will determine
whether you win or lose... The winners will be the ones who
develop a world-class digital nervous system so that information can
easily flow through their companies for maximum and constant
learning.'

Certainly the standard of financial stewardship that this book promotes, the financial management methodology that is described and the uncertain environment in which it assumes charities now have to operate, all place heavy demands on the quality of the information systems. Financial stewardship should be based on using up-to-date information about the current financial position and latest thinking about the future in the context of defined targets or goals. This information will be continually changing and eight characteristics that the financial information required must exhibit in order to be of value have been identified (see Box 9.3, page 117). Timeliness, accuracy, and the other 'fit for purpose' characteristics of the management accounting information provide the criteria for judging the adequacy of the financial information systems.

The efficiency with which a charity can understand where it is now and what is ahead of it, and make appropriate decisions that contribute to furthering its objects depends on the quality of information, which in turn depends on the quality of the systems which generate the information. What is certain is that there needs to be an urgency, a dynamism, associated with information management in an uncertain operating environment. The whole emphasis of the financial management methodology of Part 3 is directed to looking forwards from where the financial steward is now and reacting to what is ahead. Out-of-date, incomprehensible, inaccurate information invalidates the whole process.

Stewarding IT-based financial information systems

Haeckel (1999 ch.9) calls it 'managing by wire', Gates (1999 p.xvii) 'a digital nervous system'. Irrespective of the label that it is given, there is universal acceptance that organisations now have the technical capacity through information technology (IT) to generate and exchange appropriate information between appropriate parties at the appropriate time. Whilst non-IT systems will continue to play a part in the provision of the financial information required, even the smallest and least resourced organisation is likely to find itself placing increasing reliance on IT. 'Any data on any desk', whether local, regional, national or worldwide, is the enticing prospect for any charity if the strategic vision for information management and the political will to achieve that vision are in place. Parts 2 and 3 of the book have detailed the information management requirements of good financial stewardship: what information is needed, when it is needed, in what form and to what level of detail. But what are the implications of this for information systems? How can the charity ensure it harnesses the capability of IT to provide excellent financial stewardship information systems? Before considering the systems management process that needs to be in place, it is necessary first of all to acknowledge the strategic importance that must be attached to such systems.

17.1 A digital nervous system

You know you have built an excellent digital nervous system when information flows through your organization as quickly and naturally as thought in a human being and when you use technology to marshal and coordinate teams of people as quickly as you can focus an individual on an issue. It's business at the speed of thought.

Source: Gates (1999) p.37

IT as a strategic resource

Gates (1999 p.317) is among many to recognise the importance of treating IT as a strategic resource to the extent, in his opinion, that chief executives and other senior managers 'should become as engaged in IT as in any other important business function'. A survey of IT use in the not-for-profit sector by financial software consultants Tate Bramald found that the strategic role that IT can play in organisations is not often appreciated by chief executives and senior finance executives (Tate, 2001).

It is important that an organisation articulate its philosophy with regard to information technology: it must be clear how committed it is to investment in information systems, not least in relation to the financial resources at its disposal. Sight Savers International, for one, aims to be 'just behind the crest of the wave', maintaining a high level of investment in IT, recognising its strategic importance to the delivery of business objectives without wishing to be right at the leading edge of IT development. It is a question of risk assessment, of understanding the relationship between the quality of information management (generation and communication) and IT investment. Pressure to upgrade the quality of IT must be accompanied by the business case for doing so, and tempered by an acknowledgement that good enough *is* good enough. In relation to finance systems there is no need for charities to be right on the crest of the wave. There are tried and tested 'off-the-shelf' IT solutions available and it should not be necessary to opt for bespoke systems with all the costs and difficulties of ongoing support that accompany them.

Ensuring IT meets financial stewardship needs

If appropriate resources are to be devoted to the management of finance systems, a high degree of mutual understanding needs to be developed and maintained between the financial stewards and the IT specialists. The former must understand enough about IT and its capability to contribute to deliberations about IT solutions and their management. The latter need sufficient appreciation of the requirements of financial stewardship to ensure that the IT solutions are designed *exclusively* to meet those requirements. Careful consideration and energy must be given to developing working practices that foster and, if necessary, force that mutual understanding. Williams *et al.* (1999, p.20) encourage organisations to establish a Staff and Systems Development Group to support the chief executive in taking account of the needs of the whole organisation in managing technology developments (see Box 17.2). Such a group should be able to rank the IT needs of financial steward-ship against the other organisational priorities, and ensure that the IT solutions for each business need dovetail technically.

17.2 Staff and Systems Development Group responsibilities

- Steering the organisation's use of technology.
- Identifying and prioritising critical business issues.
- Ensuring that these issues are linked to the organisation's objectives.
- Prioritising projects to form a credible one-year development plan.
- Initiating activities that will increase the organisation's ability to support new systems once approved and working.

Source: Williams *et al.* (1999) p.20

In practice, however, the capacity for non-IT specialists to develop suffi-cient understanding of information technology to offer adequate guidance may be stretched. This can result in over-reliance on possibly only one IT specialist, but this risk can be countered by establishing access to other IT expertise to advise the charity on matters ranging from IT strategy to technical detail (see Box 17.3). Such expertise could be accessed in many ways: from a specialist on the trustee body, from a charity supporter, within a network of charities, as a member of a software user group, from a group of advisers on an IT panel or in a more formal rela-tionship with external IT advisers. Whilst the latter can appear expensive, it may prove to be cost-effective, certainly in comparison to the cost of recruiting the equivalent expertise full-time into the organisation.

17.3 Possible areas of involvement for external IT advisers

- Guiding the determination and implementation of the charity's IT strategy.
- Advising the management team of a major IT-based project.
- Completing an audit (a health-check) of the IT systems, procedures and capabilities.
- Acting as a technical mentor to the IT staff.

Managing IT-related costs

It is important to recognise that IT solutions to business requirements such as financial stewardship absorb sizeable financial resources. Expectations internally, from the board of trustees down, therefore need to be managed. IT-related costs are likely to form an increasingly high element of a charity's total costs, and to be consistently high. Culturally, it is important that, where possible, such expenditure is perceived as an essential component of the activities undertaken for income generation or to further the objects of the charity, not as a central overhead. The classification of costs on the SOFA should also reflect this.

The information systems management cycle

The operation of high-quality finance systems needs to follow a continuous cycle of five activities – design, implementation, maintenance, use and review (see Figure 17a). The charity must be clear how each stage is to be completed.

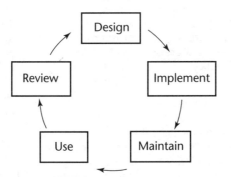

Figure 17a Systems management cycle

Design

'Design' refers to the construction of systems to enable the agreed policies and procedures to be implemented. The successful design of finance systems depends on understanding the objectives of the system (outcomes), the origin of data (inputs) and the process by which that data is handled to deliver the objectives (processes). A formal project management methodology should be used to manage the process of design and implementation of major systems developments. This includes writing a formal specification of requirements, defining as precisely as possible the outcomes required from the system (such as reports) and any design features that the system must have (for example to reflect the sources of data). All the tasks that need to be completed in order to design and implement the new system successfully are logged and mapped, on a Gantt chart for example. Such a chart enables the

231

project management to identify a realistic timetable, confirm which tasks are on the critical path, assign responsibilities and appreciate the resource requirements. Very careful consideration needs to be given to systems design, particularly over tasks such as designing a coding structure. Williams *et al.* (1999 pp.21–9) lay out one framework that can be used for any system development (see Figure 17b). The design phase of systems management must determine how data will be input/gathered, analysed and converted into information, and then communicated. The framework very usefully distinguishes between, and stresses the importance of, both information and communication systems. Information must not only be generated, but also communicated if it is to reach the decision-makers that will use it.

Data Gathering	Analysis	Information & Communication Systems	Implementation
1 Identify the **critical business issue**	1 **Re-design** the way work is done to address identified shortcomings	1 Determine the **information needs and IT solutions** that are now required as a result of the Analysis phase	1 Identify and record **benefits** of implementing the Information and Communications solutions arrived at the previous phase. This will be used to measure achievements
2 Be clear about the related **business objectives**	2 Explore whether changes will be required at the **organisational level** in light of the re-designed process and established goals	2 Determine the **communications needs and communications technology solutions** that are now required as a result of the Analysis phase	2 Establish the **cost** of implementing the Information and Communications solutions arrived at the previous phase. This will become the project's budget
3 Set down in detail the **current process for undertaking this work**	3 Explore whether changes will be required to **individual(s) roles and responsibilities** in the light of the above	3 Compare solutions in 1 and 2 to existing systems and equipment	3 **Installation**
			4 **Evaluate** performance improvements by measuring benefits achieved and costs incurred against what was planned

Source: Adapted from Williams *et al.* (1999)

Figure 17b Framework for managing technology developments

Managing the development of a system using such a framework is a time-consuming activity but it is essential if the charity is to enjoy the benefits of excellent financial information, appropriately communicated. A project manager must be defined to co-ordinate the project, either from the existing staffing (with consequent implications on workload) or externally sourced. A project management team with suitable representation from the finance and IT functions, together with key users/customers, must jointly steward the project's progress if it is to be successful in meeting the various information needs within the charity whilst complying with its IT strategy. When establishing a project management team, it would be unwise to assume that staff necessarily have the project management capabilities needed to manage the successful implementation of a new finance or communications systems on time and within financial projections. Some professional development in project management techniques may be needed. Involvement of consultants can also be considered in some project management or support capacity.

For multi-site operations the design stage must also determine whether each site is to use standardised finance systems, where responsibility for the design must ultimately rest with one individual, or whether each site has discretion to tailor systems for its own purpose within the constraints of any corporate requirements. There are considerable advantages to standardising the finance systems such as cash and banking arrangements, purchase ordering, invoicing and receipting, and data entry. The level of corporate familiarity and expertise in the systems should be significant if all users are maintaining common systems. This increases the organisation's ability to design appropriate systems, implement them, resolve queries/faults, and train staff. Users on different sites can support each other, and the charity has scope to cover temporary staffing gaps from a pool of competent users.

Choosing an appropriate software product deserves careful consideration. The complexity of charity accounting can easily be underestimated. Reference to Figure 9a on page 121 quickly illustrates the demands that must be made in terms of coding and reporting. All charities will want to be able to classify their income and expenditure in various dimensions such as by cost type, SOFA activity and fund. The criteria by which products will be assessed must include functionality (i.e. ability to capture, analyse and report information as required), cost, supportability, compatability with the charity's other systems and IT infrastructure, and breadth of use by other organisations.

Implementation

Williams *et al.* (1999 pp.103–6) break down this phase into six elements – installation of equipment, staff training, data conversion, parallel running, security and technical support with sensible bullet-point advice on each (see Figure 17c). Each clearly needs to be considered and have responsibilities assigned. As the previous chapter has discussed, building capability internally requires commitment on the part of the charity and individuals. There is much to be said for developing capacity to conduct core training on finance systems within the internal workforce. This can be supported by access to external support in the form of supplier helpdesks, user groups, etc. Similarly on the technical side, involving in-house staff in the resolution of installation issues can only improve the charity's corporate knowledge of such matters.

Installation	■ Assure system performance by testing with expected volumes of data and in proposed permanent location
Training	■ Arrange training on newly installed equipment before going 'live'
Data conversion	■ Use test data to verify the effectiveness of the proposed solution
	■ Devise checks to verify the success of the conversion procedure
Parallel running	■ Consistent results for reports need to be checked using data and procedure simulations
Security	■ Check procedures in a controlled manner to ensure that they will recover the system to the nominated state
Technical support	■ Minimise teething problems by keeping technical expertise on hand initially, by documenting problems, and by involving relevant staff in their resolution

Source: Adapted from Williams *et al.* (1999)

Figure 17c Implementation advice

Use

For good financial stewardship in a dynamic environment both the decision-makers and those who support them must be competent users of the finance systems albeit in very different ways. The information management vision of 'any data on any desk' implies an environment in which decision-makers can access relevant, up-to-date information when they need it, wherever they are. The spread of responsibility described in Chapter 15 demands an open philosophy with regard to information access. All financial stewards must therefore receive some training in how to use the key information systems, even if their skills extend no further than being able to generate or access essential financial reports. Ideally, their systems competency will enable them not only to access key information, but also to use technology-based systems to analyse data, track trends, conduct sensitivity testing, and, if necessary, 'drill-down' into the database to audit the trail of particular data. This implies a minimum level of competency with the finance information database (e.g. accounting software), analytical tools such as spreadsheets, and communications tools such as e-mail and Internet.

For each financial steward a personal training programme for their particular responsibilties could be devised based on a comparison of their current systems competencies with those demanded of the position. In reaching conclusions the charity must decide the extent to which it wishes to devolve responsibility to users for tasks such as data entry and report design that historically may have been the preserve of the finance department (see pages 208–9 on the role of the manager). Devolvement of responsibility, whilst in keeping with the need for the charity to be adaptable and responsive, must however not compromise the integrity of the information. Data security and other systems controls must be addressed.

Maintenance

Without financial information, no financial stewardship can be undertaken. Maintenance of the finance systems to ensure their reliability is therefore essential. Two forms of support are required:

- *technical* design and installation support (i.e. how the system has been built, what operating conditions should be in place for it to function properly, what assumptions underpin it, etc.)
- *functional* support (i.e. how the user should use the system so that it functions properly).

In the spirit of financial stewardship developed in this book the aim should be to create an information system which is as easy as possible for every user to understand. If this is the case then on the functional support side users can often help themselves and each other, as well as relying on IT expertise. The sources of expertise when required could include knowledgeable users, in addition to the system's designers, and external helpdesk facilities.

It is essential, however, for a defined job-holder, who is probably a member of the central finance team, to take responsibility for system maintenance, as well as performing general system tasks such as setting up definitions (e.g. new ledger codes). Technical support for this role is likely to come from the product's developer or supplier.

Review

Review is an essential part of the systems management cycle (see Figure 17a, page 231). It is necessary to ensure that, periodically, the adequacy of the systems from both a functional and technical point of view, including the controls, is assessed. This may lead to systems, or the processes associated with those systems, being redesigned. Functional assurance testing can be undertaken by the users themselves, by internal audit or as part of external audit. Technical assurance testing is more difficult for most organisations to undertake simply because of the specialist nature of the subject. Receiving assurance on the adequacy of the IT infrastructure or the overall IT strategy, for example, may well require outside help. Consideration should be given to commissioning an overall IT health-check and/or to developing a long-term relationship with IT consultants to provide ongoing and specific support, advice or review.

Key stewardship questions – systems

1 What philosophy does the charity have with regard to information access?
2 Is the value of information and communication technology (ICT) recognised at a strategic level?
3 Are the systems that are developed and used in support of financial stewardship managed in line with the systems management cycle?

Bibliography

Aldrich, Tobin (1999) 'How much are new donors worth? Making donor recruitment investment decisions based on lifetime value analysis', *International Journal of Nonprofit and Voluntary Sector Marketing*, Vol. 5, No. 1, pp.81–9

Argenti, John (1993) *Your Organization: What is it for?* McGraw-Hill

Armstrong, Michael and Angela Baron (1995) *The Job Evaluation Handbook,* Institute of Personnel and Development

Belbin, Meredith (1996) *The Coming Shape of Organizations,* Butterworth-Heinemann

Belbin, Meredith (1997) *Changing the Way We Work,* Butterworth-Heinemann

Binder Hamlyn (1986) *Economic Resource Management*

Blackmore, Becky, Richard Hardy and Christina Hogg (1998) *Partners in Leadership,* ACEVO

Bryson, John M. (1995) *Strategic Planning for Public and Nonprofit Organizations,* rev. ed., Jossey-Bass

Charity Commission (1997) *Charities' Reserves,* CC19, HMSO, May

Charity Commission (1999) *Responsibilities of Charity Trustees,* CC3, HMSO, September

Charity Commission (2000) *Accounting and Reporting by Charities, Statement of Recommended Practice,* HMSO, October

Chartered Institute of Management Accountants, The (2000) *Management Accounting: Official Terminology,* CIMA Publications

Drucker, Peter (1990) *Managing the Non-Profit Organization,* Butterworth-Heinemann

Gates, Bill (1999) *Business @ the Speed of Thought,* Penguin

Gillingham, Shirley and John Tame (1997) *Not Just for a Rainy Day?* NCVO

Haeckel, Stephan (1999) *Adaptive Enterprise,* Harvard Business School Press

Herzlinger, Regina and Denise Nitterhouse (1994) *Financial Accounting and Managerial Control for Nonprofit Organizations,* South-Western Publishing Co.

HM Home Office (2000) 'Compact on Relations between the Government and the Voluntary and Community Sector in England', *Funding: a Code of Good Practice,* HMSO

Hind, Andrew (1995) *The Governance and Management of Charities,* Voluntary Sector Press

Hope, Jeremy and Robin Fraser (1999) *The BBRT Guide to Managing Without Budgets,* CAM-I Inc., Release V3.01

Hope, Jeremy and Robin Fraser (2001) *Beyond Budgeting,* Harvard Business School Press.

Hudson, Mike (1999) *Managing without Profit,* Penguin

Kaplan, Robert and David Norton (1996) *The Balanced Scorecard,* Harvard Business School Press

Kaplan, Robert and David Norton (2001) *The Strategy-Focused Organization,* Harvard Business School Press

Kirkland, Kate (1995) *The Good Trustee Guide,* NCVO

Lynch, David (1994) *Quality in the Finance Function*, CIMA/Kogan Page

Mainelli, Michael (1999) 'Organisational enhancement: viable risk management systems', *Risk Management Briefing*, No. 27, pp.6–8, Kluwer

McBride, Neil (1999) Chaos Theory and Information Systems [Internet], De Montfort University. Available from: http://www.cms.dmu.ac.uk/~nkm/CHAOS.html [Accessed 18 Feb 2002]

Peters, Tom (1992) *Liberation Management*, Macmillan

Poffley, Adrian (1997) 'Power tools – how to build better management accounts', *NGO Finance*, January/February, pp.32–3

Poffley, Adrian (1997) 'Super structures – how to engineer a better blueprint', *NGO Finance*, March/April, pp.32–4

Poffley, Adrian (1997) 'Shall I compare thee to the best in the business – or to the budget?', *NGO Finance*, May/June, pp.26–7

Poffley, Adrian (1997) 'Preaching the gospel – spreading the word about management accounts', *NGO Finance*, July/August, pp.34–5

Poffley, Adrian (1999) 'An effort worthy of development', *NGO Finance*, October, p.58

Poffley, Adrian (2000) 'Global concerns – aid in uncertainty', *NGO Finance*, June, pp.44–7

Poffley, Adrian (2001) 'Moving beyond budgeting', *Charity Finance*, July, pp.26–9

Porter, Michael (1996) 'What is strategy?', *Harvard Business Review*, November/December, pp.61–78,

Powell, Mike (1999) *Information Management for Development Organisations*, Oxfam

Refugee Council, The (2001) *Strategy 2001–2006*

Semler, Ricardo (1994) *Maverick*, Arrow

St John Price, A (1979) *Understand Your Accounts*, rev. ed. Kogan Page

Sight Savers International (2001a) *Strategic Framework 2001–2003*

Sight Savers International (2001b) *Strategic Review of Integrated Education*, August

Sizer, John (1985) *Management Accounting*, 2nd ed., Penguin

Stacey, Ralph (1993) 'Strategy as order emerging from chaos', *Long Range Planning*, Vol. 26, No.1, pp.10–17

Tate, John (2001) 'Time to rise to the challenge', *Charity Finance*, June, p.59

Turney, Peter (1996) *Activity Based Costing: The Performance Breakthrough*, Kogan Page

Unwin, Julia (2001) *Funding our Future: Core Costs Revisited*, ACEVO

Warnes, Brian (1984) *The Genghis Khan Guide to Business*, Osmosis Publications

Warnes, Brian (1985) *The Genghis Khan Guide to Business: Cash Flow Handbook*, Osmosis Publications

Weighell, Richard (2001), 'SORP 2000: Making the risk disclosures and using them to your advantage', *Charity Matters*, February, PKF

Williams, Clyde, Chris Nunn, Tasleem Chaudary and Terry Mitchell (1999) *Computers can be managed – A CEO's guide*, Sho-net Systems

Wise, David (1998) *Accounting and Finance for Charities*, ICSA Publishing Prentice Hall Europe

Index